THE ALPHA FILE:
The Story Barry Goldwater Didn't Intend to Tell

I shared the agony and frustration of President Eisenhower when he was abused for the U-2.

I was present in the Oval Office when President Kennedy faced the reality of the Bay of Pigs.

I heard Lyndon Johnson confess his failure and frustration.

I was commissioned to inform Richard Nixon that he must resign.

I am aware of the risks in speaking frankly and candidly. It had been my earlier intention to postpone the publication of my recollections and judgments of the past twenty-six years until I left public office. I am now convinced I cannot hold to that decision.

WITH NO APOLOGIES

BARRY M. GOLDWATER

WITH NO APOLOGIES

The Personal and Political Memoirs

of

UNITED STATES SENATOR

BARRY M. GOLDWATER

BERKLEY BOOKS, NEW YORK

This Berkley book contains the complete
text of the original hardcover edition.
It has been completely reset in a type face
designed for easy reading, and was printed
from new film.

WITH NO APOLOGIES:
The Personal and Political Memoirs of
United States Senator Barry M. Goldwater

A Berkley Book / published by arrangement with
William Morrow and Company, Inc.

PRINTING HISTORY
William Morrow edition published 1979
Berkley edition / September 1980

ISBN: 0-425-04663-X

A BERKLEY BOOK ® TM 757,375
Berkley Books are published by Berkley Publishing Corporation,
200 Madison Avenue, New York, New York 10016.
PRINTED IN THE UNITED STATES OF AMERICA

*Dedicated to my parents and their parents
whose courage and strength in helping to settle the Far West
have been an inspiration to me over the years*

Contents

This is the oath required by the Constitution and by law to be taken by Senators under Rule 2:

"I do solemnly swear or affirm that I will support and defend the Constitution of the United States against all enemies, foreign and domestic; that I will bear true faith and allegiance to the same; that I will take this obligation freely without any mental reservation or purpose of evasion; and that I will well and faithfully discharge the duties of the office on which I am about to enter, so help me God."

CHAPTER 1

Why Now?

On the day President Gerald Ford opened his campaign for the Republican nomination in New Hampshire, former President Richard Nixon announced from his forced retirement in San Clemente that he was going to visit China again. Either deliberately or inadvertently, Nixon had monopolized the attention of the media—to the possible detriment of the man who may have injured his own political future by granting Nixon a presidential pardon. I happened to be on NBC's *Today Show*. Asked to comment about the China visit, I said, "As far as I'm concerned, Mr. Nixon can go to China and stay there."

Once, in a moment of frustration over an impractical, wasteful program being pushed by the eastern liberals, I said, "It would be a good thing to saw off the eastern seaboard and let it float out into the Atlantic." Doyle Dane Bernbach made a TV commercial from that remark. They used it against me when I was running for President.

At no time during that campaign or at any point in my public life have I ever advocated or suggested the use of atomic weaponry. But the media said I did. Every time I saw that hideous Johnson TV commercial with the little girl, it saddened me to realize that all involved—the reporter, the spot writer, the producers, the advertising agency, and the candidate who was then the incumbent President of the United States—valued political victory more than personal honesty.

I was elected to the United States Senate in 1952, riding on Dwight Eisenhower's coattails. I have always acknowledged my indebtedness to Ike for that first victory. He was my President—a member of my party. I treasure my association with "Ike" as a memorable and rewarding experience. Yet in May 1960, in a speech on the Senate floor, I called Ike's proposed budget, with a projected $5 billion increase, a "dime-store New Deal."

In 1952 I said continuous expansion of the federal establishment would make us the slaves of bureaucratic masters. Today every individual's business or personal decision is grossly influenced by some agency of the federal government. Throughout my career I have been saying that reckless expansion of the federal budget would produce unbearable taxation. Today forty-six cents of every dollar earned are claimed by the tax collectors—federal, state, and local.

I said the average Joe Citizen who went to work every day, paid his taxes, obeyed the law, and saved to educate his children had become the forgotten American—the victim of federal taxes. Twenty-five years later the forgotten Americans in California approved Proposition 13.

It's not pleasant to be the bearer of bad news. In 1964 I tried to warn people what would happen eventually to the Social Security system. Almost no one believed me because no one wanted to believe. In 1977 the President of the United States admitted that unless draconian measures were adopted, the Social Security system would soon be insolvent. I take no satisfaction in saying, "I told you so."

I warned that continuous deficit financing would destroy the purchasing power of the dollar and initiate an inflationary spiral capable of destroying the American economic system. If we didn't stop government intrusion in the private sector, we would surreptitiously create a socialistic state. Today the government subsidizes and operates Amtrak, Conrail, and scores of other businesses—most of them at a loss.

In 1962, speaking at the War College in Montgomery, Alabama, I said that in war there is no substitute for victory. In Vietnam we fought a twelve-year war which could have been ended in twelve weeks. Our political masters were afraid to acknowledge defeat and wouldn't let our military win a victory.

As a result of those and other remarks, I have achieved certain prominence as a "shoot-from-the-hip, tell-it-like-it-is, uncompromising public figure." I make no apologies for what I've done or for what I've said in twenty-five years spent in the company of the rulers of America. I confess having made mistakes. For most of them I have been adequately punished.

It had been my earlier intention to postpone the publication of my recollections and judgments of the past twenty-six years until I left public office. I am now convinced I cannot hold to that decision.

Shortly after my election to the U.S. Senate I initiated a practice which I have continued throughout the years. I recorded my observations of major events as they occurred. I dictated my personal evaluation of the people I met. I kept copies of important correspondence. This material went into what came to be called my Alpha File—strictly personal and very private. I had no special purpose in mind beyond the recognition that memory should not be trusted to preserve detail—that the passage of time blurs and distorts the present.

The Alpha File is the indispensable support upon which this book rests. Without it I could not offer an examination of the changes that have taken place in our society since the day long ago when I became the Republican U.S. Senator from Arizona. In addition to my personal recollections preserved in the Alpha File, I have drawn on the writings of others to illuminate our errors and to suggest the reforms which I feel are necessary if the Republic is to be preserved.

I am not so vain as to presume that my personal participation in the national political arena has given me the credentials to speak for anyone other than Barry Goldwater, but:

I was privy to the secret development and utilization of the U-2, which permitted us to know precisely what our potential enemies were planning. I shared the agony and frustration of President Dwight Eisenhower when he was abused by certain pundits who didn't know and couldn't know what they were talking about.

I was present in the Oval Office at the White House when President John Kennedy faced the reality of the Bay of Pigs. This charming young man, who put his name on a book entitled *Profiles in Courage,* lost his nerve and conveyed to world communism its first outpost in the Western Hemisphere.

I was at Camp David with politician Richard Nixon when he vowed to abandon politics and assume the role of responsible statesman. And then I watched that vow broken on the wheel of political expediency.

On almost his last day in the White House, I spent a very private hour with President Lyndon Johnson to hear his confessions of failure and frustration and confusion.

Only one man in all of history has resigned from the most powerful office in the free world. I was commissioned by my fellow Republicans to inform Richard Nixon that we could not and would not prevent his impeachment, that he must resign.

In the Bible story of David and Goliath we are told that David's brothers, who were older and bigger than he, ordered David to stay home while they went into the valley to confront the enemy. When David joined them a day or so later, they rebuked him. He replied with a question: "Is there not a cause?"

To my mind there is a cause. That cause is freedom. We stand in danger of losing that freedom—not to a foreign tyrant, but to those well-intentioned but misguided elitist utopians who stubbornly refuse to profit from the errors of the past.

If I am right, if the Republic is in danger, then time is short. I must take this opportunity to share what I have seen and experienced as a member of the U.S. Senate, as my party's nominee for the presidency, as a man whose only aspiration has been to serve the cause of freedom.

If I am wrong, time will display my error and reprimand me. If what I have to say strikes a response in the hearts and minds of other Americans, perhaps they will enlist in the cause to keep our country strong and to restrain those who seek to diminish the importance and significance of the individual.

Informed opinion is sharply divided. Merely to line up as a partisan supporter of one side or the other will contribute nothing toward finding a true solution to our present dilemma.

We have conjured up all manner of devils responsible for our present discontent. It is the unchecked bureaucracy in government, it is the selfishness of multinational corporate giants, it is the failure of the schools to teach and the students to learn, it is overpopulation, it is wasteful extravagance, it is squandering our national resources, it is racism, it is capitalism, it is our material affluence, or if we want a convenient foreign devil, we can say it is communism. But when we scrape away the varnish of wealth, education, class, ethnic origin, parochial loyalties, we discover that however much we've changed the shape of man's physical environment, man himself is still sinful, vain, greedy, ambitious, lustful, self-centered, unrepentant, and requiring of restraint.

I cannot change what I am, nor would I wish to do so. I am quite aware of the risks in speaking frankly and candidly. My appraisal of the great figures of my time will certainly be challenged. I must question certain notions which have been authenticated by a vast amount of intellectual authority. My opinions expressed here may once again make me a target of scorn and ridicule.

I do not plan to offer a chronological political history of the past thirty years. What I do intend is an insider's view of the great changes which have taken place in our society and the role of government and the men who have wrought these changes.

It is my ambition to share with you my experiences as I tried to establish a balanced authority, to maintain and support the ordered and just society. It is inevitable, I think, that if you peer at the world through the windows of my mind, we will disagree on some matters. Believing the American people possess the courage to face the truth and will find the strength to overcome the habits which threaten our destruction, I cannot keep silent.

When I was born, Arizona was still a territory. The automobile was a newfangled invention. Steam locomotives and horses pulled our conveyances. For personal transportation we had the horse and the street railway. There was no federal welfare system, no federally mandated unemployment insurance, no federal agency to monitor the purity of the air, the food we ate, or the water we drank. There were not enough federal marshals to control the outlaws. My grandfather came to Arizona before the cavalry had ended the attacks of hostile Indians on white pioneers.

The exponents of social change have taken charge of government. They have expanded the power of the federal establishment to satisfy what they claim are the needs and aspirations of each succeeding generation. It is the trade-off which bothers me—the surrender of independence, of individual personal choice. Even the most casual student of history is forced to confess that in this eighth decade of the twentieth century, the role of government has been expanded to a point where government influence and government decisions exert an overwhelming control over our daily lives.

Manners, morals, and dress may not be true indicators of a society's worth. But when the people become a mob, surly and indifferent, when the ancient moral values are relegated to the ash heap, when dress respects no situation, we may be experiencing a decline in the prescriptive values which has preceded the fall of every great civilization in history. We can find a mass of social critics who will tell us our present discontent can be traced to past failures to respond with sufficient speed to the need for change in social structure, governmental organization, and the ambitions of the Third World.

We have, through the application of mechanical energy and the discoveries of science, expanded our dominion over nature to a staggering degree. But have we improved our conceptual understanding? Are we more enlightened? Have we determined our proper responsibility to translate this wondrous new power for the benefit of present and future generations?

I have been influenced by my encounters with men and events to revise some of my earlier persuasions and at the same time, some of the understandings which were more intuitive than reasoned have been reinforced.

As a candidate for the presidency I was categorized as an extremist, uninformed, insensitive, obstinate, quick to call an untruth a lie. Yet I hold no malice for any man. My anger is directed against those proposals for change in our established institutions which, in my opinion, threaten our freedom.

CHAPTER 2

Roots

My grandfather, Michael Goldwasser, was a Polish-Jewish refugee. He was born in the city of Konin in 1823, one of twenty-two children of Elizabeth and Hirsch Goldwasser. Under the oppressive rule of the Russian czars, Jews in Poland were denied educational opportunities, their employment was restricted, boys were conscripted into the Russian Army.

When my grandfather was fourteen years old, he was involved in some sort of revolutionary activity serious enough to cause him to believe his life was in jeopardy. He crossed the border at night in to Germany and never returned to Poland. He never again saw Elizabeth or Hirsch.

Once safe across the border in Germany, where the political climate was much more tolerant of Jews, my grandfather decided to travel to Paris, where he found employment at the tailor's trade. He mastered the language and saved his money. When the French government collapsed on February 24, 1848, Mike gathered his belongings and crossed the Channel to London.

Whenever I encounter some passionate advocate of bilingual education arguing the necessity of offering instruction in both Spanish and English in the public schools of Arizona, I invariably think of my grandfather, the French-speaking Polish immigrant boy who cheerfully learned English because it was a social and economic necessity when he moved to London.

Michael Goldwasser was twenty-six years old when he met a seamstress named Sarah Nathan. Two years later, on March 6, 1850, they were married.

In 1851 Michael's younger brother, Joseph, then twenty-one years old, fled from Poland to avoid conscription in the Russian Army. He came to London. Mike and Sarah took him in.

The brothers were remarkably different. Mike was tall and fair, an easy mixer who made friends everywhere. Joe, dark and swarthy, was a head shorter than his brother. Today we would call him an introvert or a loner. It was Joe who talked his brother Mike into seeking their fortune in the New World.

News of the gold strike at Sutter's Mill in California had reached England. In the United States, Joe argued, there was no discrimination against Jews. There they would find unlimited opportunity. Joe didn't propose the brothers should become gold miners—let others dig the precious metal out of the rocks. He and Mike would be merchants.

Finally, it was agreed that Mike and Joe would go to California. Sarah and the two children, Carolyn and Morris, would remain in London. She would support the family working in the seamstress trade. Mike, the thrifty one, had put by enough to enable the brothers to go into some kind of retail business in California.

Mike and Joe Goldwasser arrived in San Francisco in November 1852. They journeyed by stagecoach to the newest bonanza town, Sonora, in the foothills of the high Sierras. Mike had planned on opening a general store. He soon discovered his meager capital would not permit the acquisition of a stock of merchandise sufficient to compete with the existing stores.

Gambling, whiskey, and wild, wild women were an inseparable part of the American West. The Goldwasser brothers opened a saloon on the ground floor of a two-story building which housed the camp's most popular bordello.

In fifteen months Mike saved enough money to pay the passage for Sarah, their two children, and to finance the trip for Sarah's recently widowed sister, Esther. On July 2, 1854, Big Mike was reunited with his wife and children in San Francisco.

Sarah was a city girl. She found the crudities of life in a mining camp intolerable. After three years in Sonora, during which time she gave birth to two children, Elizabeth and Samuel, she moved back to San Francisco with the four children and her sister.

The gold boom in Sonora faded. Miners moved on to new strikes. The saloon business suffered. Joe went to one of the new towns, opened a saloon, and in six months was broke. He moved again, this time to Los Angeles, where he opened a tobacco and notions store in the Bella Union Hotel.

In 1855 creditors put a padlock on Big Mike's Sonora Saloon. He joined Sarah and the children in San Francisco and spent the next three years working in a variety of jobs, earning enough to pay all his debts. In 1858 he moved his family to Los Angeles and went to work with Joe.

In 1859 overland travelers brought news of gold discoveries in the western portion of the territory of New Mexico, the area which was to become Arizona. Big Mike brought the Goldwater name (the brothers had anglicized the spelling by this time) to Arizona in a two-horse spring wagon loaded with tinware and Yankee notions.

To reach the placer fields east of the Colorado River, Mike had to cross 300 miles of desert. Watering holes were few and far between. He ferried the Colorado at Yuma, then made his way north on the Arizona side to La Paz, which was located some fifteen miles to the northeast of the present city of Blythe, California.

The Southern Pacific Railroad completed its line from Los Angeles to Tucson in 1880. Prior to that date most of the supplies for the western part of the area were carried up the Colorado on river steamers and then freighted overland from the port of La Paz.

Joe moved from Los Angeles to join Mike. In partnership with Dr. E. B. Jones they developed and operated the largest wagon freight line in the territory. They hauled supplies under contract to most of the Army forts during the government's campaign against the Apaches. They operated businesses in Tucson, Phoenix, Yuma, Prescott, Bisbee, and Wickenburg.

The river currents at La Paz hampered the docking and offloading of the paddle-wheel boats. A new site was selected a few miles downstream, and Mike Goldwater built an entire new town. He named the new port Ehrenberg in honor of a German mining engineer who had become his best friend. On my uncle Morris's first trip to Arizona he and Mike found Ehrenberg's body near the Dos Palmas Store, which was operated by a character known as Bottle-ass Smith. The murder was never solved, but thanks to Mike, Ehrenberg's name is still on the map of Arizona.

McKenney's Pacific Coast Directory for 1880–81 has only two entries under the heading "Ehrenberg." My uncle Henry was the postmaster, and J. Goldwater and brother were listed as operating a general store.

Ultimately Mike and Joe established a mercantile headquarters in Prescott when that city was the capital of the new Territory of Arizona. They handled general merchandise, hardware, agriculture implements, furniture, and carpets.

Sarah and the children moved from Los Angeles to San Francisco. Joe joined them. He negotiated the freight contracts, bought the merchandise, was the resident agent for the Arizona enterprises.

Mike stayed on in Arizona. He financed and built a gold stamping mill on the Hassayampa River to handle ore from the fabulously rich Vulture Mine. When the owners of the mine ran up a $35,000 debt they said they couldn't pay, Mike took over the mine and operated it until the obligation was liquidated. Then he gave the mine back to the owners.

This fugitive immigrant who traveled halfway around the world to establish a mercantile business was not seeking riches or power or the easy life. He endured hardship and privation. He survived the attacks of hostile Indians. He was separated from Sarah and his children almost continuously for the first twenty-seven years of his married life. What he sought was freedom and independence. He found it.

They called my grandfather Big Mike not because of his physical stature, but because, as my uncle Morris once explained to me, he was big in courage, big in vision, big in heart. He died before I was born. His story is not unique.

In 1877 Mike turned over the active management of the Arizona properties to his sons, Morris and Henry, and joined Sarah in San Francisco.

My father, Baron, was sixteen years old when he came to Prescott from San Francisco in October 1882 to work in the family store. I cherish many pleasant memories of my father, but I never really knew him. What I know about him I learned from my mother and my uncle Morris. He was five feet six inches tall, slender, cosmopolitan in his habits, devoted to providing for his family, but never really one of us. Uncle Morris said my father worked hard at pleasing customers, served his apprenticeship without complaint but was often critical of the merchandise and the selling methods.

At the end of that first year in Arizona my father went back to San Francisco to visit Mike and Sarah. When he returned, he brought with him a magnificent square piano, which he promptly sold at a handsome profit. He purchased the piano with his own savings—he never brought it to the store. He refused to divide the profits of that initial sale with his brothers. He made his point. Goldwater's started handling pianos. In the next twelve months they sold fifteen. As a result of this first independent venture, Morris and Henry let Baron expand the lines of the merchandise they handled far beyond the staple necessities originally featured.

About three years before Baron came to Arizona, M. Goldwater & Sons had tried to open a store in Phoenix, a new farming community in the central part of the state. For some reason the store didn't go and was closed. Now Baron wanted to enter this market again. He argued that mines around Prescott would someday be worked out. He said the state's economic future would be built on agriculture. He thought the population of Phoenix was bound to grow faster than Prescott's.

Morris and Henry were opposed to the opening of a branch in Phoenix. Baron was insistent. They finally played a game of casino to settle the matter. Baron won. In 1896, with Baron in charge, a branch of M. Goldwater & Sons was opened in the valley community.

My mother, Josephine Williams, grew up in the sand hills of Nebraska, moved to Chicago, and went through nurses' training. In 1903 her doctors told her she had lung fever and recommended she go to Arizona. She came by herself, keeping her medical problem a secret from her parents. She told them she was going west with a patient and would write when she was established—an explanation literally true. She was the patient.

Not too much was known about tuberculosis at this period, but it was believed the dry air of western deserts had an exceptional healing quality. Most of the "lungers" lived in tents on the outskirts of Phoenix, seeking maximum exposure to the sun and the air.

My mother never discussed her illness or her recovery with us, but I do know that within three years after she came, she was doing special duty as a surgical nurse at the old St. Joseph's Hospital.

My father made the Phoenix Goldwater store the leading fashion center of the territory. He traveled frequently to San Francisco and New York on buying trips. He sold high-quality merchandise at high prices. He established the motto which was the guideline we all followed until our family sold the store in the late 1950s. It was: "The Best Always."

Baron Goldwater was one of the most eligible bachelors in the territory. Josephine Williams was "that new trained nurse from Nebraska." My mother says she met my father at the store. They were married in 1907. She was twenty-nine; he, forty-one.

My father had been living with two other bachelors, Dr. George E. Goodrich and Gus Hershfeld, a highly respected professional gambler. They had an adobe house about two blocks from the store. When I was a boy, it had a green door and green shutters. My father's first proposal wasn't an offer of marriage. He invited Jo to move in with him, an offer she rejected scornfully.

According to Uncle Morris, the wedding took place in Prescott during a snowstorm, the ceremony performed by an Episcopal priest. Following a reception at the boardinghouse where bachelor Morris lived, the newlyweds left on the Santa Fe train for a honeymoon trip to New York City. I was the first child of Baron and Josephine Goldwater.

Arizona was admitted as the forty-eighth state of the Union on February 14, 1912. My uncle Morris was vice-president of the Constitutional Convention which preceded that event. He was elected to represent Yavapai County in the first session of the new state legislature.

My father was a very private man, almost solitary. His pattern of life was rigidly followed, day after day. My mother says he wanted children but never knew quite how to cope with us. My brother, Bob, who is fifteen months younger than I am, was born on the Fourth of July; my sister, Carolyn, on April 15, 1912, the day the *Titanic* went down.

Uncle Morris was gregarious, impulsive, a leader of the Democratic party and a highly respected citizen. He became my friend and my instructor.

Mother loved the out-of-doors, absorbed the culture and the history of her adopted home. My father was a city man. He had his store, his card games in the afternoon with cronies at the Arizona Club, and the companionship of his male friends, who often stopped on their way home to have a drink at Baron Goldwater's house. When Prohibition became the law of the land, my father bought the bar, the back bar, and the brass footrail of his favorite saloon and had them installed in the basement of our house. The country went dry, but that bar was always wet.

My first year in high school I was not a scholastic success. The prinicipal diplomatically informed my father that I probably would do much better in a private school. The following fall I was enrolled at Staunton Military Academy in Virginia. It was probably the best thing that ever happened to me.

Looking back on this period, I now understand the friends of my childhood were all the sons of successful fathers. But to be a success in that period didn't mean you had to be rich or white collar, black or white, Gentile or Jew. To be respectable meant respecting others, keeping your word, paying your way. The kind of work a man did wasn't important.

I realize now the Goldwaters were somebodies in the social and economic circles of that dusty little frontier town. But when I was growing up, I never thought I was different from anyone else. I was a poorer scholar than some of my friends, better at athletics. Thanks to my courageous, remarkable mother, I knew a lot more about Arizona than many of my friends.

Before I was ten years old, "Mun" took us on camping trips to every remote corner; to the Grand Canyon, to the Navajo and Hopi reservations, to the border towns of Douglas and Nogales, to the high mountain places—Flagstaff, Show Low, and Springerville. We had a Chalmers touring car with boxes built on the running boards to carry food, cooking utensils, and other camping gear. Mun did the driving and the bossing. Bob gathered the wood and built the campfires; Carolyn washed the dishes. Mother did the cooking. And when we got stuck on those primitive roads, it was my job to take the shovel and dig us out.

Mun told us the history of the places we visited. We had to learn and identify all the vegetation. She read to us from books about geology so that we could understand how the mountains and valleys were formed.

History and literature fascinated me. The military training at Staunton was physical and mental. I accepted the discipline as being necessary, was absorbed by the studies of military tactics and the history of the world's great battles. I graduated as the outstanding military cadet of my class.

My instructors at Staunton urged me to pursue a military career. They said I qualified for an appointment to West Point, and their sponsorship would make it possible for me to enter the academy. The idea appealed to me, but my father was not well. Mun wanted me to come home. I enrolled as a freshman at the University of Arizona in the fall of 1928.

My mother, who, in addition to managing our pleasant household, worked for volunteer charity organizations and served on the medical auxiliary of the hospital, was a talented golfer. She mastered the game and became club champion. On the morning of March 6, 1929, Mun teed off at eight-fifteen in the second round of a women's tournament at the Phoenix Country Club. After eight holes, she was two up on her opponent. Suddenly, without offering any explanations, she walked off the course, stopped only long enough to take off her golf shoes in the locker room, and drove home. Afterward she told us, "I just knew something was wrong."

When Mun reached home, my father was still in bed—a most unusual thing for him. He appeared to be in great pain. Mun called the doctor and did what she could to make my father comfortable. He was dead when the doctor arrived.

The Goldwater store was under the capable management of our longtime associate Sam Wilson, but the first breezes of that economic windstorm the Great Depression were being felt in Arizona. It was time, I thought, to go to work.

CHAPTER 3

The Real World

My apprenticeship in the business world commenced the spring my father died. I was twenty years old. Goldwater's had fifty-five employees. The annual sales were about $400,000.

The fact that my name was Goldwater didn't cut any ice with Sam Wilson. I started as a junior clerk. Over the years my father had dropped most of the general lines. Goldwater's had become a high-fashion store catering to a clientele in the middle- and upper-income brackets.

In the piece goods section I learned the different fabrics, how to tell them apart and what they were used for. As soon as Sam thought I had mastered one line, he moved me to another department. With the exception of ladies' undergarments and shoes, I did it all. My salary was $15 a week, and I had to live on it. Bob and Carolyn both were away at school. Mun didn't charge me anything for room and board. I had been used to more spending money when I was at college, but this was different—this was earned money.

During my first campaign for U.S. Senate, my opponent referred to me in a belittling manner as a "ribbon clerk." I responded saying that I was a damned good ribbon clerk and proud of it. I said, "The people I know who work at this trade are honest and enterprising, determined to give their customers value received for every dollar spent. I want the gentleman to know that's the way I intend to conduct myself when I'm sitting in his old seat in the Senate." I don't claim that working in a store, dealing with customers, employees, manufacturers, and brokers, is the equivalent of an academic degree, but I do think that in this real world of commerce I learned some things not taught in any college.

The Depression wasn't really felt in Arizona until 1932. I have never found a satisfactory answer to explain this time lag, but 1932 was the year of most business failures. We cut the inventory, skimped on advertising, switched off lights to save electricity, and reduced deliveries. Everyone in the store, including me, took a cut in pay, but we didn't fire anybody. We never sued anyone to collect an overdue bill. We never missed a payroll.

The hard times which commenced in 1929 and continued until the beginning of World War II reinforced all my understandings of economics. Businesses go broke because they borrow more than they can repay. Interest rates eat up profits.

I am sure this early experience is responsible for my strong opposition to governmental borrowing. When individuals or corporations go broke, creditors seize all available assets, liquidate them, and then take their loss. Governments don't go broke. They just print more money. The interest we paid on the federal debt in 1977 was more than $35 billion, roughly equivalent to the total federal budget for the full nine years from 1931 to 1939.

Some of my critics in the Senate have described me as a skinflint, a pinchfist when I vote against new appropriations, new programs, and new agencies. Old habits are hard to break. I'm even more concerned about spending the taxpayers' dollars than I am about spending my own money.

Those first years at the store were exciting and rewarding. Our merchandise was higher-priced than that of our competitors, but we had better quality. Our customers recognized this. Lots of them with comparatively small incomes appeared to prefer to have one or two dresses a year from Goldwater's rather than three or four less expensive garments. With the slogan "The Best Always," our store not only kept afloat during the Depression but gradually increased our volume of sales.

The store didn't claim all my attention, and I became intensely interested in Arizona history. I went again to those out-of-the-way places we had visited with Mun when we were children and found some new ones. I ran the rapids of the Colorado River in a wooden boat, hiked or rode horseback over much of the Navajo Reservation.

Phoenix in this period was a small, semi-isolated western city. The summer heat was intense; only a few theaters and some of the stores had central air conditioning. We called the winter visitors snowbirds and rejoiced when they left in the spring, even though this would mean a lessening of commercial activity.

It may have been the Depression, our isolation, or perhaps our limited population, but there existed in those years a spirit of community which I have never encountered elsewhere. This was a part of our frontier heritage when survival depended on our neighbors.

I can remember a group of businessmen coming to our house to discuss the need for a better hospital when my father was still alive. They talked about where it should be built and how much it should cost. The next day they started raising money. In the teens and the twenties, the institution they built was the equal of anything in a city ten times our size.

In 1930 I decided to learn to fly. My instructor, Jack Thornburg, had a Great Lakes biplane with an inverted four-cylinder air-cooled engine. It was the only time I ever kept a secret from Mun.

Because there is considerable turbulence in Arizona the year around, especially during the hot summer months, the best flying conditions for a neophyte pilot are just at daybreak. I would slip out of the house and meet Jack at an unpaved airstrip east of the city.

Flying has been a major part of my life. Perhaps it is the splendid isolation of being alone in the air which fascinates me, or it might be the perspective which comes from looking down on every part of the world—rivers and oceans and cities and hamlets. I prefer night flying to day flying. I see the lights, and I wonder where they are burning—in a young couple's home where they have just put the babies to bed, in a widow's lonely house, or perhaps in a store like Goldwater's when I was a boy. In the daylight hours the landscapes change, are marked by rivers, by luxuriant growth in areas of heavy rainfall. At night even the mountains are blurred. Only the lights indicate the presence of other human beings.

It was a new world for me, partially mechanical, having to do with airspeed, lift, and pressure altitude. Any pilot can describe the mechanics of flying. What it can do for the spirit of man is beyond description. When you are flying at night in a modern jet at 30,000 feet, the skies and stars are infinite. The entire universe seems to be saying, "Oh, God, how great thou art." The heavens endure; men come and go.

Some pilots claim flying gives them a sense of power or mastery over obstacles on the ground. My feelings in the air take me an opposite direction. When man conquered the sky, he didn't create anything. All he did was take advantage of the laws of physics. Our piston engines are an example of this, and our jet engines an extension of that example, and all of it made possible by Him who created this orderly, always consistent universe.

My faith in the future rests squarely on the belief that man, if he doesn't first destroy himself, will find new answers in the universe, new technologies, new disciplines, which will contribute to a vastly different and better world in the twenty-first century. Recalling what has happened in my short lifetime in the fields of communication and transportation and the life sciences, I marvel at the shortsighted pessimists who tell us we have reached our productive capacity, who project a future consisting primarily of dividing what we now have and making do with less. To my mind, the single essential element on which all new discoveries are dependent is human freedom.

All history is the record of man's quest for freedom. At the moment to fly an airplane is the ultimate extension of individual freedom. We have penetrated outer space. We have sent men to the moon and brought them home. But in this apparently limitless world of the sky, nature's immutable laws must be obeyed. And man is still subservient to the dictates of his Creator.

I wasn't breaking any law when I sneaked off to learn to fly, but Mun knew I wasn't going to the store at that early hour. She didn't ask any questions. I didn't offer any explanations.

After my first solo flight, the owner of the ground where the strip was located decided it would be more profitable to plant lettuce then to serve aviation. The airplanes which had been using the strip moved to a new field on the west side of town. Some years later the 27th Pursuit Squadron from North Island, San Diego, was named winner of the Frank Luke, Jr., trophy for aerial gunnery. Luke, one of the aerial heroes of World War I, was a native Phoenician. The squadron wanted to fly into Phoenix and receive the trophy. The owner of the ground where I learned to fly had given up on lettuce and was ready to reestablish an airport, but the strip hadn't been graded.

When the city was slow to act, I borrowed a tractor and a drag from a Japanese gardener I knew. With the help of Lee Moore, a local mortician, who had learned to fly about the same time I did, the strip was graded. The runway which resulted from our efforts is now eight left, two-six right of the international airport operated by the city of Phoenix, named Sky Harbor.

In 1978 more than 5 million passengers arrived and departed from that field, which is only twenty-four blocks from City Hall. The only other major city in the United States with an airport so close to the downtown area is San Diego. When I visit other cities and have to spend forty-five minutes to an hour in a cab or a bus traveling from the airport to downtown, I think how lucky we are in Phoenix. It gives me considerable personal satisfaction to remember my part in the location of Sky Harbor.

When I earned my private pilot's license, there was a one-paragraph story in the Arizona Republic. Mun clipped it out and handed it to me at breakfast. "If you had told me," she said, "I would have learned with you." I believe she would.

Since that day I have logged more than 12,000 hours of time in 165 different types of aircraft, helicopters, and gliders. I was the first nonrated test pilot to fly the U-2. I have flown the B-1 bomber, the F-104, the French Mirage, the German-French A-300. I have flown the SR-72 at a speed of Mach 3 at an altitude of 83,000 feet.

Shortly after I qualified to carry passengers, my friend Harry Rosenzweig persuaded me to take his current love, an attractive young lady named Strauss, for a ride.

In those days pilot instruction did not include spins and recovery. I had been told that if I ever got an airplane into a spin, I should let go all controls, and the aircraft would right itself.

Harry's girlfriend and I were in the Great Lakes at about 2,500 feet over her house. To attract attention, we were doing some tight 360-degree turns. The aircraft stalled; we went into a spin.

I let go of everything, said a prayer, and we recovered. Not long after that, fledgling pilots had to learn how to put their craft into a spin and recover before being permitted to solo.

When my brother, Bob, graduated from Stanford in 1932, we held a kind of family conference. Sam Wilson had married a wealthy widow and retired. I was running the store and enjoying it. It was decided Bob would go to work at the Valley National Bank and learn how bankers make money. By this time I knew we would never become millionaires running a store. Incidentally, Bob wanted to learn to fly, and Mun encouraged him.

I first met Margaret Johnson when she and her mother came into the store to do some shopping in December 1930. Her parents, the Ray Prescott Johnsons of Muncie, Indiana, had leased United States Senator Carl Hayden's home on the Country Club grounds for the winter.

The Johnsons were snowbirds. They had come down hoping the mild climate would benefit Peggy's brother, who suffered from some bronchial complications. I remember thinking she was a rather pretty girl, with very deep blue eyes and a beautiful complexion. She told me later she was depressed by the thought of missing all the good Christmas parties in Muncie. She thought Phoenix was a hick town, and I didn't make much of an impression on her. She said she was going to Mount Vernon Seminary in Washington, D.C. I told her I had graduated from Staunton in Virginia.

Herb Green, a friend of ours, brought her over to the house on Central Avenue for one party that Christmas season; but it was a big affair, and I didn't pay any particular attention to Herb's date. When I saw her again in 1932, the little girl from Mount Vernon Seminary had become a ravishingly beautiful, mature woman. She had come back to Phoenix to be with her father, who was desperately ill. I tried to see her as often as possible, but she had other things on her mind.

When her father died, Peggy and her mother returned to Muncie, and I became something of a commuter. She was fun to be with. I liked her sense of humor, her independence, her throaty laugh, her eyes. I was in love.

The Johnsons spent the summer of 1933 at their summer place in Charlevoix, Michigan. In that two-year interval between our first and second meeting, Peggy had worked as a designer for the David Crystal organization in New York City. Because they were in the apparel business, I had some contacts with the Crystals, and the people I knew there told me that Peggy had exhibited exceptional talent. About the only thing we had in common was an interest in style and fashion. Her father had been president of the Warner Gear Company. Borg-Warner is the result of a merger of Warner Gear and the Borg and Beck Clutch Company. Ray Johnson became executive vice-president, a post he held until his death.

I first proposed after a two-week visit in the summer of 1933. Peggy said she wasn't ready to get married. She wasn't sure about Arizona, and she wasn't sure about me. But I was sure, and I told her so.

Christmas is "The Season" in the dry goods business. Holiday sales can make the difference between profit and loss for a full year. I went to Muncie the day after Christmas 1933 to spend the rest of the holidays. New Year's Eve Peggy and I were at a dance. She wanted to call and wish her mother a Happy New Year. When we were in the telephone booth, I told her I was running out of money and out of patience. For the umpteenth time I asked her to marry me. She said yes.

We were married in Muncie almost ten months later on September 22, 1934. Peggy and her mother had been scheduled to embark on a long-planned world cruise in January 1934. I couldn't ask her to give it up, but I didn't want her to go. I was tormented by the thought she might meet someone on shipboard or onshore, so I made sure there was a packet of letters waiting for her whenever the cruise ship docked. She still has them.

There are many moments of triumph in a man's lifetime which he remembers. I have been to the mountaintop of victory—my first election to the Senate, and my reelection; that night in Chicago, in 1960, when the governor of Arizona put my name in nomination for the office of President of the United States; and another night in San Francisco when the delegates to the Republican Convention made me their nominee. But above all these I rate that night in Muncie, Indiana.

Peggy and I have had four children. We have known joy and sorrow together. We have encountered pain and illness. We have suffered separation for long periods of time. Through it all she has been my strength, my companion, a part of my private world where no other human beings, not even our children, have been allowed to enter. Peggy doesn't like flying or camping, but she has done a lot of both with me.

By 1937 most of the other nations in the world had recovered from the 1929 Depression. The United States was lagging behind. Things at the store were going very well. My brother, Bob, had been named to the board of directors at the bank. My sister, Carolyn, had married her childhood sweetheart, Paul Sexson, and Mun was in reasonably good health. But I was disturbed.

I had read Hitler's *Mein Kampf*. My grandfather had been forced to flee Poland, and the Jewish community was probably the first to recognize the full horror of the Nazi program.

When Lindbergh went to Germany to make his appraisal of Hitler's Air Force, I was pleased. When he attempted to tell the American people about the real purpose of the Nazi glider schools and detailed the technological superiority of the new aircraft the Germans had developed, I hoped it would awaken our nation to its peril.

The official reaction, supported by the media, was the exact opposite. Lindbergh was categorized as a Nazi sympathizer. His loyalty to the United States was questioned. We know now that President Franklin D. Roosevelt put Lindbergh on his personal enemies list.

Perhaps World War II was inevitable, but there are some unanswered questions. If the Western allies had maintained their military strength after World War I, would Chamberlain have made that trip to Munich? If a strong West had made it clear to Hitler and to Mussolini and to all other conquest-minded world leaders that the use of military force against a neighbor would be met instantly with superior force, would Hitler have crossed the border into the Low Countries? Perhaps my commitment through the years to maintaining weapons systems superior to any potential enemy is only the natural outcome of my frustrations and disappointments in this period just prior to World War II.

I don't mean to imply that all my attention or even a major portion of it during these years was occupied with world strategy. I had the store, I had Peggy and our family, and I had all the wonderful attractions of outdoor Arizona to occupy my mind.

Our first child, a girl, was born on January 1, 1936. We

combined the names of her two grandmothers and called her Joanne. Our second child, a boy, Barry, Jr., who now serves in the Congress from California, was born July 15, 1938. Our third child, a boy, was born in 1940, and we named him after his great-grandfather, Michael. I was overseas in the Burma-India Theater when little Peggy was born in 1944.

Despite the war clouds gathering over Europe and our confused domestic situation, these were good years. There hadn't been enough elapsed time to prove that all of the New Deal's social legislation was the true answer to our discontent, but they weren't yet demonstrable failures.

CHAPTER 4

World War II

Nineteen-forty was a presidential year. Roosevelt had served two terms. The threat of the international situation became his excuse for ignoring the two-term tradition. On September 3 we traded fifty destroyers to Great Britain in return for naval bases in Newfoundland and the West Indies. On September 16 Congress passed the first peace-time draft in our history. In November Roosevelt was reelected.

On December 7, 1941, Japanese carrier-based aircraft attacked and virtually destroyed our Pacific fleet at Pearl Harbor in the Hawaiian Islands. While millions of Americans were genuinely surprised by the bombing of Pearl Harbor, which precipitated our legal entry into World War II, they shouldn't have been. Ignorance, or perhaps wishful thinking, had closed our eyes to events in Nazi Germany, Fascist Italy, Imperial Japan, and Communist Russia. Hitler's Germany had absorbed Austria and threatened Czechoslovakia. Mussolini's Italy had invaded Ethiopia. Japan had been waging war on China. Communist Russia, Nazi Germany, and Fascist Italy had been deeply involved in the so-called civil war in Spain.

Clare Boothe Luce insists President Roosevelt had advance information about the Japanese attack. Her construction of events may be correct, but President Roosevelt does deserve credit for the action he took in 1939 and 1940 to rebuild our military capabilities.

It was obvious that air power held the key to the new military strategy. In 1940 and early 1941, the U.S. began training pilots on a scale never attempted anywhere before. Arizona's dry, cloudless skies provide the best flying weather in the nation. In February 1941 the Air Corps opened a single-engine advanced training school at Luke Field, about thirty miles west of Phoenix.

Primary schools operated by civilians taught new cadets how to fly in two-place Stearmans. Three of these schools were in the Phoenix area.

In July 1941, as chairman of the Armed Services Committee of the Phoenix Chamber of Commerce, I paid a courtesy call on Lieutenant Colonel Ennis C. Whitehead, commandant of Luke. My purpose was to inquire if there was anything we could do, as the business community of Phoenix, to make the colonel's job easier. A new base, a new program, a staff composed of officers who had never heard of Arizona until they got their assignment orders—what Colonel Whitehead needed was an officer who knew his way around Arizona.

In 1932 I had attempted to enter the Air Corps as a cadet. My eyesight didn't meet the military standards, and I was rejected. Now I was overage for the Air Corps, and my vision hadn't improved. But I told Colonel Whitehead that I was a reserve first lieutenant in the infantry—if he could use me in any way, I was available. I said I thought I knew something about how to get things done in Arizona.

Colonel Whitehead took me to a typewriter, handed me an application for active duty, and told me to fill it out. I typed out the form and signed it. It was for a term of one year. I believed that barring a miracle, we would be involved in a war, and I would be in for the duration. The important thing to me at the moment was that Colonel Whitehead needed me.

When I told Peggy what I had done, she approved. She predicted I would find a way to move from a desk job into an airplane. Four weeks later I was back on the base—this time in uniform as First Lieutenant Goldwater, assigned to the ground school and Officer's Club Officer.

One of the great and lasting disappointments of my lifetime

is that I never made it into combat. My eyesight and my age were against me. But I didn't sit out the war as somebody's PR officer in a stateside base.

Every second lieutenant who won his wings at Luke wanted a picture of himself in his airplane—pictures to send to the folks at home, to his girl. I took my camera to the base and traded pictures of these young officers for unauthorized flight time. They wanted more than snapshots of themselves standing beside their craft on the ground. When they flew, I had to go along in an accompanying plane to make the airborne shots. When I did, the pilots let me do the flying and log the flying time.

It wasn't a question of learning how to fly. I wanted to become familiar with the military aircraft. I was determined to qualify for some kind of flying assignment in the Air Corps.

After about six weeks I was sent to the Air Corps Supply School at Wright-Patterson Field in Dayton, Ohio, for three months. This permitted me to become acquainted with all the current aircraft being used, not only at Luke but at other fields. Knowledge of the Air Corps inventory was something I put to good use later on.

When I returned to Luke, I went through channels and again requested admission to the aviation cadet program. I was turned down. The training command decided to open a new school at Yuma, Arizona. I was assigned the task of overseeing construction, requisitioning inventory, and doing everything else necessary to put the new school in operation. I was still a junior officer. When the field opened, our assignment was to teach aerial gunnery. The methods of instruction the Air Corps gave us had not been particularly successful. Fewer than 10 percent of the cadets were being graduated as proficient.

With the help of Captain Walter Clark, who was assigned to Luke, and Group Captain Teddy Donaldson of the Royal Air Force, we set out to improve the techniques. Clark was a mathematical genius. This was before the age of computers, which could probably equal our efforts in a few seconds. What we developed came to be known in gunnery training as the curve of pursuit, a theory that all bullets fired at an enemy aircraft, starting at 90 degrees and following through to zero, would hit the target. Ninety-four percent of the pilots in our first graduating class at Yuma were declared qualified for gunnery.

The training command in Washington was so skeptical of our reported results they sent a colonel out to investigate us. I think they thought we were cheating or lying. After a short classroom indoctrination, I showed the visitor the accuracy of our theory. It was made standard practice. It is still used.

When the function at Yuma was changed from aerial gunnery to twin-engine pilot instruction, I asked for and received assignment to the Ferry Command in New Castle, Delaware. This was a new group composed of overage pilots organized to deliver aircraft and supplies to every war theater. It wasn't a very glamorous job, but I was still trying to pull strings to get into the four-engine Bomber Command. At least I got to the war zones.

I think I was among the first to qualify as a service pilot because of my familiarity with the AT-6. I took a test ride and passed. Later in the same year I received my regular Army wings, which made it possible for me to become a command pilot eventually.

The Ferry Command established two airlines to deliver supplies to all the European theaters. One was known as Crescent; the other, Fireball.

Crescent operated out of LaGuardia Field, New York. Our equipment was the C-54—the military version of the DC-4. We flew to Newfoundland, then to the Azores, across North Africa, to Karachi and Pakistan.

Fireball operated from Miami, using the C-87, a cargo version of the four-engine B-24 bomber. Fireball flew the South Atlantic route from Miami to Natal, Brazil, to Lagos, Nigeria, and across Central Africa to Karachi.

From Karachi, Crescent went to Kharagpur, India, and Fireball to Chabua. The first B-29s were based at Kharagpur, which is about seventy miles west of Calcutta. Our mission was to supply engines and other equipment. Eventually I became chief pilot for both these supply airlines.

At Luke and in Yuma we trained many Chinese cadets. Some of them became my fast friends. When I eventually reached the India-Burma Theater, I discovered to my delight that many of the Chinese pilots we had trained in Arizona were flying combat here.

In the European, African, and Far East theaters, there was an urgent need for fighter aircraft—single-engine, high-performance pursuit planes to protect our bombers from the enemy's attacking fighters. The Ferry Command was asked to help with this problem.

Auxiliary fuel tanks were designed to increase the range of the single-engine airplanes. I volunteered to participate in the first aerial delivery of what was then our newest fighting plane, the P-47 Thunderbolt, to England. This airplane was powered with a single Pratt-Whitney radial engine. The frontal resistance of the big engine was a drawback. The 47's high performance was due entirely to its horsepower.

I'll never forget the briefing we got before that flight. The Ferry Command had been delivering twin-engine aricraft across the North Atlantic, but this was to be the first attempt to ferry a pursuit plane. Our instructor explained how we could use the life raft if it became necessary. He told us about the nice warm clothing we would be wearing and what great protection the accompanying aircraft would provide. Then he said, "Well, fellas, if you have to bail out or if you have to put her down in the ocean, don't worry too much. You'll have about twenty minutes to live, and there's no way we can rescue you."

Nine of us left New York in nine P-47s just off the production line. Our route took us over the North Atlantic to Newfoundland, from there to Greenland, then to Iceland, to our destination in northern Scotland. By today's standards our navigational aids were extremely primitive, but we made it. We did lose one plane when the pilot ground-looped landing at a refueling stop, but he wasn't hurt.

We thought this first experimental ferry delivery was a success, but apparently the Air Forces brass thought otherwise, and all the rest of the single-engine pursuit planes we sent to the European theater were delivered by ship.

On the Crescent and Fireball we had our share of problems with instruments that malfunctioned, inaccurate weather forecasts, and the autopilots, which never seemed to work just right. But for anyone who enjoys flying as much as I do, it was pretty routine. In retrospect, I can now recognize that I was a very brash, nonconforming chief pilot. I did some things which were strictly against the rules. Our planes went over loaded with supplies and then flew home empty. When I discovered that servicemen returning home from this faraway theater were frequently delayed for as much as three months in Karachi waiting for sea transport, I offered them space on our empty return flights to the States. A senior inspector in the Air Forces whom I had first met at Yuma came through to examine our operation and was horrified. He ordered me to send the planes home empty. I followed orders as long as he was at our base. When he left, we let the weary home-bound troops hitchhike rides whenever we had space available.

When I arrived in India, we were under orders to use native mechanics to service the planes. There were incredible delays and snafus. A senior officer came into Kharagpur in a C-54 to inspect and review our operations. As he was preparing to leave, we saw an Indian mechanic—a member of the flight line crew—pumping gasoline into the oil reservoirs on the colonel's aircraft. He was outraged. I told him it was not unusual for these untrained native mechanics to make such errors.

He wanted to know how long it would take us to restore the C-54 to flying condition. I said that with the native help available it would probably take a month. The colonel immediately requisitioned one of our standby C-54s. Within two weeks we had a full complement of GI mechanics assigned to service our aircraft.

I first met General Curtis LeMay at Kharagpur. I had come in with a C-54 carrying two replacement engines for the B-29s. There was no forklift at the field to unload my cargo. I walked along the flight line until I encountered a rather short, heavyset fellow with a cigar in his mouth. I introduced myself and explained the problem.

He said he was Curt LeMay and not to worry about unloading those engines, just wait a few minutes.

LeMay climbed into a C-46, flew to Calcutta, and returned in about three hours with two forklifts. If ever an officer personified the can-do motto of the Air Force, that man was General Curtis Lemay—a tremendous pilot, a superior tactician, and a totally dedicated patriot.

In the Burma Theater I helped train Chinese pilots to fly our newest pursuit aircraft, the P-40. I was qualified to fly the B-29s. I repeatedly requested a transfer to the Bomber Command, but no one would listen to me.

At the end of my tour in India, I was reassigned to a fighter replacement and retraining unit in California, where I served until the end of the war. I was mustered out in November 1945 with the request that I form an Air National Guard Unit in Arizona. To serve in the Guard, I had to take a reduction in rank from colonel to captain. We organized the 197th Fighter Squadron. I requested that we be permitted to make it a nonsegregated military unit. This request was granted.

For almost five years military affairs had occupied my undivided attention. When one sits at the controls of an aircraft on a long ferry flight or cargo run, there is time to think. How did we blunder into the bloodshed and waste of war? How could it be avoided in the future?

I became convinced the isolationist mood of the country after World War I, not the harsh terms of the Treaty of Versailles, had made World War II inevitable. If we had maintained our military superiority throughout the twenties and thirties, President Roosevelt could have warned Hitler not to invade any neutral countries, and that warning would have been heeded.

Throughout history civilian populations and political rulers have talked of peace. We have never been free of war. The soldier, whose profession is war, understands that peace must be enforced by superior military might. The certainty of defeat is the only effective deterrent we can use to maintain peace. Furthermore, we can be strong without being aggressive.

As a member of the victorious alliance after World War I, we made no claim for new territory. We didn't demand or extract reparations. After World War II we provided the money and the know-how to rebuild the economies of Western Europe and Japan. To label the United States of America as an aggressor is a distortion of history.

CHAPTER 5

One Thing Led to Another

When I came home in 1945, it took some time to appreciate all the subtle changes which had taken place during the war years I was away. There weren't any new buildings. There had been no major expansion in the residential areas. But Phoenix wasn't the same. There was a change in attitude, in spirit. We had lost our isolated parochialism and some of that casual *mañana* attitude which had been a part of our inheritance. The population hadn't increased. In fact, there were 12,000 fewer Arizonans registered to vote in 1946 than there had been in 1940.

Activating the Arizona wing of the Air National Guard, getting reacquainted with my family, and trying to adjust to the role of a civilian merchant occupied all my time that first year. In 1946 Governor Sidney P. Osborn, a Democrat, asked me to serve on the Arizona Colorado River Commission. Our goal was to secure congresssional authorization for the Central Arizona Project.

I was thirty-seven years old. Every soldier who has ever served in time of war has cause to speculate about the politics which produced the conflict. Because of my uncle Morris and my admiration for him, I had been privileged to know something about the inner workings of our political system. I had never been involved in a purely political dispute between two factions, in which

respectable men of good conscience adopted opposite positions
and then employed all the tools available to achieve their objective—money, passion, prejudice, and at times outright falsehoods.

To understand the magnitude of the political war for water in
which I found myself a participant, it is necessary to review briefly
the history of reclamation in the western half of this nation. All
the Rocky Mountain states and California are dependent on stored
water for the irrigation of agriculture. Seven states—Wyoming,
Colorado, Utah, Nevada, New Mexico, Arizona, and California—
contribute to or divert water from the Colorado River system. It
is the Southwest's last great water hole.

In 1919 the governor of Utah called a conference of representatives of basin states to discuss utilization of this regional re-
source. Two years later Congress authorized the formation of an
interstate pact. Delegates gathered in Washington in 1922 to organize; Secretary of Commerce Herbert Hoover was named chairman. They then adjourned to Santa Fe, New Mexico, to write the
law of the river now known as the Santa Fe Compact.

This interstate agreement attempted to divide the water equi-
tably among the basin states, but the conferees did not feel competent to make specific allocations to any state. So what they did
was to allocate 7.5 million acre-feet of mainstream flow to the
three lower basin states—Arizona, California, and Nevada—and
set aside an equal amount for the upper basin. (An acre-foot of
water is enough to cover an acre of ground to a depth of one foot,
approximately 325,000 gallons.)

The compact did not really settle anything. The individual
states were left to fight it out for their share. The controversy
claimed headlines in the first three months of 1977, when newly
elected President Jimmy Carter threatened to halt funding for the
Central Arizona Project, which had been authorized by Congress
in 1967.

When the Boulder Canyon Project Act authorizing the construction of Hoover Dam was passed by the Congress in December
1928, Carl Hayden was a powerful figure in the U.S. Senate. He
insisted the legislation contain a binding covenant between the
United States and the State of California requiring California to
limit its use of water from the river to an amount not exceeding
4.4 million acre-feet of the water allocated to the lower basin
states and not more than one-half of any excess or surplus water

unapportioned by the compact. Hayden maintained this self-limitation was essential to protect the interests of the other six basin states, including Arizona.

When I was appointed to the Colorado River Commission, Hayden was chairman of the Senate Interior Committee. He provided me with an extensive background on the history of the Santa Fe Compact and our struggle with California. My task was to help mobilize public sentiment throughout Arizona in support of our delegation's efforts in Congress to secure authorization of the Central Arizona Project for diversion of Arizona's share of Colorado water into central Arizona.

The California interests, seeking to prevent diversion of any Colorado River water to Arizona, employed gross exaggeration and outright falsehood. For almost twenty-five years their delaying tactics were successful. Then the Supreme Court decided in favor of Arizona. The Central Arizona Project was authorized by Congress in 1967. It is under construction and will be completed in the early 1980s.

This was my first exposure to the world of real politics. It led me to understand that in such struggles equity and truth are relatively impotent. It is power at the ballot box, power in the banking circles, and power in the halls of academia which determine the outcome of such disputes.

My first participation in matters political was on a grand scale, embracing two states directly, the other five basin states indirectly, and reaching into the Congress of the United States. My next step took me into the rather limited theater of municipal politics.

Before the war Phoenix was an isolated desert community. The population was less than 50,000. The city covered seven square miles. Municipal government was conducted by five city commissioners, who elected one of their members to serve as mayor. The mayor, with the support of two members of the Council, could hire or fire the city manager, the chief of police, or anyone else. As a result of this arrangement, there was a new coalition coming to power every few months. The average term of a city manager was less than twelve months. There had been some graft and some scandal.

In common with most western cities in the days of my youth, Phoenix had a segregated red-light district. The madams and their pimps were well known to the local citizens and to the police.

The community was not scandalized by the presence of these "working girls." There was no connection with organized crime.

Four pilot training schools were established adjacent to Phoenix at the outset of the war. The whorehouses expanded to take care of this new clientele. An alarming high incidence of venereal disease resulted in Phoenix's being placed off limits to military personnel in 1943.

According to local insiders, some members of the City Council demanded and received under-the-table protection payoffs. Nowadays, when anyone in Phoenix talks about the reform movement we started in 1947, they invariably mention open prostitution. This was only one minor manifestation of the problems that existed. What we set out to correct was inefficient city management, totally incapable of delivering the kind of police protection, fire protection, and sanitary services required by our exploding population.

The mayor of Phoenix, a Democrat named Ray Busey, directed public attention to the instability of civil government and the opportunities presented for graft and corruption. Busey, a likable man, appointed a citizen's committee to revise the charter. Charles Bernstein, a prominent jurist who was later to serve on the Arizona State Supreme Court, was named chairman.

This was the beginning of municipal reform and my introduction to local politics. The forty members of the Charter Government Committee were representative of the community—doctors, farmers, lawyers, bankers, and real estate men. I was named to serve, along with my friends Harry and Newt Rosenzweig.

It didn't take us long to discover the Phoenix city charter was woefully deficient. It might have been adequate for a city of 20,000, but our population was rapidly approaching 100,000.

The old charter vested complete control of city operations in the Council. The one we wrote transferred responsibility for the day-to-day activities of the city administration to a professional manager. Under the old charter the manager had served at the whim of the Council. We said he could only be fired for cause. Then we provided for the election of six councilmen at large and a mayor to be chosen by the voters. We said no councilman, not even the mayor, could directly approach a city employee with a request for service or for a favor. We established a separate finance department to oversee tax collections and disbursements. It was a good, solid piece of work. The people of Phoenix adopted the new charter in a special election in 1948. We then elected a new mayor, a new Council, and I thought our job was done. It wasn't.

The new mayor, a competent, principled attorney, tried to implement the provisions of the new charter. His Council would have none of it. They preferred the old political system.

We had been naïve. We had thought it necessary only to reform the charter; in truth, no written document is of much value unless the people elected to power are faithful to that document. This conclusion, reached at the beginning of my entrance into the political world, has been reinforced by my experience in the Congress. In the past thirty years, we have, as a result of executive action, congressional inattention, and a passel of Supreme Court decisions, radically altered the intention of the Founding Fathers expressed in the Constitution of the United States.

Dismayed at this turn of events, but not willing to concede defeat, we reconvened the citizen group, named it the Charter Government Committee, and prepared to nominate six new candidates for Council who would be committed to the new charter. The committee approached a number of men and women we thought competent to serve on the Council. Most of them turned us down. The time grew short. Other members of the committee urged me to agree to be a candidate.

The war had been over for four years. I was nominally president of Goldwater's, but the problems of merchandising no longer commanded my interest as they had in those early days. Public questions occupied my mind. I was disturbed by my discoveries that greed and power oftentimes made the wheels go around. Because the decision I made then was the true turning point in my life, I have reflected many times on that moment. I had no intentions of devoting my life to public service. I certainly didn't think I was any more competent than the man next door to serve on the City Council. I was angered at the people who had turned us down. I remembered, "All that is necesaary for evil to triumph is for good men to do nothing." I agreed to become a candidate. We won. The city government of Phoenix is now respected nationwide for its excellence, its impartiality, its efficiency, and its economy.

I enjoyed the campaigning, and there was considerable satisfaction in winning; but my plan was to serve two years, perhaps four, and then return to the store. I was a registered Republican, and the Democrats outnumbered us about ten to one. Since statehood in 1912, the Democratic party had held a monopoly on political power. In that thirty-eight-year period only two Republicans had been elected governor, and only one Republican was sent to the national Congress. The Democratic party primaries held in September were bloody free-for-alls with the winner coasting to victory in the general election.

At the end of World War II Arizona's population began to increase as a result of immigration from the eastern states. Many of the newcomers had learned to fly at one of the military airfields in Arizona and returned when the war was over. Old-timers advised these newcomers to register in the Democratic party because the Democratic primaries were the only real contests. This was an accepted fact of life. As a consequence of this very practical, conventional wisdom, registration in the Democratic party showed sizable increases during those years of growth following the war. But the figures were misleading—there were a lot of good Republicans masquerading under the Democratic party label in order to participate in the primaries.

In 1950 there was considerable dissatisfaction over the Korean War, which had started in June of that year. The Republican state chairman for Arizona was a former Illinois mayor named Charlie Garland, who was unwilling to accept as an article of faith that a Republican could never win statewide office. Garland had come to Phoenix to manage a newly established radio station. He got the job of state chairman by breathing new life into the few diehards who stubbornly registered Republican and perhaps because no one else really wanted it.

Garland and author Clarence Budington Kelland, who was our Republican national committeeman, called attention to the obvious fact that a lot of registered Democrats had voted for Republican presidential candidates. They also thought there was an opportunity to take advantage of a local conflict which might divide the normal Democratic majority. The Democrats had a full field of aspirants for the nomination for governor. The front-runner was an attractive lady named Ana Frohmiller, who had earned quite a following as a result of her long and excellent service as state auditor.

Garland and Kelland didn't believe the Arizona electorate was quite ready for a woman governor. They thought it was time to nominate a strong, serious Republican candidate. If Mrs. Frohmiller won the Democratic nomination, they argued, we might have a chance to capture the state's highest office for the first time since 1928, when a Republican, John C. Phillips, rode into office on the coattails of Herbert Hoover.

My uncle Morris, the only active politician in the Goldwater family, had been a leader in the Democratic party most of his life. My father, although not politically active, was a registered Democrat. My Midwestern mother was a staunch Republican. A number of people have attributed my decision to register in the Republican party as a result of maternal influence. Not so. All my life I have had strong sympathy for the underdog. The Democratic party had ruled Arizona with an arrogance that offended me. My decision to register as a Republican was an act of defiance.

If I hadn't been a registered Republican, my dissatisfaction with President Roosevelt would have caused me to change my registration. His programs never quite lived up to his promises. As a merchant I deeply resented the provisions in the National Recovery Act which gave the federal government the power to impose its will on private business. I think the foundations of my political philosophy were rooted in my resentment against the New Deal, but it was an instinctive rather than a reasoned reaction. The philosophical convictions which have guided my life were acquired over a period of years commencing with my first experience in city government.

Despite the fact we used to say facetiously the Republicans could hold their state convention in a telephone booth, Garland and Kelland were determined to find a gubernatorial candidate who would offer more than token opposition to the Democratic nominee. The man they had in mind was a local broadcaster named Howard Pyle. Pyle had gone overseas as a war correspondent. He had a twenty-year history as a radio newscaster on the most important station in the state. He had a beautiful speaking voice; he was articulate and very high in name identification.

Pyle agreed to become a candidate, and he asked me to help with his campaign. Mostly my help consisted in flying him all over the state and introducing him to the people I had met when I was promoting the Central Arizona Project.

Some writers of local political history have suggested that Pyle really wanted to be a candidate for the United States Senate in 1952 and that I wanted to run for governor in 1950. There is no truth in this construction. At the time I had no plans for seeking higher political office.

Charlie Garland's predictions turned out to be correct. After a bitter primary fight, the Democrats nominated Ana Frohmiller. Pyle never mentioned her name, waged no campaign against her personally. The voters just weren't ready for a woman governor. Pyle won.

When Pyle took office, both houses of the state legislature were controlled by the Democratic party. Three months later he told me he had picked the wrong target. He said the power was in the legislature. He said any one of the cow-county senators could do more to help or harm state government than the governor could do.

As the months went by, I began to believe Pyle was right in his assessment. The Arizona Constitution was purposely written to place authority for state government in the hands of the legislature. But most Republicans were so pleased to have a member of their party in the governor's office they didn't complain. Perhaps they didn't even notice that nothing much had changed except the name of the man in the governor's chair.

When I was flying Pyle around the state, it did occur to me that I might like to be governor of Arizona one day. But after watching his programs frustrated by Democrats in control of the legislature, I recognized that the executive branch of government was powerless to act when confronted by a hostile legislative branch.

As the Korean War dragged on, more and more of the people I talked with in Arizona expressed dissatisfaction with the national government. They didn't like the no-win war we were fighting in Korea. They objected to the giveaways of the Marshall Plan.

The Reconstruction Finance Corporation, a governmental agency created under Franklin D. Roosevelt to make loans to businesses hard hit by the Depression, was operated until 1945 by Texas banker Jesse Jones. Jones was a hard-nosed, practical, knowledgeable financier. For the years he was in control, there was never a hint of scandal; but Jones had left in 1945, and appointees of Harry S. Truman took over.

In 1951 Democratic Senator J. William Fulbright of Arkansas was named chairman of a subcommittee of the Banking and Currency Committee to investigate alleged irregularities in the RFC and one of its subsidiaries, the Defense Plants Corporation. The President first condemned the Fulbright committee and then belatedly promised to reorganize the RFC, but not until it had been revealed that some politicians close to the White House had benefited financially.

Senator John J. Williams of Delaware did some digging into the IRS and discovered that a number of the collectors of internal revenue were involved in tax fixing and bribery. The list of five-percenters and bribe takers increased almost daily. Fifteen top officials of IRS were finally indicted or removed for their mishandling of tax collections. Public indignation was constantly fed with the revelations of new crimes and the names of new perpetrators.

I had developed considerable admiration for President Harry Truman after his decisive action to bring World War II to an end. I think what I found most attractive about the man was that when confronted with a problem, he made quick, positive decisions without any attempt to equivocate or rationalize. I felt we always knew where we stood with Harry in the White House. I don't know whether he actually condoned all the graft that took place during his administration or whether his reaction was just a demonstration of loyalty to his friends and appointees, but the thievery, the cover-up, the proprietary attitude of the people close to Truman were more than I could tolerate.

Our rapid liquidation and dismantlement of the most powerful military machine ever assembled distressed me. Perfectly good, usable war matériel was declared surplus and disposed of at give-away prices. The favored purchasers of war surplus made millions, and all those I knew personally were members of the Democratic party power clique.

To appreciate the magnitude of the tragedy of the Korean War, it is necessary to understand how the conflict started. As early as 1905 Japan had gained control of Korea. In 1910 the formal treaty was signed that annexed the Korean peninsula to Japan. At the Potsdam Conference, July, 1945, the thirty-eighth parallel was designated as the line dividing the Soviet and the American occupation of Korea. Russian troops entered the country on August 10, 1945. Our troops entered in September, 1945. When the Russian and American troops withdrew in 1949 the country was divided. North Korea was openly communist; South Korea was a democratic republic seeking to emulate the Western nations.

Although the Japanese had surrendered to MacArthur in 1946, the war in China had continued. We were told that Chou En-lai and Mao Tse-tung were amiable, benevolent reformers determined to free the Chinese people from the oppressive, corrupt government of Chiang Kai-shek. General George C. Marshall ordered Chiang to admit Chou and Mao into a coalition government. When Chiang refused, we withdrew American logistic support. Chiang was forced to flee to Formosa, and mainland China came under communist rule. The agrarian reformers, Mao and Chou, executed at least 50 million Chinese who refused to cooperate with the communists.

The success of the Red Chinese, coupled with the declaration by our State Department that the island of Formosa and Korea were outside the defense perimeters of the United States, encouraged the North Koreans to attack the South. This they did on Sunday, June 25, 1950. The Reds in North Korea had an army of more than 200,000 equipped with the latest Russian offensive weapons. South Korea had only about 100,000 poorly equipped militiamen.

The Security Council of the UN met in emergency session. The United States proposed a resolution condemning the actions of the North Korean forces and calling for immediate cessation of hostilities and the withdrawal of North Korean troops to the thirty-eighth parallel. The resolution requested that the United Nations' temporary commission on Korea communicate its full considered recommendations on the situation at once and called on every member to render every assistance to the United Nations in the execution of the resolution and to refrain from giving assistance to the North Koreans.

President Harry Truman interpreted the UN action as an authorization to assist the South Koreans militarily. General MacArthur was ordered to use the Navy and the Air Force to assist South Korean defenses and to isolate the Nationalist-held island of Formosa from the Chinese mainland.

As the fighting continued, with the United States providing most of the men and material, it became apparent the politicians in Washington and the UN were committed to a no-win policy. General MacArthur's brilliant end run to Inchon, considered by many military experts the greatest strategic success of modern times, cut the invader's supply lines and foreclosed the possibility of a communist victory. The Red Chinese, who along with the Russians had been supplying weapons and other material to the North Koreans, entered the war. They operated from sanctuaries north of the Yalu River—bases which MacArthur was not permitted to destroy.

We could have taken all of Korea and reunited this divided country. The politicians, fearful of provoking a full-scale conflict with the Red Chinese and Russia, refused to let MacArthur pursue victory.

It should be remembered we were the sole possessors of the atomic bomb. Our air and sea power was vastly superior to anything the communists had. Most of the military leaders I served with during World War II were bitterly critical of our desertion of Chiang. They saw the invasion of South Korea by the communists as an opportunity to reestablish freedom and democracy in that part of the world.

When Harry Truman relieved General Douglas MacArthur of his command on April 11, 1951, because the general was committed to victory, not stalemate, I suddenly realized the future of freedom was in the hands of the Washington politicians. I didn't question the President's right to fire MacArthur. I believe the Commander in Chief and the civilian authority is and should be paramount to any military commander. What troubled me was the apparent loss of our once-strong commitment to defend freedom at any cost.

The Korean War cost us 137,051 casualties—25,604 killed; 103,492 wounded; 7,955 missing. In our history the President has called out the troops some two hundred times. We have officially declared war only five times. Two of these declarations had to do with World War II. Never before in our history had we refused to pursue victory.

It appeared to me that American foreign policy had embraced appeasement and deserted principle. Was it the result of poor judgment, or was it by design? Deeply dissatisfied with the conduct of American policy, both foreign and domestic, I began to think about running for the United States Senate.

CHAPTER 6

I Decide to Pay the Rent

In the 1964 presidential election President Lyndon Johnson's hatchet men pictured me as a reckless, "spur-of-the-moment activist," a man motivated more by impulse than by reason. A goodly number of political railbirds in Arizona classified my decision to run for the United States Senate in 1952 as a rash, quixotic, unreasoned act. They cited the Democratic party's numerical superiority, said the election of Howard Pyle in 1950 had been a fluke, and called my candidacy a lost cause. I didn't think so— a long shot certainly, but winning was not an impossibility.

When I told Peggy in the fall of 1951 I was seriously considering becoming a candidate for the Senate, she said she hoped I wouldn't do it. She said all my political beliefs were on the wrong side of the fence, that New Deal Democrats were in control of the nation and the national press. Gentle, reserved, almost shy, my wife is, and always has been, a very private person. She avoids arguments, never harbors a grudge, and is extremely charitable in her attitude toward others.

She pointed out that politics divides families and destroys friendships. She said I was too direct in my manner of thinking and speaking to make a success in public office. She thought she would find the social life in Washington, D.C., personally distasteful. She would much rather live in Arizona. She said I had demonstrated great talent as a merchandiser of women's fashions. She wasn't at all sure my ideas about government would sell.

I told her we are all required to pay rent for the space we occupy on this earth. I said the good Lord had been most gracious to us, and perhaps by helping to preserve our freedoms, I could make a real contribution. She said if I really felt that way about it to go ahead. She would do whatever she could to help.

The first move was to hire a campaign manager. My experience with Howard Pyle taught me that a candidate who must always be on the go—speaking, shaking hands, traveling—has no time to manage his own campaign. He can't make objective judgments. He can't even schedule his own appearances to the best advantage. The man I wanted was Steve Shadegg. We weren't close personal friends, but in the Phoenix of the 1940s it was possible to know a lot of people even if you didn't see them very often.

I knew Steve had helped Carl Hayden win reelection to the United States Senate in 1950. I also knew he had handled the election campaigns for all the men who had been elected sheriff since 1936. In those years the race for sheriff of Maricopa County was the hottest political contest in the state. Steve was active in community affairs, owned and operated a small manufacturing business, and had written for radio, motion pictures, and magazines. He had written the booklet on the Central Arizona Project when I was working on that project. His wife worked with Peggy in the establishment of a Planned Parenthood clinic in Phoenix. They both were members of the Junior League. In 1951 the Phoenix Advertising Club had named Steve "Phoenix Man of the year," an honor which they had given to me in 1949 and to Howard Pyle in 1950.

In the spring of 1952, late February or early March, I went to Steve's office and told him I thought I would run for the United States Senate as a Republican if he would run my campaign. We talked for more than two hours. Although Steve was a registered Democrat, he shared my political opinions, was concerned about the enlargement of federal government and the diminution of personal freedom.

He told me he had been approached by Joseph Duke, then the sergeant at arms of the United States Senate, with a request to run

Senator Ernest McFarland's campaign. Steve had worked with Duke on the Hayden campaign in 1950, and enjoyed that association, but he wasn't impressed with McFarland's support of the New Deal and the Fair Deal. He told Duke he wouldn't take the job.

I gave him a couple of days to think it over; then I went back to see him. Before I left his office that afternoon, Steve said he would run my campaign if I would agree not to make any off-the-cuff speeches or adopt any positions we hadn't discussed in advance.

I remember asking him if he was afraid that in some moment of stress I might say something which would damage the campaign. He said yes, but that was only a part of it, that Bob Creighton and Senator Hayden had taught him to weigh every proposed statement or action against the questions: Is this necessary? What can we expect to gain politically if we do it? What is the liability or potential loss?

Bob Creighton was the publisher of a political weekly newspaper and a longtime friend of mine; Hayden, Arizona's most successful politician. Their advice seemed worth taking.

The popularity of Harry Truman was on a steady decline. The people didn't like the Korean War or the firing of MacArthur. McFarland was Truman's Majority Leader in the U.S. Senate. The strategy we finally adopted was simple and straightforward—tie McFarland to Truman, condemn the no-win war in Korea, expose the scandals in Truman's official family, and talk about high taxes and government waste.

In my visits with Republicans around the state I discovered a great deal of sentiment favoring Senator Robert A. Taft of Ohio for the presidential nomination. A lot of old-time Republicans regarded General Eisenhower as a Johnny-come-lately to both the Republican party and to politics.

When we held our state convention to select delegates to go to Chicago, I believed they should go uninstructed. I argued that if we tied their hands, made them commit their vote in advance to a particular candidate, it would defeat the purpose of the national convention. I had never attended the nominating convention of a political party, and I had some very idealistic notions about open conventions and delegates making personal decisions.

This is one area where I have changed my mind. I now understand how important it is to be for the winner before the winner is nominated. This is particularly true of a small state with few electoral votes. If the man nominated goes on to win the office, he will always remember those early supporters.

I now realize my opposition to instructing the delegates for Taft was a political blunder which might have damaged my own chances for election. At the time I had great respect for the accomplishments of Senator Taft; and after serving with him in the Senate and becoming better acquainted with all his talents, I truly believe he was one of the ablest men ever to serve in that body.

I suppose I had some natural leanings toward Eisenhower, acquired during my five years in the military service. But junior officers rarely have that same awestruck attitude toward a Commander in Chief which is usually exhibited by the general public.

Ike's great talent was in his ability to get along with people. Ike would be a stronger candidate. He was a fresh face, an authentic hero, and, from what I had read of his public positions, I couldn't disagree with him. The results of that convention are ancient history.

Twelve years later, when I was nominated at San Francisco, my primary and convention opponents went home and sulked in their tents. In 1952 Taft urged all his supporters to help make Ike the next President. I have often wondered what might have happened if Bob Taft had chosen a different course. I am sure it was Taft's words of advice to his friends in Arizona which helped heal the wounds and unite the party.

I opened my general election campaign with a speech on the courthouse steps in Prescott on the evening of September 18, 1952. Prescott was more than a sentimental choice. This seat of Yavapai County is still a supply center for the ranchers in northern Arizona. Cattlemen are an independent, hardy lot. If I could win their support, we knew it would spill over into all the other counties.

We also knew we could get a good crowd. The Prescott people are accustomed to outdoor events at the courthouse, which is distinguished by a statue of Bucky O'Neill, Arizona's hero of the Spanish-American War, who rode with Teddy Roosevelt's Rough Riders. I guess I thought that in this community where Uncle Morris had lived for so long, where my father and mother had been married, I would be among friends.

At that time there was only one TV station in Arizona, and most of the people listened to the radio. We had arranged to have my opening speech broadcast on a statewide network. Because of the time requirements of the radio, I used a script, and I opened with praise for some of the social programs of the New Deal. I mentioned the Securities and Exchange Commission, the FDIC, Social Security, unemployment insurance, old age assistance, aid to dependent children and the blind, and the FHA. I said that "no responsible Republican, and especially not this Republican, has any intention or desire to abolish any one of them." I did point out some deficiencies such as the maladministration in the FHA, and then I talked about the presidential candidates.

Midway in the speech the light on the podium failed. I finished with the aid of a flashlight. When the lights went out, I ad-libbed something to the effect that it wasn't very nice of "Mac," to shut off the electricity. The remark got a laugh from the crowd, but, of course, my opponent had nothing to do with it.

In his appearances around the state McFarland had boasted he was one of the four most powerful men in government, being the Majority Leader of the majority party in the United States Senate. So I asked that night if he was willing to take 25 percent of the blame for the St. Louis collector of internal revenue who had been accused of misconduct or 25 percent of the blame for the Justice Department's criminal lawyer who had accepted a gift from a law firm representing a defendant in a government case? Would my opponent, the junior Senator, accept 25 percent of the responsibility for the increase in federal taxes, which had gone up 800 percent since 1941?

About thirty minutes before we were due to go on the air from the courthouse steps we learned from a reliable source that McFarland, speaking to a service club in his hometown, had defended the Korean War by saying it was a "cheap war." It wasn't costing much money, and we were killing nine Chinese for every American boy who died. In that same speech he said it was the Korean War which was making us prosperous. The friend who brought this information to us had been present when McFarland made the statements. He had managed to get a tape recording of the speech, which he played for us in the hotel room.

Everything McFarland said was true. Our casualties were infinitely less than those of the Chinese and North Koreans. The war had stimulated the economy, but Arizona boys were fighting and dying in Korea. My opponent had made a monumental error. I cut out some of the paragraphs I had planned to use and inserted the McFarland quote.

Federal spending, federal waste, high taxes, misbehavior in public office, and the war we weren't trying to win—these were the issues in 1952.

In the National Archives building in Washington, D.C., this message is carved in stone: "What is past is prologue." From my perspective of twenty-six years in public life, it is a bitter thing to realize that nothing has changed, although the spending and the taxing and the waste and the misbehavior have been on a much grander scale. Those reforms I talked about twenty-six years ago have not been implemented. Government now confiscates more than 46 percent of the national income. The bureaucracy is bloated with new employees, and the threat of war has not materially diminished.

Whenever I get to thinking that perhaps I would be a happier man today had I stayed in Phoenix to merchandise ladies' fashions, I come up against this solid truth: I have tried. No one ever said that life should be easy or that we must succeed in everything we undertake. But to recognize a wrong and not do anything about it is the coward's way out. Then I am comforted by the thought that perhaps by being here, by swimming upstream against the popular notions, I may have delayed the final disaster. Perhaps by my speaking of these things with utter candor, the people may yet be aroused to face the dangers confronting us.

It is never reasonable to attribute political victory to any single circumstance. In 1952 we had Ike and his wonderful grin and his warm, straightforward talk. The people of Arizona, despite the lopsided registration in the Democratic party, went for Ike. Ike's strong showing made it possible for me to win that first election by a little more than 7,000 votes. I also acquired some new enemies. As the Majority Leader of the Democratic party in the United States Senate, McFarland had attracted the support of the Washington press corps. They had predicted he would easily win re-election. I had upset their predictions and their plans. They resented me.

CHAPTER 7

To Support and Defend

The Constitution of the United States is one of the most radical documents ever offered to the world. It severely restricts the authority and power of he who governs and bestows a high degree of sovereignty on the governed. The Declaration of Independence declares that all men were intended by their Creator to be free.

On the third day of January, 1953, I swore before Almighty God to support and defend the Constitution of the United States. I have made other solemn promises in my life—when Peggy and I were married, when I entered the military service, when I joined the City Council—but this one moment stands out in my mind. My life has never been quite the same since that day.

Standing in that historic place with the venerable Carl Hayden as my sponsor, I felt an awesome kinship with the giants of our past whose debates and decisions shaped the nation. Hayden was seventy-six years old. My father and my uncle had counted him friend and supported him in all his campaigns. I had been only three years old when he was first elected to the Congress. Now I was forty-four.

The campaign for election had been a challenge, a contest. For me it had become a cause. Now I was here, a member of the United States Senate. The realization of this new responsibility overwhelmed me. Both fear and doubt were present in my mind. What did I know about the workings of this august legislative body? I wasn't a lawyer; I had never seriously studied political science. As an outsider, it had been easy enough to criticize. Could I now make my voice be heard? Or was I Don Quixote tilting at windmills?

Most of my life I have been blessed with abundant energy and a commitment to excellence in the activities which engaged my interest. I had been an indifferent scholar until I went to Staunton. When I got my first camera, I didn't just want to take pictures; I wanted to be a good photographer. The same with flying and merchandising.

On that long-ago Tuesday it came to me that I had spent the years of my life in pursuit of relatively unimportant goals. That I had been a good merchandiser was of importance only to me; that my photographs earned critical acclaim, that other skillful pilots counted me proficient had been pleasant and satisfying. This was reality. I had, as Edmund Burke once expressed it, assumed an obligation to and made a contract with the generations long since dead and generations not yet born.

With a Republican President in the White House and a Republican majority in both houses of the Congress, I had hoped to be named to the Senate Armed Services Committee. Styles Bridges of New Hampshire and Everett Dirksen of Illinois, along with Bob Taft of Ohio, explained to me that was too ambitious for a freshman. I was named to the committees on Banking and Commerce, Labor and Public Welfare.

Bob was the banker in our family. There was very little industry in Arizona. We had no labor problems, and I was sympathetic with the trade union movement. I wasn't at all pleased, but these were my assignments. I was determined to do the best I could.

The rules and traditions of the United States Senate are frequently criticized. In common with many other outside observers, I had some preconceptions. I thought the filibuster a dreadful waste of time. I couldn't understand senatorial courtesy. It seemed to me the seniority system of committee assignment gave unwarranted privilege to longevity and denied opportunity to the bright, young, more vigorous members.

Experience has changed my opinion. The filibuster does waste time, but the basic concept of our Constitution is to protect mi-

nority rights, to make all citizens equal before the law. The filibuster is the court of last resort for a minority. Like the sea anchor
of a sailing vessel in stormy weather, it prevents the momentary
majority from steamrolling over men of good conscience who hold
an opposite view. Without senatorial courtesy, which I had thought
hypocritical, debates in the body would be in danger of becoming
vindictive, vituperative outbursts, deserting reason and appealing
to passion.

The seniority system does promote some incompetents to positions of power only because of their length of service, but stability is vital to government. Along with Edmund Burke, I admire
gradualism, and, while the seniority system has kept some men
in power long after their energies were exhausted and their faculties
diminished, it does provide continuity.

Bob Taft, who had persuaded me to take the position on the
Labor Committee because he said we needed a conservative to
balance all the liberals, died on July 31, 1953. In the seven months
I had been privileged to serve with him I acquired a tremendous
respect for the man. I am forever indebted to Bob Taft, perhaps
most of all for his insistence that I serve on the Labor Committee,
which ultimately led to my appointment as a member of the Senate
Select Committee to Investigate Improper Activities in Labor/
Management Relations under the chairmanship of John McClellan
of Arkansas.

Being a member of the United States Senate is a learning
experience. It is inevitably disillusioning. I had expected the calling would ennoble the members. I encountered scholars and
dunces, rascals and egotists. The quality is not divided by the aisle
which separates Republican from Democrat.

There were pretenders and performers. Some were warm and
friendly; others, distant and aloof. Over the years I have developed
some admiration for the good qualities I found in those whose
performance was, in my view, unsatisfactory. I disagreed almost
violently with the political philosophy of Hubert Humphrey. But
he was warm and wonderful and, for the most part, a very direct
man. In our colloquies on the floor and in private discussions,
Hubert was an agile, resourceful opponent. He was never vindictive. After one of his long-winded harangues I suggested, "He had
probably been vaccinated with a phonograph needle." He responded by saying that I "would have been a great success in the

movies working for Eighteenth Century-Fox."

In the Senate I kept my mouth shut for the first four months. When we began debate on a proposal for price controls, I could no longer keep silent. Almost every page of history refutes the effectiveness of such governmental dictation. I told my colleagues such controls were first tried under the Code of Hammurabi, c. 1750 B.C., and were a failure. They had been tried again under the Roman Empire and in the Middle Ages. I am not vain enough to believe my maiden speech had much to do with the Senate's decision not to adopt price controls, but at least my personal views were on the record.

In July of the same year I again claimed the attention of my fellow Senators to speak out against deficit spending. This was in opposition to the requests of a Republican administration. Our national debt at that point was $272 billion; our gross national income only $340 billion. I predicted there would be a day of reckoning, that deficit spending would produce inflation, that wages would increase, and then prices would increase, and that never-ending spiral would ultimately lead to the collapse of the Republic.

I had come to Washington to try to correct what I considered to be the grievous errors of some people in the Truman administration. I thought their misbehavior deserved to be exposed and punished. I believed Ike's election had been more of a personal triumph than a victory for the Republican party and Republican principles. I thought the people should be told in a very emphatic way about all the failures of government under Roosevelt and Truman.

Some of the scandalous actions involved the misuse of public funds. Others, which I considered far more grievous, were in the area of national security. I believed the whole complex apparatus which had led us into what, in my opinion, amounted to a betrayal of the Nationalist forces of mainland China had been a tremendous concession to the communists and needed to be investigated.

Many of the postmortems of the 1952 election credited Ike's promise to go to Korea as one of the determining factors in his election, but the cease-fire which he produced was not a settlement. We experienced the long agony over the exchange of prisoners of war and became a party to the division of Korea.

As a freshman senator I was in no position to force such an

investigation of the foreign policy of the previous administration, but for the first time in our national history we had lost a war. Our prisoners had been brutally mishandled, brainwashed, and I considered the expansion of communism a major threat to the freedom of the world.

The one man in the United States Senate endeavoring to focus congessional attention on the foreign policy decisions of the Truman administration was Joe McCarthy of Wisconsin. I couldn't approve of some of the charges McCarthy was making, but there was a tremendous amount of evidence to support his allegations about the Institute of Pacific Relations. I supported McCarthy's efforts to bring this out in the open. He also called attention to the *Amerasia* case. In 1945 the FBI raided the magazine office in New York City and recovered some 1,700 secret and top secret documents obviously stolen or given to the magazine by some traitor in the State Department. Owen Lattimore, the academic who headed the IPR, was judged to be a "top Soviet espionage agent."

Joe McCarthy was unquestionably the most controversial man I ever served with in the Senate. The anti-anticommunists were outraged at his claims that some of the principals in the Truman and Roosevelt administrations actively served the communist cause.

McCarthy was supported by a strong, nationwide constituency, which included among others, Joseph P. Kennedy, the father of John, Bob, and Edward. A variety of respected, creditable federal employees disturbed by security risks in the national government provided McCarthy with a steady stream of inside information.

Two small examples of the hysteria of the time are offered here.

Mrs. Annie Lee Moss, a middle-aged black woman who worked for the federal government, was brought before the McCarthy committee and questioned about her communist affiliation. The eastern press featured bitter condemnations of McCarthy for his abuse of this obscure and "obviously innocent" government worker. Four years later the Subversive Activities Control Board, after assessing the data, concluded that Mrs. Moss was "an active member of the Communist Party." By this time McCarthy was dead.

The Peress case, which eventually led to McCarthy's downfall, arose out of charges that Dr. Irving M. Peress, an Army dentist who was openly sympathetic with the communist cause, had been given an honorable discharge.

The liberals mounted a skillfully orchestrated campaign of criticism against Joe McCarthy. And in the Army-McCarthy hearings the President sided with the Army. Substantive issues were lost. The hearing degenerated into a recital of personality failures. Some of the indivuduals on McCarthy's staff had gone overboard. The Senator himself appeared unable to temper his accusations. Under the pressure of criticism, he reacted angrily. It is probably true that McCarthy drank too much, overstated his case, and refused to compromise, but he wasn't alone in his beliefs.

When Senator Ralph Flanders introduced his resolution to censure McCarthy, I voted with twenty-one other Republicans against the adoption of that resolution. It passed. John Kennedy, who some say owed his election to McCarthy's refusal to come into Massachusetts and campaign for Lodge, did not vote.

McCarthy was destroyed. The liberals added a new adjective to our lexicon—McCarthyism.

No one seemed to notice that after the furor faded the Army's top secret operations at Fort Monmouth, New Jersey, which had been the subject of one of McCarthy's attacks, were quietly moved to Fort Huachuca, Arizona. Carl Hayden, who in January 1955 became chairman of the powerful Appropriations Committee of the United States Senate, told me privately Monmouth had been moved because he and other members of the majority Democratic party were convinced security at Monmouth had been penetrated. They didn't want to admit that McCarthy was right in his accusations. Their only alternative was to move the installation from New Jersey to a new location in Arizona.

I can now reveal without danger of embarrassing others that it was McCarthy's stubborn refusal to make any compromise which finally led to his downfall. When the motion to censure McCarthy was being debated on the floor, I was approached by Senator Price Daniel of Texas. The Senator told me that if I could persuade McCarthy to sign letters of apology to two members of the Senate who believed McCarthy had insulted them, the South would vote against the censure.

I contacted McCarthy's attorney, Edward Bennett Williams. The two of us drove out to Bethesda Hospital, where McCarthy was undergoing treatment. Because our mission was a very sensitive one, we thought it best to attempt to avoid being seen. We walked up thirteen flights of stairs, slipped past the nurses' station, and entered McCarthy's room. I repeated what Price Daniel had said and offered him the two letters of apology Edward Bennett Williams had written for his signature.

I told Joe that if he signed one of the letters, it might be sufficient; if he signed them both, I had the word of Senator Daniel that the southern bloc would stand by him. McCarthy read the letters carefully. They were short, mild in their language, and regretted a discourtesy without really conceding any substantive error on McCarthy's part.

Williams urged him to sign, arguing that it really wasn't a retreat from principle and warning that his critics in the Senate probably had enough votes to pass the censure resolution. This upset McCarthy. He threw the pen across the room, started swearing at both of us, and pounded the table.

The commotion brought the floor nurse. She called the doctor, who, in turn, called the admiral in charge of the hospital. The admiral demanded to know what in the hell we were doing in his hospital and threatened to have us arrested by the Shore Patrol.

I finally convinced him I was a United States Senator by the name of Goldwater, that Mr. Williams was Senator McCarthy's lawyer, and that we were there in the interest of Senator McCarthy. He didn't call the Shore Patrol, but he did tell us to get out of his hospital and not to come back and not to try to see his patient without first securing permission.

In the Eighty-third Congress I consistently voted against spending programs, agency enlargement, many times against bills sponsored by fellow Republicans.

I had reluctantly accepted assignment to the Senate Labor Committee. As I attended the meetings and listened to discussions, my interest increased. Michael J. Bernstein, a lawyer and Republican counsel on the committee, with what I now recognize as great patience, introduced me to the hard, brutal inside story. I became persuaded that certain labor bosses in their insatiable reach for greater power were abusing the rank and file of their unions.

In general this abuse took two directions—one, the wrongful conversion of union funds for the enrichment of labor bosses,

Jimmy Hoffa, president of the powerful Teamsters Union, being an example of this group; and the other, the utilization of union money and union manpower for political purposes. In this field Walter Reuther was the dominant figure.

I have instinctively and consistently resisted compulsion whenever and wherever it has been employed against individual Americans. Now I discovered that men were being forced to join unions against their will, forced to pay dues with the rates established by the union hierarchy, and prevented from having any voice in how union dues should be spent. This was especially true when unions supported political candidates. I discovered that labor unions were a special privileged class, operating outside the rules which control most of industry and all individuals.

The strike against the Kohler Company of Wisconsin was an unnecessary display of brutal, destructive union power. It was financed by funds from Reuther's United Auto Workers Union and disfigured by repeated acts of violence and defiance of the courts.

This outrageous, and to me quite clearly criminal, behavior was something I would not tolerate. Apparently the Senate was of the same opinion. A special subcommittee was named to investigate the alleged improper activities in the labor or management field. John McClellan of Arkansas was named chairman; Irving Ives of New York, vice-chairman. Other members were Patrick McNamara, John F. Kennedy, Sam J. Ervin, and Republicans Karl Mundt and Barry Goldwater.

Jack Kennedy had come to the Senate at the same time I did. We were on the opposite sides of the aisle, but I found him likable, aggressive, and consistent in his support of the liberal Democratic policies. His brother Robert was named chief counsel to the select committee. The Kennedys were after Jimmy Hoffa, and they pursued him relentlessly. I was never able to interest the committee counsel in making a full investigation of what I regarded as the transgressions of Walter Reuther and the United Auto Workers.

At first I attributed the Kennedys' position on this matter as a reflection of their long association with the Americans for Democratic Action. Reuther was well tailored, well spoken, a man who would be at ease in the cultured drawing rooms of the wealthy. Hoffa was blunt, coarse, lacking in grace and grammar. He wanted money for himself and for his members; Walter Reuther lusted for power. Hoffa was the muscle man; Reuther, the politician.

The reason Bobby and Jack were protecting Walter Reuther became obvious to me. Their plan was to make Jack President. Reuther and the UAW could help them gain that objective.

In the Eighty-third Congress, January 3, 1953, to January 3, 1955, the Republicans held a majority in both houses. When the Senate met to organize in January 1955, Wayne Morse of Oregon, who had been elected as a Republican in 1950, voted with the Democrats. This single switch vote gave the Democrats control of the Senate and the chairmanships of all committees. The Republicans have never been able to regain a majority.

Ike served six more years in the White House. In 1968, after eight years of Kennedy-Johnson, Nixon was elected, and we had Rebublican Presidents for eight more years. But throughout this entire period the Democrats have controlled the Congress. This one-party rule is, to my mind, the most significant political fact essential to understanding the history of the past three decades. The White House may recommend and execute policy—the Congress runs the country.

I had not wanted to serve on the Labor Committee. Now I was embroiled in a struggle distinctly not of my own choosing. Because of my criticism of Reuther, the press branded me as antilabor. My disagreements with John Kennedy were philosophical; with Bobby they were technical and procedural. This adversary role suddenly gave me unexpected new visibility in Washington, and, in that respect, it was all very beneficial to my career.

In early 1957 I received a call from the White House. I was told the President wanted me to come to lunch so that we could discuss ways in which he could help me in my campaign for reelection in 1958.

I have never minimized the beneficial effect of Ike's coattails in 1952. Ike had carried Arizona when he ran for reelection in 1956. His help in 1958 would be a magnificent plus in my campaign for reelection. But I politely declined the luncheon invitation. The reason? I had prepared and planned to deliver a speech on the Senate floor strongly critical of the Eisenhower administration.

I opened the speech with an expression of regret that I was compelled to wage a battle against the same elements of fiscal irresponsibility which had so long been the sole property of the

Democratic administrations. I said that until quite recently I was personally satisfied this administration was providing responsible, realistic leadership. I could no longer be confident.

I said, "A seventy-one-point-eight-billion-dollar budget not only shocks me, it weakens my faith in the constant assurances we have received from this administration that its aim was to cut spending, balance the budget, reduce debt, cut taxes—in short, live within our means." I said, "It is disillusioning to see the Republican party plunging headlong into the same dismal state experienced by the liberal Democrats." I reminded our President that in 1952 he had said, "We must eliminate deficits and waste, cut crazy spending programs."

I said every item in the President's budget could and must be reduced. And then I said, "If the junior Senator from Arizona is not a member of the Eighty-sixth Congress, it will not be because he has broken faith with either the American people or the principles of the Republican party in this almost frenzied rush to give away the resources and freedoms of America, whether in federal spending programs at home or economic aid efforts abroad."

I didn't personally blame Ike. I knew that many of the modern liberal Republicans close to him believed the administration must turn left to regain public approval.

The press said that speech was my "bill of divorcement" from the modern Republicans. I was greatly reassured when I discovered that Ike had not taken offense at my remarks. In private he almost agreed with me. I had planted my flag. I had no regrets.

CHAPTER 8

Ike—Mr. President

It was impossible to dislike Dwight David Eisenhower. I first met him at a political rally in Phoenix, Arizona, in September 1952. He was General of the Armies, the victorious commander of Allied forces in World War II. I was a former transport command pilot and the operator of a local family-owned store.

He was the Republican candidate for the office of President. I was a candidate for the United States Senate. Ike shook my hand, called me Colonel Goldwater, and made me feel my race for the U.S. Senate was just as important as his race for the presidency.

It was an outdoor rally at a high school stadium. About 10,000 Arizonans had come to listen to Ike. The speech he made that day was a short one, his delivery uneven, but his words and his manner conveyed a love of country, a belief in the goodness and greatness of America. He touched on our past mistakes, condemned the stale-mated Korean War, and urged the people to accept their responsibilities as voters to shape the years ahead.

The first Republican to be elected to the presidency in twenty years, Ike built up a plurality of more than 6.5 million votes over his urbane, literate challenger, Adlai Stevenson. My margin of victory was just a few over 7,000. I was the first Republican elected to the Senate from Arizona in thirty-two years.

The most memorable episode of the 1952 presidential campaign was the revelation of the existence of the so-called Nixon Fund. On September 18 the New York *Post* banner-headlined the story "Secret Rich Man's Trust Fund Keeps Nixon in Style Beyond His Salary."

The scandalous misuse of public funds under the Truman administration was a major campaign issue. The Democrats immediately attempted to exploit what they hoped would prove to be a serious weakness in the heretofore-unblemished Eisenhower image. The AP and UPI distributed the *Post* story, and for the next five days the alleged misbehavior of the vice presidential candidate filled the front pages of the American newspapers.

There were press reports that Eisenhower was considering asking Nixon to withdraw from the ticket. Members of the Republican National Committee were presented as favoring a Nixon withdrawal.

On September 21 Harold Stassen, the self-appointed Galahad of the Republican party, sent Nixon a wire. "After a thoughtful review of the entire situation, Dick, I have regretfully reached the conclusion you should offer your resignation from the ticket to General Eisenhower."

The Democratic National Committee piously quoted federal statutes on bribery and graft by members of Congress.

Ike held an off-the-record news conference. He refused to make any final judgments. He wanted the facts.

Richard Nixon had won election to the U.S. Senate in 1950 after a hard-fought, expensive campaign. A group of Nixon supporters headed by Dana C. Smith, a Pasadena lawyer, urged the need for a political fund to finance future activities designed to keep Nixon's name before the California voters.

At that time members of the Senate received a salary of $12,500 a year. They were allowed $2,500 for telephone, telegraph, and stationery bills. The government paid for one round trip home per session. The group wanted funds available to permit Nixon to make more than one trip home per session, to travel to other parts of the nation, to speak in behalf of other Republican candidates, to use the mails, the telephone, and the telegraph to keep in touch with his California supporters.

Today members of Congress have a salary of $54,000 a year.

They have un-limited use of long-distance telephone, can transmit documents between Washington and their home states by tele-copier, are permitted twenty-six round trips home per year, can send frequent newsletters to every voter in their constituency, all at federal expense.

The Nixon committee projected a budget need of $15,000 per year. It solicited contributions in amounts from $100 to a maxi-mum of $500. A special trust fund was opened in a Pasadena bank. Bills for these purely political activities were paid directly from the trust. Not one dollar was ever paid to Nixon, his wife, or members of his staff. In that period some members of Congress who were lawyers continued to receive fees from their old firms. Nixon had refused to do so. Other members put their wives and relatives on congressional payrolls. John Sparkman, the Demo-cratic vice presidential candidate in 1952, had long had his wife on his senatorial payroll.

On Tuesday, September 23, Nixon appeared on a national hookup of 64 NBC television stations, 194 CBS radio stations, and practically all 560 stations of the mutual Broadcasting System radio network. This was the famous Checkers Speech. Nixon said the funds raised amounted to about $18,000. It all had been used to finance legitimate political activity. Not one dime had come to him. He mentioned Pat Nixon's good Republican cloth coat. He concluded with a story of the man from Texas who had given the Nixon family a black and white spotted cocker spaniel. He said Tricia had named the dog Checkers. He said the family in-tended to keep it.

As to whether or not he should withdraw from the Republican ticket, that decision was up to the Republican National Committee and to General Eisenhower. He urged the people to wire and write the national committee and express their views. He pledged he would abide by their decision.

In Cleveland, Ohio, where Eisenhower had watched the per-formance on television, he praised Nixon as a brave and coura-geous patriotic American—"the kind of man we want for Vice President." Nixon's supporters were bitterly critical of Ike for not coming immediately to the defense of his running mate. I think Nixon himself was deeply resentful.

In my opinion, this episode reveals a great deal about Ike's approach to a problem and his habit of thinking. He wanted to know all the facts before he reached a decision. He just wouldn't make a snap judgment.

When Ike took office, Republicans were in the majority in both the House and the Senate. Joe Martin of Massachusetts was Speaker of the House; Charles Halleck of Indiana, Majority Leader; and Les Arends, Whip. In the Senate, Styles Bridges of New Hampshire was President pro Tempore, a largely ceremonial position; Robert Taft of Ohio was Majority Leader; and William Knowland of California, Whip. All these party leaders were experienced and knowledgeable. They understood politics. They were committed to the principles Ike had enunciated in his campaign.

At White House policy sessions Ike would listen attentively to Bob Taft when we were talking about legislative programs. When the conversations turned to political strategy having to do with the passage of legislation, the President seemed to lose interest.

I don't think Ike ever really understood that he got the nomination as the result of the ruthless convention politics engineered by Henry Cabot Lodge and Herb Brownell, who accused the Taft forces of being underhanded, dishonest, and dictatorial. I say this because in matters political I found Ike to be extremely naïve. He was a product of the military.

In the military the commander depends on staff decisions. The staff analyzes, then reports, offering certain alternatives. After a course is chosen, the staff carries out whatever strategy the commander considers necessary to achieve the objective. When Ike's name was first suggested as a potential candidate, no one knew whether he was a Democrat or a Republican. He told me once the first person ever to suggest that he should run for President was Harry Truman.

Ike's attitude toward Taft was not deferential. It was certainly respectful. And Taft, although he had every reason to be bitter over the treatment he received from Ike's lieutenants in Chicago, never exhibited any resentment. I asked Bob Taft about this one time. He told me a good Senator's priorities must put the country first, the party next, and personal ambition at the bottom of the totem pole.

Taft made it easier for Ike to overlook what had happened at the convention. He was always patiently respectful of the President. Had Bob Taft lived, the Eisenhower administration might have chosen a different path.

Senator Bill Knowland of California, who became Majority Leader when Taft died, was far more dogmatic in his positions and his presentations than Taft. Bill Knowland was a great Senator and a great patriot, but he was more inclined to tell people what they should do than he was to persuade them to follow a particular course.

I don't mean to suggest that Ike wasn't aware of the struggles in Congress. There is an unwritten rule in all legislatures that new members should be seen but not heard. Four months after I entered the Senate I broke that rule to speak against standby authority for the President to impose price and wage controls. Ike sent me a two-word message: "Atta Boy."

There was no pretense about Ike. That wonderfully infectious grin could totally disarm his critics. He and Mamie were as American as apple pie. His career validated the American Dream.

Old-timers in the party strongly resented Ike's failure to investigate and reveal the misbehavior of those in the Truman administration who had been responsible for the national scandals. Political parties grew fat and healthy on patronage. At one early Republican caucus Ike told us there were some 18,000 jobs filled with political appointees of Harry Truman. He said Truman told him he didn't expect these people to stay. Our impression was that Ike intended to replace them with Republicans.

Senator Paul Douglas of Illinois, who naturally wanted to keep the jobs for Democrats, successfully blocked Ike's efforts. Douglas knew the bureaucratic ropes. Ike didn't. Some of my more experienced Republican colleagues expressed great disappointment.

As chairman of the Senatorial Campaign Committee in 1955 and 1956 I ordered some exhaustive surveys in an effort to identify areas of potential Republican strength. We interviewed party leaders and party workers to find out what they liked or didn't like about Ike's administration.

When I took the results to Ike, he told me bluntly he thought the Senatorial and Congressional Campaign Committees should be abolished, absorbed by the Republican National Committee. I explained this couldn't be done because these two campaign committees are creations of the Congress.

It was after our third or fourth meeting on this subject that I finally recognized the President's problem. He listened to my reports, looked at the charts with great interest, but he wouldn't accept his role as the political leader. In his mind it was a problem for staff to handle. It was something I should take up with Sherman Adams.

Adams, who had served one term in the House of Representatives and been governor of New Hampshire, was an early supporter of Ike's bid for the presidency. In 1953 he was installed in the White House as chief of staff. Adams wouldn't forgive anyone who had supported Taft. When these Republicans came to the White House to offer advice or seek favors, Adams would ask, "Where were you before Chicago?"

These state party leaders weren't concerned with the humdrum bread-and-butter jobs. What they wanted were the prestigious appointments in foreign service or on domestic commissions—assignments which oftentimes cost the holder more than the salary attached to the job. Sherman Adams awarded these strictly on the basis of early personal loyalty to Ike with no thought whatsoever to building the regular party.

In the elections of 1954 which determined the makeup of the Eighty-fourth Congress, Republicans lost eighteen House seats, and the Democrats became the majority. In the Senate, Wayne Morse deserted the Republican party to give the Democrats the one vote they needed for control. The opportunity for the Republicans under Ike to institute any major reforms was lost.

In 1955 Ike suffered his heart attack in Denver. While the President recovered and recuperated, Richard Nixon was in command. His conduct during this trying period was admirable. He functioned as an efficient housekeeper to maintain the status quo. For a time it was believed Ike's health would prevent him from seeking a second term. The party had divided between those who wanted Nixon to be the candidate and those who hated Nixon.

During this period, when Ike was at Gettsburg, Republican National Chairman Leonard Hall visited the President frequently. Len told me that Ike didn't really want to run for a second term. His failure to take command in the first two years, which Hall told me Ike recognized, and his inability to make the reforms he thought necessary were the source of his great frustration.

If the party leaders had been united on Nixon as a candidate in 1956, I believe Ike would have been happy to step aside. But the party was so divided on Nixon, Ike was persuaded to run again. A true measure of Ike's personal popularity is to be found in the results of that 1956 election. Ike increased his plurality by almost 2.2 percent of the popular vote and received fifteen more electoral votes than he had in 1952.

In his second term Ike was a much stronger President. He sent U. S. troops to Lebanon, took a strong stand against Russian penetration in the Middle East, intervened when the Red Chinese appeared to be planning an invasion of Taiwan, proposed the nuclear test ban, and stood up to Khrushchev in Geneva and at Camp David.

Domestically he resisted efforts to expand the role of the federal government. He vetoed a bill to make the federal government responsible for cleaning up the pollution of rivers, saying, "That responsibility should be assumed by state and local governments and by industry." In view of the excessive costs imposed on our economy by legislation subsequently passed, it appears Ike was correct in his judgment.

Ike despised segregation, but he was philosophically opposed to making the federal government the policeman in this area. This did not prevent him from sending troops to Little Rock to enforce the laws Congress had passed.

Ike was accused by his opponents of catering to business. This was because he believed in private enterprise. He deplored the thought of an all-powerful, benevolent federal government managing the lives of the people. He did believe there was a role for government in the highly controversial area of social reforms.

Ike's cabinet reflected this devotion to the principles of personal liberty and private initiative. His Secretary of the Treasury, George Humphrey, and his Secretary of Defense, Charlie Wilson, were passionate exponents of private enterprise. Their opinions were shared by Ezra Taft Benson in Agriculture, Sinclair Weeks in Commerce, and Douglas McKay at Interior. Of the men in Ike's first Cabinet, only Art Summerfield, Postmaster General, and Herbert Brownell, Attorney General, could be classified as politicians.

It was Lodge and Brownell who made the deal with Earl Warren. In return for the California governor's support in Chicago, they promised him an appointment as Chief Justice of the Supreme Court. Ike kept that commitment. He was never happy about it.

When I reflect on the character, talents, and performance in office of the men who have occupied the White House during my adult lifetime, it is easy to understand why the term "politician" has earned such a derogatory connotation.

Harry Truman may have been victimized by some of his greedy political allies who thought being close to the President was a license to steal. Truman's personal life was above reproach. His most vigorous critics rate him high in courage and love of country. He had the guts to make the decision to drop atomic bombs on Japan and end World War II with an Allied victory, but he was less resolute when faced with the threat of Red Chinese intervention in Korea.

Dwight D. Eisenhower never really grasped the political complexities of his office. His courage, his quality, his wholesomeness helped greatly to restore our faith in the institution of government. He could be alarmingly profane—never vulgar.

Ike gave us eight years of relative peace in the world and relative prosperity here at home. It was within his power to undo some of the mischief resulting from errors in national judgment under Roosevelt and Truman. He was ambitious to bring reform— his political talent was unequal to the task.

As Commander in Chief he was superb. He was responsible for developing the CIA into the most efficient intelligence system in the world. Ike kept us ahead of the Russians in science and technology as related to defense capabilities. Many of us did not agree with some of his domestic decisions, but during the years of the Eisenhower presidency, the military superiority of the U.S. was never questioned, especially not by the Russians.

Ike's major concern was for the country. He detested the infighting, the manipulations, the intrigue of partisan politics. I have served in the Senate of the United States during the terms of six Presidents—three Republican and three Democratic. I think Dwight Eisenhower was the best of the lot and least understood. Years from now students of the twentieth century may agree. Ike was a product of his military background, but he didn't radiate that aura of condescending, imperial authority which everyone recognized in George C. Marshall and Douglas MacArthur.

MacArthur died in 1964. A year earlier I went to see him at his suite in the Waldorf Towers. I had hoped for a thirty-minute visit. We spent all day together and had dinner before I left.

We talked about the war in the Pacific. MacArthur believed the politicians in Washington had deliberately subordinated Asia to Europe. He was extremely critical of our neglect of the defense of the Philippines in the years prior to Pearl Harbor. He said that as early as 1935 we should have recognized Japan's expansionist policies would eventually lead to a confrontation in the Pacific.

Douglas MacArthur had never considered anything other than a military career. His father had served with distinction during the Civil War, fought the Indians in Arizona, and was in command of the troops that quelled the Philippine insurrection. MacArthur graduated from West Point in 1907, twelve years ahead of Ike. He was one of our brilliant commanders in World War I. But there was more in his head than military tactics. He thought in terms of global strategy.

I remember he admitted to me he was not very skillful at Army politics. He said the best man he ever knew at that game was Ike. This puzzled me. I said, in my opinion, Ike had been a poor political President, unable to persuade the Congress to follow his lead.

MacArthur said he intended his remark to be complimentary. The general had followed Eisenhower's career from the time Ike entered the academy. He said Ike was a determined student and extremely popular with his classmates and his instructors. He said Ike first won an appointment to the Naval Academy at Annapolis, was disqualified because of his age, and entered West Point in 1911. "You know, Goldwater," he said, "it takes a pretty good politician to get an appointment to just one of the academies." He said that after graduating as a second lieutenant in 1915, Ike was assigned to the 19th Infantry at Fort Sam Houston, Texas, and didn't go overseas in World War I.

MacArthur said Ike went to all the proper staff schools, worked hard, and never rocked the boat. "He served on my staff in the Philippines from '35 to '39, and he was good." To illustrate this point, MacArthur recalled one staff problem he had assigned to Ike—a theoretical situation calling for a tactical conclusion.

"Eisenhower came back the next morning with his first recommendation. It was neatly typed, well organized, and cited a number of military authorities to support the conclusion. I told him I didn't agree. He said he'd come back with an alternative. That afternoon he did. I said his second solution was an improvement on the first, but I thought he could do better. He grinned and said, 'Perhaps I have, General,' and handed me a third paper. This is what a staff officer is supposed to do—analyze a situation and provide the commander with a number of workable alternatives. Not just out of his own head, mind you, but alternatives which can be supported by reference to similar situations."

MacArthur said Ike knew the system, but until George Marshall selected him to be Commander in Chief in Europe, he had never commanded troops in battle or even served in an active theater. I pointed out that since Ike missed World War I, there hadn't been any other wars for him to gain command experience.

MacArthur admitted this. I asked him why he thought Roosevelt and Marshall had picked Ike.

MacArthur said, "Eisenhower was probably the best staff man in the Army. He had a magnificent talent for getting along with people. He could get Patton and Montgomery and Bradley in the room, and before they left, they would be in agreement. Ike had a positive genius for resolving differences. Perhaps it was because you couldn't dislike him even when he disagreed with you."

I told the general that when I was just eighteen I had attended the Reserve Officers' Training Camp at Fort Meade, Maryland. "You, sir, came to speak to the cadet class, and I was very impressed."

MacArthur leaned back in his chair, smiled, and said, "You should have been, Goldwater, I was the major general in command of the Third Corps area."

A number of points the general made that day are pertinent to the problems the United States will face in the years ahead: Timidity breeds conflict, and courage often prevents it. Never enter a conflict unless you are committed to victory.

A nation controlling the sea lanes can rule the world, and a nation controlling the crucial straits, Morocco, Formosa, Gibraltar, the Dardanelles, Bab el Mandeb, and Hormoz, will control the North and South China Seas, the Mediterranean, the Black Sea, the Gulf of Aden and the Red Sea, and the Persian Gulf. MacArthur mentioned two other vital geographical locations, the Cape of Good Hope and the Panama Canal.

MacArthur expressed admiration for the Japanese military commanders, but he said Japanese intelligence had never penetrated American strategy in the South Pacific. It was different in Korea.

MacArthur said, "The North Koreans and the Chinese seemed to know every move we were going to make. At first this puzzled me. Then I realized all battle plans were known to the United Nations. The Russians reported them to the Chinese field commanders. General Lin Piao stated publicly that he did not move his troops into Korea until he had been assured that Washington would 'restrain General MacArthur from taking adequate retaliatory measures against my lines of supply and communication.'"

I told MacArthur that Truman's act relieving him of command in Korea was one of the things which had heightened my interest in politics. He said he harbored no resentment against Truman, explaining that the President really had no other choice.

"I didn't agree with the politicians who were running that war. I wouldn't fight a stalemate, nor did I want to command a losing cause. When we were forbidden to go beyond the Yalu to wipe out the bases of the Red Chinese, I knew somebody had decided against winning. Hell, we couldn't even bomb the bridges over the river. When I complained about that, they said I could bomb the south half of the bridges. I knew it was time for me to get out, and I did."

In my relationship with President Eisenhower there were three moments of crisis.

My first significant confrontation with Ike occurred in April 1959. After two years of investigation into the corrupt practices of certain labor leaders, we commenced debate on Senate Bill 1555, which was to become known as the Kennedy-Ervin Bill after its sponsors, Senators Jack Kennedy of Massachusetts and Sam Ervin of North Carolina.

The measure was represented as an effective labor law reform. It wasn't. I offered some eighteen amendments, all of which were turned down. I said, "This bill, as now developed by this body, in terms of its effect on the evil conditions it professes to cure, is like a flea bite to a bull elephant."

President Eisenhower was on record as favoring corrective labor legislation. The bill came to a vote on Saturday, April 25. I voted "nay" and left the chamber before the count was tallied to fly to a speaking engagement in Philadelphia. I got the results of the vote on radio. Ninety "yeas," one "nay." I was the only member of the United States Senate to vote against the bill.

The following Monday I was summoned to the White House

for an early-morning meeting with the President. Ike wanted to know why in the hell I had voted against a measure which was badly needed to correct the abuses of organized labor. He asked sarcastically if I thought everyone in the Senate was out of step but me.

I said, "Mr. President, this bill is a sham and a farce. Have you read the measure?"

Ike replied testily that he didn't have the time to read every bill that passed the Congress. He said his staff had told him it was a good measure and would do the job, and apparently ninety members of the United States Senate had thought so, too.

I told him either he had been deliberately deceived or else his staffers were too damn dumb to understand the English language. The President's ears began to take on a crimson hue. I knew I was in trouble. Before he could say anything more, I said, "Mr. President, please listen to me for just a minute. This bill won't prevent blackmail picketing, and let me tell you just what that is. A union representative comes to management with a proposed labor contract. He issues an ultimatum—sign or be picketed. The owner refuses because his employees don't want to join the union. A picket line is set up manned by professional pickets who are not employees of the company. Deliveries are cut off; customers, intimidated. That's blackmail picketing, Mr. President.

"This bill doesn't prevent secondary boycott, and let me tell you just what that is. The employees of a company decide not to join a union. Instead of picketing the company's plant, unions picket the stores which sell the product.

"This bill ignores the right of union members to have a voice in the affairs of their union's operations. It won't prevent union bosses from looting union treasuries. It's a bad bill, Mr. President, and that's why I voted against it."

Ike grinned. "Thank you, Barry," he said, "you've given me a lot to think about, and I'm going to think about it."

At the end of the week my friend at the White House General Jerry Persons told me Ike had ordered a new team to make a careful study of the provisions of the Kennedy-Ervin Bill. Fourteen weeks and three days later, on August 6, President Eisenhower went on national television to catalogue all the deficiencies of the Kennedy-Ervin Bill and to call on the Congress to pass an effective labor reform bill.

On September 3, 1959, the Senate of the United States, which prides itself on being the world's greatest deliberative body, reversed itself by a vote of 95 to 2. Kennedy-Ervin was scuttled, and the Landrum-Griffin Act was passed. I gave Ike the credit for that turnaround and tried to thank him for it, but at the time he was very unhappy with me because I had made a Senate speech calling his budget a "dime-store version of the New Deal."

The third time the President thought he had reason to be unhappy with me he was right. It was all my fault.

At a press interview following a speech in Boston a reporter had asked me what I thought about Milton Eisenhower, the President's brother, as a potential presidential candidate. I replied, "One Eisenhower is enough." It was a tactless thing to say. What I meant was that I was satisfied with Dwight Eisenhower, and I wasn't thinking about Milton for the future. I apologized to the President.

After Nixon was nominated in Chicago in 1960, I had regular political conferences with President Eisenhower. He was keenly interested in the work of my Senatorial Campaign Committee. I know he wanted to play a role in the presidential campaign. Nixon didn't ask his help. Those of us who were working so hard to help the Vice President win the presidency understood the reasons. Nixon was a loner. He had been deeply troubled when Ike didn't come immediately to his defense in 1952 and by Ike's response to that reporter's question as to just what Nixon had contributed to the Eisenhower administration. Caught off guard, Ike said, "Give me a day or two, and I'll think of something."

After I was defeated by Lyndon Johnson in 1964, Ike organized a small ad hoc committee of Republicans to meet and review with him the in-office performance of President Johnson. Whatever cohesive policy the party had in that period was the result of this political effort by Ike. He was indignant about the growth of government bureaucracy and government spending. No one ever had the temerity to say, "Well, Mr. President, you had the chance to correct these things, and you blew it." No one had to say it. He knew it.

It seems the rage nowadays to debunk our national leaders—to focus public attention on the moments of their lives when they were a little less than wise or prudent. I resent this. Ike wasn't a gifted political manipulator, but what right did we have to expect him to be?

Ike's belief in the virtue of the American Republic never wavered. He believed in the goodness of the American people and trusted them. He devoted all his energy and all his talents to the preservation of the American Republic. It was a blessed privilege to know him and to serve with him this country we both have loved so long and so well.

CHAPTER 9

Disappointment and Distortion

On October 4, 1957, the Russians launched the world's first earth satellite, Sputnik I. To some Americans it was as great a shock as the Japanese attack on Pearl Harbor. The flight of this, by present standards, crude device questioned two widely held presumptions: (1) that the Soviets were backward and clumsy; and (2) that American science and technology were supreme.

When the Russians followed up with their first intercontinental ballistic missile, American confidence was truly shattered. We had been outraged by the knowledge the Soviets either had stolen our atomic secrets or had received them through the connivance of traitors in our own government. It was one thing to have a potential enemy copy our technology, but Sputnik and the Russian ICBM appeared to be a Russian breakthrough which left the United States far behind. This distortion of fact was skillfully exploited by John F. Kennedy in his campaign for the presidency in 1960.

In the Congress we heard a chorus of partisan critics condemn the Eisenhower administration. In private, the President exercised the full range of his barracks-room vocabulary to express his opinion of those he called "sanctimonious, hypocritical bastards," who, even though they knew the truth, were making political capital in the headlines.

In 1954 the Killian Committee on Surprise Attack, an advisory agency created by President Eisenhower, proposed the construction of a high-altitude reconnaisance aircraft, one which would be capable of overflying Russia to provide current information on the progress of the Soviet ICBM development. This aircraft, the U-2, was first flown in 1956. Three men responsible for its development and deployment were Kelly Johnson of Lockheed Aircraft, E. H. Land of the Polaroid Company, and Richard M. Bissell, Jr., of the CIA. Because the U-2 was built and flown in secrecy—its mission to spy on a nation with which we were technically at peace—the American public has never been fully informed about the magnificent capabilities of this aircraft.

The sophisticated camera gear developed for the project could look down on Russia from an altitude of 14 miles and photograph a strip of earth 125 miles wide and 3,000 miles long. The pictures were vastly superior to any of our former aerial photographs—definitions so clear it was possible to read the headlines of a newspaper photographed from an altitude of 8 miles. Relatively slow and extremely efficient, the U-2 could fly 4,000 miles and return to land at one of our bases in Europe.

When Gary Francis Powers came down on May 1, 1960, the U-2 program became an embarrassment to the United States. But in the four years of its operation it provided precise, uncontradictable evidence of the Soviets' military weakness. The truth was that photographs taken during our overflights of Russia had given the CIA detailed information in advance about Sputnik and the first Russian ICBM.

Ike could not respond to his critics without compromising our own intelligence. Despite the vast network of Russian spies operating in the United States, we had been able to keep the existence of the U-2 and our developing space technology a secret. Ike took the heat, grinned, and kept his mouth shut.

During this period I had an opportunity to fly the U-2—not as the first pilot; I had an instructor with me. Because it was necessary to wear pressure suits, and the one they provided me didn't quite fit, we were able to climb only to about 50,000 feet. The U-2 was a very fragile airplane with a fast rate of climb and great fuel economy. At its operating altitude of 80,000 feet it was out of reach of the enemy's pursuit aircraft.

I used the words "came down," not "shot down," in reference

to the capture of Powers because I do not believe the Russians had a missile capable of hitting a U-2 at its operating altitudes. But the aircraft was fragile. It was stressed to withstand a load of 3g's, nothing more. A forgetful pilot, or one whose attention was distracted momentarily, could easily permit the aircraft to enter into a dive. Unless the pullout was slow and deliberate, the wings would come off. The other U-2s we had lost were the result of structural failure.

I asked Gary Powers about this after his return to the United States. He gave an evasive answer, forcing me to conclude it was pilot error, rather than a Russian air-launched defense weapon, which caused the U-2 to crash.

I have flown the successor to the U-2, the SR-71, from the pilot's seat—performed a midair refueling, reached 83,000 feet above sea level, and cruised at a speed in excess of Mach 3, somewhat over 2,000 miles an hour. On that flight I made the return trip from Billings, Montana, over to Edwards Air Force Base in Southern California in twenty-four minutes.

In 1957 Ike proclaimed what came to be known as the Eisenhower Doctrine in the Middle East. He said the U.S. would respond to requests for military aid from any Middle East nation menaced by international communism. In the following year he landed our Marines in Lebanon. The Russians backed down.

Ike delivered a strong diplomatic ultimatum to Red China when it attacked Quemoy and Matsu with long-range artillery. The shelling stopped. On balance, I believe the Sputnik launching was really a plus for the United States. It resulted in increased congressional support for the space program then underway. It certainly influenced Ike to make a tough stand in the Middle East and the Strait of Formosa.

To my mind, these two positive actions by President Eisenhower in 1957 and 1958 did not receive proper recognition. The landing of U.S. Marines in Lebanon frustrated communist plans in the Middle East. Red China, which had achieved a significant victory in Korea, bringing half that country into the communist hegemony, abandoned its belligerency toward free China in response to Eisenhower's firm policy.

Immediately following the explosion of the first Soviet atomic bomb, the Russians launched a propaganda campaign to convince the world that any confrontation between the U.S. and the Soviets must inevitably lead to a nuclear holocaust. This proposition has attracted many supporters in the United States and in other capitals of the free world. Followers of this doomsday theory argue that American restraint in its dealings with Russia is necessary to preserve the world from atomic incineration. Advocates of unilateral disarmament as the only alternative to nuclear destruction rest their justification of Truman's decision on Korea, Kennedy's concessions on Cuba, and our no-win war in Vietnam on this doomsday theory.

Along with a respectable number of military experts, I hold an opposite view. I believe the possibility of an atomic confrontation has been increased by the dramatic turnaround in American strategic policy commencing with the death of John Foster Dulles in 1959. From 1950 until at least 1970 the United States enjoyed unquestioned superiority in atomic weapons and delivery systems. This is no longer true. The policy decision of Secretary of Defense Robert McNamara was to seek parity and abandon superiority.

We should remember that in Korea and Vietnam the Russians relied on conventional weapons. They made no response to the landing of Marines in Lebanon. It can be argued that since the Russians were successful in both Korea and Vietnam and came out ahead in the Cuban missiles crisis, there was just no need to employ atomic weaponry. This brings up another generally held misconception which needs to be corrected.

President John F. Kennedy has been lavishly praised for standing eyeball to eyeball with Khrushchev and staring him down when the Russians attempted to install ballistic missiles on the island of Cuba. President Kennedy put the nation on war alert.

I believe it is more realistic to attribute Russian restraint during this period to their recognition of our nuclear superiority. I find no evidence suggesting the communists have abandoned their ambition to rule the world. A wise man once told us, "Those who will not learn from the errors of history are bound to repeat them."

As a candidate for Congress in 1952 I discovered a great many Arizonans were dismayed over the waste and misapplication of foreign aid funds. Examples are too numerous to mention, ranging from technological advancements transmitted to the Russians to airports constructed in countries where they had no airlines, hospitals where there were no doctors.

American foreign aid is the result of two decisions reached in 1947—one, remembered as the Marshall Plan; the other, the so-called Truman Doctrine. Specifically, President Truman asked Congress for $400 million in aid to be given to Greece and Turkey to help the governments of those countries combat communism—a request the Congress granted. The Marshall Plan, adopted later in that same year, authorized the spending of $12 billion to help rebuild the economies of Western European countries and Japan. By January 1953, when I came to the Senate, the total amount of foreign aid authorization was $31 billion.

It is historically inaccurate to give full credit or blame to either Truman or Marshall for these policies. Before the end of World War II there was considerable discussion in the Congress concerning the proper postwar U.S. attitude toward our allies and our enemies. At Potsdam and Yalta President Roosevelt had made substantial concessions to the Russians. The expansion of communist influence in Eastern Europe provoked great alarm in the United States. There was public support for the proposal to use our economic strength to resist and counter any further communist expansion.

What we today call foreign aid, the transfer of money and goods from our government to other governments as a gift, is a practice old to the world but new to the United States. We had responded generously to other nations after a disaster, but the deliberate giving of economic resources to other nations with an intention of influencing the recipient nation's internal and external policies was a new departure. Hans J. Morgenthau, the distinguished German-born educator who was director of the Center for Study of American Foreign Policy from 1963 to 1968, says, "Bribes proffered by one government to another for political advantage were, until the beginning of the nineteenth century, an integral part of the armory of diplomacy, and much of what goes by the name of foreign aid today is in the nature of such bribes."

We gave to our allies in both World War I and World War II. The theory behind post-World War II foreign aid rests on a number of assumptions: (1) that if we arm friendly nations, they will help us fight the spread of communism; (2) that all underdeveloped nations yearn for industrialization; (3) that if we provide the capital and the know-how, all the backward peoples will benefit materially, and their improved condition will cause them to opt for something like representative government; and (4) that if we don't elevate the standard of living in these backward nations, they will seek to take by conquest what they cannot produce themselves.

The giver of a bribe does so on the clear understanding the recipient will deliver some specific quid pro quo. The receiver of a bribe accepts payment with a clear understanding of what is expected and in most cases carries out his part of the bargain.

Nations justify such direct payments or bribes on the grounds that the ensuing procured action benefits peace or improves trade or achieves some other generally desirable objective. In a discussion of this problem Hans Morgenthau says, "The government of Nation A, trying to buy political advantage from the government of Nation B, for, say, twenty million dollars, not only must pretend but also must act out in elaborate fashion the pretense that what it is actually doing is giving aid for economic development to the government of Nation B—old-fashioned bribery is a straightforward transaction; services are to be rendered at a price, and both sides know what to expect. Bribery, disguised as aid for economic development, makes of giver and recipient actors in the play which, in the end, they can no longer distinguish from reality."

Both the Truman Doctrine and the Marshall Plan accomplished their early objectives in a much shorter time than was anticipated. Our aid to Turkey and Greece blocked communist expansion short of the Mediterranean. The economies of West Germany and Japan, along with those of France and England, displayed great improvement. The noncommunist government in Italy was preserved.

Feeding on its early successes, the program of American foreign aid was enlarged to include both military and economic assistance to dozens of countries not directly involved in World War II—all of it justified as being essential to the containment of communism. A number of influential international associations, such as the Council on Foreign Relations, the United World Federalists, and the Atlantic Union, supported a continuance of the foreign aid program as essential to the maintenance of world peace. We were told that unless the have-not nations (the term "Third World" had not come into popular use) were given access to the material benefits enjoyed by the people of the United States, they would be forced to try to fight their way out of poverty.

A first-term junior Senator doesn't have much clout in the Congress. But I did have access to the Republican President,

Dwight Eisenhower, and to the Republican Secretary of State, John Foster Dulles. Much to my satisfaction, I discovered Dulles was dismayed by the proliferation of foreign aid, and, in my opinion, he would have been pleased to see the program phased out. Eisenhower, who had been instructed by his years in the military service to rely on staff judgments, had no strong opinions of his own on foreign aid and was prepared to follow whatever suggestions his Secretary of State might offer.

Had the Republicans not lost control of the Congress as a result of the defection of Wayne Morse, I believe the Eisenhower administration would have gradually ended the economic aid part of the program. We were giving money to a number of nondemocratic governments, and substantial sums were going to enemy countries where the rulers deliberately promoted anti-American, anticapitalist sentiment.

I favored the continuation of military aid. The funds for the development and manufacture of new weapons systems all were spent in the United States. The production facilities and technological advances strengthened our own military capability. By providing arms and other material directly related to defense, we were able to inhibit and sometimes prevent communist takeovers. Perhaps even more important, we had an opportunity to observe these new weapons systems in operation and, thus, appraise their true capabilities.

On the other hand, much of our economic aid was going to enemy countries or countries whose public policy statements were not compatible with our concepts of freedom. Example: We have given more than $10 billion to India. The government of Mrs. Indira Gandhi was far more supportive of Marxism than of capitalism. Our foreign aid has enriched individual rulers of many countries while doing nothing at all for the poor or the underprivileged we were sincerely hoping to help.

Cicero once told us that "every good and perfect thing has within itself the seeds of its own destruction through an excess of its virtue." To my mind this is what has happened to the American foreign aid program. It has been continued year after year. The true amount of monies thus distributed has been concealed from the American public.

By July 1978 the total cost of the foreign aid program—outright gifts, unsound loans with no expectation for repayment, and interest costs—totaled about $325 billion. The program has been in existence for thirty-one years. In all but two of those years the federal government has incurred a deficit. Most of the money we have sent overseas for foreign aid has been borrowed. During the same period of time the United States' gold reserves have declined from $20.3 billion in 1946 to $11.5 billion in 1978. Since federal deficit spending is clearly responsible for the major portion of the disastrous inflation which threatens the solvency of every American family, we must recognize that the foreign giveaway program is responsible for as much as one-half of that inflation charge.

At first our motives were noble, humanitarian, and defensive. This is no longer true. The international bankers and the multinational corporations are the principle beneficiaries of American foreign aid. The most frightening aspect of this whole program is to be found in the fact that American taxpayers are contributing American capital to subsidize our implacable enemy, the Russian communist.

When we sell wheat to the Russians, they don't pay us in cash. The deal is accomplished with a system of credits. We lend the money under very favorable terms. If the borrower doesn't make his payments, the taxpayer is stuck. Congressman Ben Blackburn, who made a study of the 1972 sale of grain to the Soviets, has declared that this one deal cost the American public $3.2 billion in a nine-month period.

The private Chase Manhattan Bank and the Export-Import Bank, which operates with your tax dollars, contributed 90 percent of the $2 billion Kama River truck factory recently completed in Russia. Repayment of the loan made by Chase Manhattan is guaranteed by the U.S. taxpayer through government agencies such as the Overseas Private Investment Corporation and the Foreign Credit Insurance Association.

The Kama River truck plant is equipped with the world's largest American industrial computer system. It will ultimately have an annual production capacity of 150,000 to 200,000 ten-ton multiple-axle trucks. This American-built, American-paid-for manufacturing facility is capable of producing tanks, military scout cars, trucks for military transport, and rocket launchers.

When the Soviets wanted a new fertilizer plant, we built it for them. With the plant designed to cost $400 million, the Soviets put up only $40 million. The Export-Import Bank and private American banks put up the balance.

When American exporters sign a contract with some unstable Third World country and deliver the goods, they know that if the buyer defaults, the American taxpayer, under the foreign aid program, will pick up the tab. All these complicated commercial transactions have been conducted in a manner calculated to deceive the American people. Less than 25 percent of the American tax dollars going overseas are publicly identified as foreign aid. The rest of the money is concealed under different titles and dispersed by a variety of federal agencies.

The Truman Doctrine and the Marshall program had great merit at the time of their inception. They served their purpose well. It is the continuation and the expansion of this giveaway which threaten to bankrupt the United States.

In 1977 the Congress did stop the delivery of our most advanced scientific computer to the Russians. This was done when it became widely understood that this computer would greatly improve the guidance systems of Russian ICBMs. But we had already given them a Control Data Corporation Model 6200, which is installed at the Dubna Research Institute.

Confronted with an energy shortage in this country, we have exported millions of dollars in drilling equipment, pipe, and other supplies to Russia. This we did at a time when oil drillers in the U.S. were unable to purchase what they needed for exploration and development here at home.

The convergence theory, supported by Kissinger during the Nixon and Ford administrations and now by Brzezinski in the Carter administration, assumes that as the Russians increase their industrial and agricultural output, the standard of living will rise, and having an equal share in material rewards, the two peoples, the Americans and the Russians, will draw so close together that armed conflict will become highly improbable, if not impossible. They see foreign aid as a tool to bring the Russian production economy up to the level of ours.

John P. Roche, a liberal professor with impeccable credentials who served in the White House under Lyndon Johnson, wrote a column on Moscow's manipulation of the American businessman which he compares to "rolling a drunk." Mr. Roche said:

Does anybody really appreciate the cosmic irony involved in the present deals between the Soviet government and various American manufacturers? At the American end, the enterprise is justified by everybody from Secretary of State Henry Kissinger down, as a technique of cementing political relations.

The theory is that once the Russians get thoroughly dependent on us for spare parts, their ideological compulsions will wither away. In short, the American protagonists have adopted the quintessential Marxist logic that economic relationships determine the behavior of political superstructures.

As the United States Chamber of Commerce prepares to hang a portrait of Karl Marx over the mantel in the director's room, the Soviet spokesmen are busy asserting the primacy of political power. In this they can draw sustenance from Lenin's 1921 New Economic Policy and from his improvisation of a category known as Progressive Capitalists.

Lenin, who never let little theoretical problems interfere, kept assuring his distressed colleagues, notably the compulsively abstract Trotsky, that if it ever came to the crunch, the Bolsheviks could seize the foreign assets—that is, Lenin asserted the supremacy of the political over the economic relationship.

Stalin said, "As long as capitalism and socialism exist, we cannot live in peace. In the end one or the other will triumph—a funeral dirge will be sung either over the Soviet Republic or over world capitalism." He also said something to this effect: "When it comes time to hang the capitalists, they will sell us the rope."

The foreign aid program has robbed the American citizen by sending money and products overseas on credit, in direct subsidy, and indirectly by the clearly established increase in inflation. We can't buy our friends—we can't inspire other men to fight for freedom when they are willing to settle for slavery. The foreign aid program has increased economic uncertainties now facing us in the United States. It has strengthened our enemies. It must be ended.

CHAPTER 10

The Second Time Around

Ernest McFarland, the Democrat I replaced in the Senate, was elected governor of Arizona in 1954. As a candidate for reelection in 1956 he defeated his Republican opponent by 55,000 votes and immediately began organizing to run against me in 1958.

As governor McFarland was constantly in the news. He was in a position to do favors for the party faithful. The people had no reason to be dissatisfied with his performance in office.

Some Republicans were unhappy with me because I criticized Eisenhower and differed with a number of national party leaders. The economy was hesitant. In his two successful campaigns for the presidency Ike had led voters to expect a dramatic change in direction at the federal level. This had not happened.

During my five years in the Senate we Republicans had done little to correct the errors of the past. We had promised to reduce waste, put an end to deficit financing. Under the first four Eisenhower budgets, 1953 through 1956, expenditures exceeded income, but the 1957 budget provided for a $1.6 billion surplus.

My years in Washington had taught me to understand the federal behemoth is an unwieldy, unresponsive organization. Almost all of the second- and third-echelon administrators were holdovers from the Roosevelt-Truman era, many of them frozen in place by executive order from the White House. I knew that a number of top-level policy decisions had been reversed entirely or drastically modified as they moved down through the bureaucratic labyrinth.

Because I had strongly condemned the practices of certain union bosses, I was categorized in the national media as being antilabor. I was marked the number one target to be defeated by the AFL-CIO. I had voted against the resolution to censure Senator Joe McCarthy, and this infuriated the liberals.

The laws of physics tell us that for every action there is an equal and opposite reaction. This is also true in the world of politics. When the national union leaders made me their number one target, I found some new friends—men and women who had long opposed the excesses and misbehavior of union bosses.

In February 1958 the Senate Select Committee on Improper Activities in the Labor or Management Field opened hearings. Reviewing portions of that testimony, I am compelled now to question how many, if any, Americans understood the enormity of union excesses.

The Kohler Company of Sheboygan, Wisconsin, is a manufacturer of plumbing supplies. Its employees were nonunion. The UAW decided to organize the plant. Union funds, union attorneys, union thugs were sent to Sheboygan. They terrorized the community, defied the courts, virtually destroyed the company, and got away with it.

A secondary area of investigation revealed the political power of the AFL-CIO COPE organization This is the most adequately financed political operation in the United States, dominated and controlled by labor bosses, financed by dues money of individual union members.

My friends in Washington expected me to be defeated in 1958. They regarded my 1952 victory as a fluke. In 1958 the economy was depressed. The number of Republicans in the Congress had decreased in 1954 and 1956. The President was a lame duck whose popularity had diminished.

Because Congress stayed in session until almost the opening of the campaign, my initial television commercials were done in a hurry, inadequately produced, and lacking any professional shine. My opponent was on the TV with some superb, professionally made thirty-second messages which clearly established him as the father of reclamation in Arizona.

This inauspicious beginning was really a blessing. It made me the underdog, it inspired my supporters to increase their personal compaigning, and we had in reserve some innovative campaign techniques, which have since been adopted by most candidates for public office. They involved polling, volunteer recruitment, effective use of television, and coordinated display advertising in the newspapers and on billboards.

Public opinion sampling is now a refined, precise science. Data gathered from personal interviews is analyzed by computers to provide semantic profiles of the contending candidates—to measure and identify those issues which will influence the voters' decision. It is not uncommon for a senatorial candidate to spend as much as $100,000 for pollsters. In presidential races the cost runs into the millions. We spent less than $1,500 on the polling system we used.

I wrote personal letters to about 300 individuals throughout Arizona and asked them to be my eyes and ears. Some, but not all, were close friends. Some had been involved previously in politics. Others had no political identification. At least one-half were registered Democrats. We maintained frequent contact with these people by mail, seeking their judgment on the issues and the attitudes of the voters. It worked.

Door-to-door canvassing, a neighbor coming to a neighbor's house to ask support for a particular candidate, has been proved effective beyond all question of a doubt. My brother Bob's wife, Sally, took charge of our volunteer enlistment program. By election day she had recruited 6,000 men and women, some of them students, who covered their neighborhoods the week before election day to distribute my literature and ask their neighbors to vote for me.

In 1958 there were four television stations in the Phoenix area, three in Tucson, one in Yuma. The pictures were all black and white; the technology, by today's standards, was primitive. Station policy in regard to the sale of commercial time was far more flexible.

Our strategy for TV was to present three thirty-minute programs in the final ten days before the election. We were able to buy the same time segment on all four stations in Phoenix and on three in Tucson. When our programs were on the air, everyone watching television in Arizona had to see them. The only simulcast the networks and station owners will tolerate nowadays is a major presidential address. It was different in 1958.

Billboards are considered important in Arizona campaigns. Our posters were up two months, but the second month we used a snipe to alter drastically the appearance of the board and give it a new appeal. A snipe is an additional printed message pasted on a portion of the existing board. It adds a new color, changes the geometry, and its use is not uncommon in commercial circles. No one else had ever used it on a political board in Arizona.

Our newspaper advertising was done with display ads. Each was a message presented in a familiar frame or format. Thanks to our continuous amateur survey, we knew the major concerns of the Arizona voters. We dealt with each one separately. In a space six columns by fifteen inches we repeated what I had been saying in my campaign speeches, in the messages on the billboards, and in our radio commercials. Unity is essential to a successful political campaign.

The object of all campaign advertising is to make an impression on the voter. The electronic media are ephemeral. A thirty-second commercial makes an emotional impact. It is great to establish name identification. When it's off the screen, very few people can recall what was said.

When the message is presented in print, it endures. It can be quoted. The supporters of a candidate frequently tear out the proper types of message ads from the newspaper and display them to help persuade a friend.

In 1958 a great many voters in Arizona had been shocked by the abuses of a few union labor bosses. Arizona has a right-to-work law. The political arm of organized labor, AFL-CIO COPE, had earned a bad reputation in Arizona.

We knew COPE had marked me for defeat. Quite early in that campaign, we discovered the top political COPE agent, a Californian named Al Green, had set up shop in Arizona. He traveled between Tucson and Phoenix, offering support for candidates for the Arizona legislature who were sympathetic to labor's view.

This activity was perfectly legal. I didn't think it would be very effective, but Al Green had chosen to conduct a covert operation. Local leaders in the Democratic party repeatedly denied the presence of any out-of-state labor lieutenants working on the Arizona election.

On the Sunday ten days before the election the *Arizona Republic* revealed the presence of Al Green in Arizona. It described his activities. It reprinted the denials of the Democratic party leaders who had been asked about out-of-state interests. And it ran a police mug shot made when Green had been arrested in connection with labor violence in California. The story attracted national attention.

On Friday, October 31, four days before election Tuesday, Mary Jane Haskins, a bright young lady who worked as a buyer at the Park Central Goldwaters store in Phoenix, looked out her office window and noticed two men putting what appeared to be handbills in the cars in the parking lot. Something about their actions aroused her curiosity. She decided to investigate. What she found was the most improbable political handbill ever devised. It was a cartoon drawing of Joseph Stalin. The headline at the top said, "Why not Goldwater?" Below the cartoon there was a paste-up message implying that the Mine, Mill and Smelter Workers Union and Goldwater would merit Stalin's support.

Mary Jane recruited some store employees, had them gather up whatever handbills they could find, then called Steve. He went to the store. Mary Jane gave him about 150 of the leaflets. I was out of Phoenix on the final campaign trip to southern Arizona. By late Friday evening it was learned a few handbills had been put in cars on East and West McDowell Road. There were no reports of any other distribution in the Phoenix area.

Both federal and state law require sponsor identification on all political literature. Newspaper ads, brochures, anything printed must have at least three names with an address. There was no such identification on the Stalin pamphlet. It was clear violation of the law.

Shadegg took samples of the handbill to the editorial rooms of the *Arizona Republic* and the *Phoenix Gazette*. He admitted he was puzzled. It was, he said, patently ridiculous to try to link Goldwater to Stalin. Why were the leaflets put in cars at Goldwater's store? It seemed obvious whoever distributed the pamphlets wanted to make sure we would find them.

Shadegg reported the affair to the Phoenix Police Department and to the FBI; then he mailed copies of the pamphlets to the editorial rooms of every daily newspaper with the simple notation that this leaflet had been distributed in the Phoenix area by persons unknown.

On Saturday morning all the Arizona daily papers carried stories about the Stalin pamphlet. They reported a new development. Senator Theodore Green (D-R. I.) was sending James H. Duffy, a staff member of his Select Committee on Privileges and Elections, to Arizona to investigate the distribution of the unsigned handbill. When I read that story, it was obvious to me Duffy must have known about the handbill before we did. My Washington staff quickly produced verification of that assumption. Duffy had ordered his airline tickets and made his reservation on Thursday, twenty-four hours before the first handbill appeared in Phoenix.

When Duffy arrived, he called on the editorial rooms of the *Arizona Republic* but made no effort to contact me. He apparently didn't want to interview the people at the store who found the handbills.

Monday morning's newspaper carried Duffy's lengthy statement, in which he charged that the only widespread distribution had been made by Stephen Shadegg, my campaign manager. Then he checked out of his hotel room and disappeared.

In 1973 and 1974 the press and the public exhibited great indignation over the Watergate affair—the break-ins, the telephone taps, the efforts to smear the innocent, and the attempt by those responsible to cover up their actions. In 1958 my campaign telephones were tapped. The office of my manager was burglarized. Professional scandalmongers were released simultaneously in four areas of the state to discredit me. There were threats against my life and the life of my campaign manager. An attempt was made to sabotage my airplane.

Would the voters of Arizona believe Shadegg had engineered the distribution of the Stalin pamphlet as a part of some Machiavellian scheme to smear McFarland by reverse inference? I didn't think so. There was no way to be certain. Fortunately we had a full thirty minutes on Monday evening before election on all the television stations in Arizona.

We condensed the planned discussion with my family to about ten minutes. Then I displayed the Stalin pamphlet. I recited where and how it had been found. I revealed that Duffy had made his airplane reservations in Washington before we knew of the existence of the pamphlet. I pointed out he had made no attempt to contact the people who found the pamphlet or to speak with me. I said that I had been trying all day long to locate Mr. Duffy and couldn't find him. I concluded that television presentation saying, "I'm here, Shadegg's here, where is Duffy?"

There is no way of telling what effect the Stalin pamphlet incident had on that election. McFarland had defeated his Republican opponent for governor in 1956 by 50,000 votes. He lost the 1958 election to me by 35,000 votes—which by any standard is a hell of a turnaround.

The Democrats kept the Stalin leaflet scandal alive in the press. There were repeated charges that Shadegg had been responsible for its creation and distribution. In June 1960 Frank Goldberg, a Democratic member of the International Association of Machinists, AFL-CIO, and Earl N. Anderson, a onetime Grand Lodge Representative for four western states of the International Association of Machinists, were convicted of printing and distributing the illegal campaign material.

The FBI investigators established that the printing cost for the pamphlets had actually been paid for in Los Angeles by the Machinists Union. After Anderson and Goldberg were convicted, the union officials said that it had been a mistake to pay for the pamphlet and that payment had been made without their knowledge.

The bizarre aspects of that campaign captured the attention of the national press. One senatorial race in a small western state, even though my reelection was considered an upset, would never have received the attention we got. The efforts of COPE to beat me—the circulation of that improbable Stalin cartoon—did as much as anything else to make me a national figure.

CHAPTER 11

The Big Leagues

When I ran for the Senate in 1952, I was a passionate, determined candidate. Despite the misbehavior of some of the men around Harry Truman and our adoption of what I believed to be a destructive foreign policy, best illustrated by the stalemate in Korea, I was still certain of the goodness and greatness of the American federal system. My personal attitude toward the Senate, the House, the presidency was almost reverential.

I was deeply disappointed when the Republican administration under President Eisenhower, with a working majority in both houses of Congress, proposed to continue the old New Deal, Fair Deal schemes, offering only a modification in scale and no change in direction.

When Republican Senator Wayne Morse switched parties in 1955 to give the Democrats control of the United States Senate, the sordid, seamy, self-centered domination of personal ambition was clearly demonstrated. Principle was forgotten; loyalty was ignored; past debts were repudiated. It was a cold-blooded trade-off for personal advantage.

Serving with Morse for two years, I had developed an attitude of toleration for his long-winded speeches, his insatiable search for personal publicity. He massaged his ego twenty-four hours a day. During one of his filibusters in April 1953 he spoke for twenty-two hours and twenty-six minutes. I wondered how he overwhelmed the commands of nature and concluded he must have had a motorman's relief tube in his trousers.

The Morse defection served to accelerate the ideological divisions within the government and the electorate. The two camps were labeled "conservative" and "liberal." To my mind, this convenient categorization concealed more than it revealed. Many of the old New Deal-Fair Deal men in government were virtually devoid of philosophical commitment. They simply asked, "What's in it for me?" Enlarging the role of government provided more patronage, permitted the distribution of special benefits to easily identified groups. This, in turn, resulted in favorable political support for their benefactors.

From 1953 to 1958 the national press paid little attention to Barry Goldwater. I wasn't seeking publicity; I didn't have a public relations officer on my senatorial staff. But after 1958 there was a not-too-subtle change. The drama of that campaign, heightened by national union opposition and a series of flamboyant events, aroused the interest of my Republican colleagues and some members of the Washington press corps.

Because I had done the unexpected and gotten myself reelected, I was immediately asked to serve again as chairman of the Republican Senatorial Campaign Committee. Traditionally the party leadership selects a new face every two years. They want a man who will not be up for reelection, one who can help the party raise money and perhaps excite some new interest. I had held the post in 1955 and 1956.

I had almost decided not to take the job again when I learned Senator Jacob Javits of New York was opposing me on the ground that "I would alienate liberal Republicans."

Privately I had been telling my friends in the party that Javits ought to go straight, reform, turn over a new leaf, and join the big-government spending Democrats . . . because that is where he belonged. On almost every substantive issue, Jack Javits had voted with the Democratic liberals in opposition to the White House proposals offered by Ike and the majority of the Republican party. I decided to take the job.

The Senatorial Campaign Committee is ostensibly committed to all Republican candidates for the Senate. Its primary purpose is to ensure the reelection of incumbent Republicans. The members who would be coming up for reelection in 1960 were Margaret Chase Smith of Maine, Leverett Saltonstall of Massachusetts, Clifford Case of New Jersey, John Sherman Cooper of Kentucky, Carl Curtis of Nebraska, Karl Mundt of South Dakota, Henry Dworshak of Idaho, Andrew Schoeppel of Kansas, Thomas Martin of Iowa, and Gordon Allott of Colorado. These Senators represented the full spectrum of Republican ideological thinking. Case and Cooper were confirmed supporters of social welfare expansion.

At one of our early meetings they all asked how I had managed to win in Arizona. I promised I would invite Steve Shadegg to Washington to tell them just how we had accomplished that victory.

We met in my office one early spring afternoon. It was a long session. After Steve left, my colleagues, whose political future would be on the block in November 1960, urged me to retain Steve to help them with their campaigns. I did. He did. And with the exception of Martin of Iowa, who decided not to run, all incumbents were reelected. With our help Keith Thompson won a Senate seat in Wyoming. Unfortunately he died before he could be sworn in.

This second time around I visited almost every state, appearing before dozens of party conventions and smaller gatherings. It was this job which resulted in my exposure to grass-roots Republicans and, I believe, ultimately made me the Republican nominee in 1964.

It would not be truthful to pretend I was entirely unaware of the opportunities available to the chairman of the Senatorial Campaign Committee, but I never once thought of it as a stepping-stone to the nomination.

What I did like about this assignment was the chance to study the face of the Republican party, to engage in thoughtful discussion about the future of the Republic. What I found encouraged me. Despite the failures of the Eisenhower administration to make any significant changes, or perhaps I should say radical changes, government spending had been checked. U.S. foreign policy was strong and determined. We had made some progress in our effort to drag racketeers out of organized labor. The economy had prospered.

My appearances before these local Republican groups convinced me they longed for a return to prudent fiscal policies, desired a reduction in the size of the federal establishment. There were times when I questioned my own judgment on this. It occurred to me their applause for the ideas I expressed was perhaps nothing more than polite appreciation given out of loyalty.

My doubts were resolved in November 1959, when I appeared before the Western Republican Conference in the Biltmore Hotel in Los Angeles. New York Governor Nelson Rockefeller, an unannounced but active candidate for the presidential nomination, spoke just ahead of me. The crowd was politely approving.

Nelson Rockefeller was a charming, urbane gentleman, a skillful politician, and a gifted public speaker. At that moment he was the spokesman for an ideological grouping within the party which I call the "Me-Tooers." They embraced most of the objectives of the New Deal and the Fair Deal and were asking voter support on the claim that Republicans could do it better and perhaps a little cheaper.

Rockefeller had increased spending for the State of New York. His rich man's approach to any problem was spend more money—buy your way out. I had no personal dislike for the governor, but I opposed the positions he had taken on most of our domestic problems.*

My reaction to Nelson's speech was probably influenced by other events of that day, having nothing to do with the governor of New York. That morning I had attended a Department of the Interior hearing on water matters in Safford, Arizona. I departed about three in the afternoon for Los Angeles in my twin-engine Bonanza, an estimated two-and-a-half-hour flight.

The weather en route was good until we reached the vicinity of San Gorgonio Pass, where a low ceiling and reduced visibility forced me to continue on instruments. I changed my VFR (visual flight rules) flight plan to IFR (instrument flight rules) with a planned landing at Burbank. When we were about forty miles out, I opened my flight case and discovered the Jeppesen plate for an instrument approach to Burbank was missing. I was confident I

* At the time I strongly disagreed with Rocky's domestic policies; but he was firm and right in his attitude toward national defense; and before his death, his attitude had changed considerably on matters of domestic policy. He was a great American and would have made a good President.

could make the approach, but not having the plate would complicate things. Fortunately, when I arrived over Burbank, the weather had improved. I was cleared for a visual approach and landing.

We got in a taxi, and I told the driver we wanted to go to the Biltmore Hotel. He left the airport, appeared to be a little uncertain, and asked me if I could tell him the way to the Biltmore. He was new on the job and had never been there before.

I claimed my reservation at the hotel desk and then decided to cash a small check for pocket money. The cashier wouldn't take the check and insisted I go to the assistant manager. I could have displayed my senatorial identification, but by this time I was a little out of sorts. The man at the desk reluctantly okayed the check, and I went back to the cashier's cage and got the money. We took the bags to the room. By this time it was after seven o'clock. I decided to go directly to the Biltmore Bowl, where the Republican meeting was already in progress. At the head of the stairs a young Republican with a band on his arm saying "Sergeant at Arms" politely told me the Bowl was full, there was no room, and he was sorry.

My companion attempted to tell the young man he had just refused entrance to Senator Goldwater, who was on the program; but I said to hell with it and decided to have dinner. Before we could order the meal, the chairman of the Western Conference came to the table to tell me that Governor Rockefeller was just being introduced and asked me to come immediately to the platform. He took me in by a back entrance just as Nelson started his talk. It was a true-to-form eastern seaboard Republican approach to the nation's problems.

When I was introduced, the crowd displayed considerable enthusiasm. I paid my respects to the people on the platform, including the governor of New York, and then I said, "For the past twenty-five years the apostles of the welfare state, some Republican, some Democrat, have been busy transforming that stern old gentleman with the top hat, the cutaway coat, the red, white, and blue trousers, from a symbol of dignity and freedom and justice for all men, into a national wet nurse, dispensing a cockeyed kind of patent medicine labeled 'something for nothing,' passing out the soothing syrup and rattles and pacifiers in return for grateful votes on election day."

I observed that Senator John F. Kennedy, who was busily campaigning for the 1960 nomination, had recently said, "Americans have gone soft." My comment: "These people, like the overindulgent guardians who spend the child's inheritance catering to adolescent whims and desires, are now naïvely amazed at what their overindulgence has produced."

I said that my kind of Republican party was committed to a free state, limited central power, a reduction in bureaucracy, and a balanced budget. Everyone there, including Nelson Rockefeller, got the message, and when I finished, the audience gave me a standing ovation. Earl Mazo, the astute political writer for the New York *Herald Tribune,* told a friend of mine in the audience that Goldwater had just challenged Nelson Rockefeller for the Republican presidential nomination. And he would put his chips on Goldwater.

As a result of that speech, I was invited by the editors of the Los Angeles *Times* to write three columns a week for their newspaper. In their announcement of the coming column they described me as "the leading conservative thinker in American public life."

I may have been the most visible conservative spokesman, but I made no claim to being the leader of conservative thinking. My understanding of the nature of man and what society and government ought to be lean heavily on the great conservative thinkers, commencing with Edmund Burke.

One reason I believe most people use labels to define philosophical positions is that full definitions vary, and they are often complex. We conservatives have great reverence for tradition. We don't think change just for the sake of change is always progress. We believe men and nations are governed by moral laws having their origin in divine justice.

I believe with Burke that each present generation has a contract with the generations which preceded it and the generations which will come after it, and by that contract we are required to preserve what we perceive to be good for society and to attempt to improve what we perceive to be evil. I understand that liberty and property are indivisible. Each one of us is entitled to the products of our own labor.

I think most conservatives commence with an understanding that human beings are not perfectable on this earth, nor can they erect and maintain perfect institutions—political, economic, or educational. We can't make heaven on earth.

We believe that all men and women must have equal rights before the law, but we regard egalitarianism as a stultifying, dehumanizing doctrine. Our great reverence for freedom requires us to resist the use of power to coerce or control the individual beyond restraining him from inflicting injury on others. We mistrust power in any establishment because we read history as an ongoing example of the abuses of power.

After three months as a local feature, the Times-Mirror Syndicate offered the column to other newspapers. Within a year 140 newspapers were buying and printing the column.

The column generated tremendous mail response. I got letters from bankers and bookkeepers, from plumbers and painters, housewives and schoolteachers, local politicians and college professors. Some writers disagreed with what I said, but for the most part, the letters echoed my concern for the future of the Republic. I didn't see the column as a vehicle for political advancement. Now I realize this new constituency helped make me the Republican nominee in 1964.

Dean Clarence Manion of Notre Dame is responsible for the writing of the book *The Conscience of a Conservative*. He suggested there was a need for a simple, straightforward delineation of conservative principles, and he helped make the arrangements with the Victor Publishing Company of Shepherdsville, Kentucky, to print the book.

I drew on my earlier speeches for much of the content of that book and put it together with the help of L. Brent Bozell and others. I didn't intend it should become a political platform. All I hoped to accomplish was to awaken the American people to a realization of how far we had moved from the old constitutional concepts toward the new welfare state.

The original print order was for 10,000 copies. Ultimately more than 3.5 million books, in hardback and paper cover, were printed and sold.

CHAPTER 12

Too Hot to Handle

When I was a boy I found inspiration in poet Ernest Henley's "Invictus," which concludes with the words: "I am the master of my fate; I am the captain of my soul." They appealed to my sense of independence. Most of us would like to take charge of life, rather than let life take charge of us. But Henley was speaking of eternity, and our lives are temporal.

Shakespeare tells of the "tide in the affairs of men." In the year 1960 I was truly caught up on a tide of events not of my own making and over which I had little control. There was a growing discontent in the great family of Republicans. The election of Dwight Eisenhower in 1952 and his reelection in 1956 had been a vote for change, an expression of protest against the increasing emphasis on social programs at the federal level.

Rank-and-file Republicans and Democrats with whom I visited on my travels were disappointed with the Eisenhower administration. The President's personal popularity had not diminished substantially, but the great expectations of 1952 had not been realized. There is an inherent rate of attrition of popular support for every national leader, but in Ike's case this had been accelerated in two specific areas. Working Republicans, the men and women who man the precincts, produce the state conventions, raise the party funds, had come to understand that although Ike wore the Republican label, he operated a nonpartisan administration. The U-2 incident and the launching of Sputnik added to Republican tribulations.

Harry Dent and the term "southern strategy" had not emerged in the political dialogue in 1960, but as chairman of the Senatorial Campaign Committee I was anxious to increase the party strength in every geographical section of the country. In March I went to South Carolina to address the Republican State Convention at the invitation of Chairman Greg Shorey. Rural parochialism had once enclosed the Solid South like a Chinese wall. This ancient barrier had been breached by a new era of industrialization. The old social and political conditions were changing. A great many southern Democrats believed they had been evicted from their party by the New Deal, Fair Deal administrations. It was a condition comparable to our experience in Arizona.

In 1952 and 1956 Eisenhower lost South Carolina to the Democratic nominee. I discovered that Ike's heir apparent, Vice President Richard Nixon, was viewed with suspicion by South Carolina Republicans.

In my speech I reminded the audience that since 1955 the Democrats had controlled the Congress, that the Congress actually runs the country, that attention should be focused on what Ike had been able to accomplish, not on his real or imagined deficiencies. I described my hopes for the Republican party. It was the kind of speech I had made at least twenty times since the first of the year.

The reaction of the audience was something I had not anticipated, the results something I did not desire. The convention pledged its delegates to the nomination of Barry Goldwater for President in 1960.

I tried to tell Shorey and National Committeeman Roger Milliken, for whom I have great affection, that their action was counterproductive. I was not seeking the nomination. I had no campaign organization, no finance committee, and no personal ambition to be President.

Milliken and Shorey ignored my claim that I had no interest in the presidency. They argued it was necessary to force Nixon to recognize reality, to make him understand that many Republicans longed for a substantial change in national directions.

Shorey thought Nixon was taking his nomination for granted. Milliken believed the action of the South Carolina Republicans would jar the Vice President's complacent attitude.

I told them in no uncertain terms I didn't enjoy being used in this manner to get their message across. I suppose I could have publicly rejected the convention's action. It would have been politically expedient to do so. But the effects on the convention would have been disastrous. From a philosophical standpoint they were practicing what I had been preaching. Despite the awkwardness of the situation they had created, I decided to let it stand. It just might work. I had been trying for seven years as a member of the United States Senate to change the public's perception of the Republicans as a party without a distinct philosophy and program of its own. Perhaps this action would further that objective. If I suffered some political injury, that really didn't matter. When I returned to Washington, I took some good-natured kidding from my colleagues.

I have characterized Nixon as a loner, a cold man with great self-confidence and a one-track mind centered on the advancement of Richard Nixon. When next I encountered him, he seemed a little colder than usual. He didn't bring up the subject of the South Carolina delegation, and I didn't bother to explain. But one thing was evident—Nixon had gotten some kind of message.

In 1960 the President's attitude toward Nixon was ambivalent. I suppose every President is reluctant to believe that his successor can outshine him. In his public appearances Nixon was more interested in advocating his own program than in paying tribute to a soon-to-be-departed President. The King is dead; long live the King.

I got the impression Ike was secretly pleased by the action of the South Carolina Republican Convention—not that he really had any interest in my nomination or that he believed it would bring about Nixon's defeat at the convention. I don't think Ike ever recognized this small ripple was in any way a reflection of discontent with his years in the White House.

The outright Nixon supporters I encountered either ignored the South Carolina action or tabled it as a small aberration. But it did require me to face up to a situation in my home state.

Congressman John Rhodes and Republican Party Chairman Richard Kleindienst of Arizona were committed to Nixon's nomination. I understood and respected their reasons for wanting the Arizona delegation to go to Chicago committed to the Vice President. In the face of the South Carolina action, I couldn't permit that to happen, even though I wasn't a serious contender, didn't want the nomination, and knew there was no chance of getting it had I wanted it. It would still be a humiliating political repudiation if my home state committed itself to Nixon in view of the South Carolina endorsement.

I explained my predicament to Rhodes and Kleindienst. They were very understanding. I told them I intended to withdraw and not permit my name to be placed before the convention, but I wanted the Arizona delegates to go to Chicago pledged to me.

It has always been my style to put the cards on the table. When the Arizona Republicans met in April, I explained privately to most of them that while I was not a serious contender, I wanted their support on the way in. Making me their favorite son selection would not, I estimated, cost them anything. I said that Nixon and his lieutenants would understand the situation and that before the nominations were made, I intended to release them and pledge my own support to the Vice President. I suppose a pure idealist would call this hypocrisy, but everyone who has engaged in practical politics must agree it was the only acceptable course of action. On April 23, 1960, the fourteen delegates from Arizona were pledged to my support.

Favorite son candidacies are frequently no more than an ego trip for the individual involved. I hoped to use whatever leverage the situation might provide to persuade the Platform Committee to recognize the aspirations of grass-roots Republicans who were not particularly happy with Richard Nixon.

I went to Chicago with two prepared statements—one to present to the Platform Committee, and the second to announce my withdrawal as an active candidate. I intended to make the second before the convention opened but not until the Platform Committee had made its decisions.

It may be difficult for anyone outside the inner world of politics to accept my statement in the preceding paragraph. I believed Nixon would be and should be the Republican nominee for President in 1960, and as a demonstration of that belief, I intend now to break my silence and describe in detail an undertaking of mine calculated to strengthen Nixon to the detriment of his opponent.

In January 1960 the front-running Democratic candidate for the nomination, Massachusetts's Senator John Kennedy, persuaded Mike DeSalle, governor of Ohio, to pledge that state's sixty-four delegate votes to him. Minnesota Senator Hubert Humphrey, Texas Senator Lyndon Johnson, and Missouri Senator Stu Symington were all candidates in the running.

But Humphrey appeared to be the only one willing to challenge Kennedy in the early primaries. Wisconsin, being next door to Minnesota, was a natural battleground. The Kennedy machine— money, organization, and the exploitation of the religious issue— made it a debacle. Poor Hubert never knew what hit him.

Joseph P. Kennedy, Sr., founder of the Kennedy dynasty, was a man of great talent and insatiable ambition, the son of an Irish saloonkeeper who had risen to a position of power in Massachusetts politics. He was an opportunistic, ruthless businessman. During World War II he was an isolationist. Winston Churchill called him an "appeaser." He admired Senator Joseph McCarthy and contributed generously to the Senator's campaign efforts. But no critic of Kennedy, Sr., has ever accused him of failing to use his money for what he believed in, and Joe Kennedy believed his son Jack should be President of the United States. If it cost him two or ten or thirty million, so what? He had the money to spare.

Enraged by his defeat, Humphrey announced there would be a rerun in the West Virginia primaries to be held on May 10. Beginning in April, the news media printed numerous reports of rigged polls, Kennedy money, and political dirty tricks taking shape in West Virginia. Candidate Kennedy invoked the image of Franklin Roosevelt and campaigned as a born-again FDR New Dealer.

Humphrey was wiped out. Kennedy came out of West Virginia with an 80,000-vote lead, in a race where only 360,000 votes were cast. The notion that Jack Kennedy would be invincible in the general election began to take shape. It was obvious that unless something were done to counteract that public perception, our Republican party candidate would have a very difficult time in November. If the stories of vote buying and political skulduggery which were being whispered could be proved, it might be possible to derail the John Kennedy bandwagon.

As chairman of the Republican Senatorial Campaign Committee I had access to certain political funds. I ordered my most trusted associate to undertake a cautious but thorough inquiry into the alleged misdeeds of the Kennedy campaign team in West Virginia.

It wouldn't do any good to concentrate on the public display of Kennedy power. It was built on charm and enthusiasm and youth and the sycophantic attitude of the national press and a Hollywood-style publicity campaign. However, if we could document some indictable offenses—not just rumors or allegations—the results of that primary could be turned to the advantage of the Republican candidate in 1960.

I didn't ask anyone's permission. I didn't tell Nixon or President Eisenhower what I planned. If we came up empty, no harm would be done. If we could find some solid facts, there would be plenty of time for action.

The investigation I authorized was carried out by a former FBI agent, a man who was extremely sensitive to the political realities. He had been involved in my Arizona campaign in 1958. I had come to respect his skill and resourcefulness, and his integrity was unquestioned.

There is an adage that where there is smoke there is fire. There had been enough smoke in the West Virginia newspapers and in the national press to encourage me to believe we might find some glowing flames. I was utterly flabbergasted when I got the results: sixteen affidavits, statements from individuals who freely confessed criminal acts on behalf of the Kennedy forces, properly witnessed and sworn to in front of West Virginia notary publics. I don't know how our man persuaded these people to confess their wrongdoings, but he did it.

Our investigator was a lawyer. The statements meet every legal requirement, were made of the witnesses' own free will, not under duress, no threats, no promises. One confessed that he had not lived in the state of West Virginia for more than ten years—said he had been brought back by the county machine to run his precinct's polls on that election day and then to count the votes in favor of John Kennedy, regardless of what the ballot said.

Another witness told of distributing 200 half-pints of Kentucky moonshine whiskey, together with $2 each, to voters who promised to cast their ballot in accordance with the county ticket, which had Kennedy at the top. There were affidavits confessing illegal voting. One man boasted he had let his relatives vote more than once. A number of statements from election officials admitted they had sold the organization strength of Kennedy supporters for a contribution to the county party and distributed tickets to the party faithful bearing Kennedy's name.

The Baltimore *Sun* had printed a by-line story by Howard Norton explaining how West Virginia county politicians delivered the vote to the candidate who made the greatest contribution to their county committee. Norton said:

> The county politicians very frankly do not care much who wins in a presidential primary. Their job is to keep their party in office in the county. The pros are apt to regard presidential primary invaders chiefly as potential sources of revenue for the county campaign chests.
>
> Once the dealing is completed the party leaders print up on little slips of paper the official slate of candidates whom they urge the voters to accept.

Editor Charles D. Hilton, Jr., of the Logan *Banner* called that primary, "one of the most corrupt elections in county history." There were allegations that Kennedy had spent up to $1 million to insure Humphrey's defeat.

The news stories were general in character. The affidavits I had were specific. I informed Richard Nixon of the content of the affidavits. He told me to give them to the Attorney General, William Rogers. I did so, fully expecting immediate action—perhaps a federal grand jury, perhaps a full-scale investigation by the FBI.

The press reports all suggested impropriety. The affidavits I gave to Rogers were evidence of specific criminal acts, committed by individuals who said they had been employed by the Kennedy campaign group, involving violations of both state and federal laws.

When a week passed and nothing happened, I began to wonder. At the end of two weeks my mind began to be filled with all sorts of dark suspicions.

The Attorney General of the United States, a man who was presumed to be a close friend of Richard Nixon, either on his own initiative or perhaps on instruction, took absolutely no action. He never mentioned the affidavits to the press. So far as I know, he made no investigation. He did not contact the agent we had sent into West Virginia. He did nothing.

When a month had passed with no action, I concluded that Rogers and Nixon had decided to hold off for a time in order to break the scandal publicly just prior to the Democratic Nominating Convention. As the weeks dragged on, I came to realize that for some unexplainable reason Rogers, or Rogers and Nixon, had decided not to use the evidence we had.

Bill Rogers was never an aggressive Attorney General. Perhaps the true explanation is that the matter was too hot for him to handle. I will always believe that had he sought indictments on the basis of those affidavits, John F. Kennedy would not have been nominated for President in 1960.

After Los Angeles, I fastened on the hope that perhaps the whole seamy, sordid mess would be displayed in the general election. When I asked Nixon about this during that campaign year, he gave me an evasive answer.

Hindsight is a wonderful thing. If I had it to do over again, I would distribute the affidavits to some member of the national press before surrendering them to the Attorney General. We live and learn.

I became further disenchanted with Bill Rogers as Attorney General following the 1960 special election in North Dakota. The incumbent Senator, William Langer, had died. State law required a special election ahead of the general election scheduled for November. The Republican candidate was then Governor John Davis; his opponent, Congressman Quentin Burdick.

Davis was a popular governor, but he did not enjoy the support of organized labor. North Dakota had the same kind of instant voter registration President Carter has advocated—that is, on election day a voter could present himself at the polls, announce his name, give an address, and sign an affidavit of qualification. He was then given a ballot and permitted to cast it.

Davis lost that special election by about 1,000 votes, even though the polls had shown him in the lead. A few days after the ballots were counted I was informed the Republicans had discovered widespread vote fraud. In the city of Minot some 535 people had cast their ballots on the basis of that affidavit of qualification, but investigators could not locate the individuals or the addresses given. Similar results were discovered in Bismarck and Fargo.

Governor Davis's campaign chairman came to Washington and delivered the results of the investigation personally to the Attorney General. In light of the narrow victory of the Democratic candidate, I believed the fraudulent votes might have made the difference. It seemed altogether proper for the Attorney General of the United States to invalidate the special election and order a rerun in November. Rogers refused to act.

CHAPTER 13

The American Munich

There is a widespread misconception that party politicians, the men and women who serve on state and national committees, are hard-nosed pros. The truth is, most of them are quite average men and women. Some get involved in party affairs to enhance their own identities. Others have strong convictions, resting on idealism and devotion to a particular political philosophy. The cement which holds them together is more often the genuine desire to serve the nation's interest than it is a reach for personal power.

What followed my selection as a favorite son candidate by the Arizona Republicans illustrates this point. These citizen party leaders from all across the nation called to offer their support if I intended to be a serious candidadate. When I explained the reality of the situation, they appeared to be disappointed, and this disturbed me. Were these callers, I wondered, just trying to butter me up? Or could it be they really believed there was any chance of blocking Nixon's nomination? Had I, by not rejecting the South Carolina action, set in motion a movement which might seriously injure Republican chances for victory in November?

When some of my close supporters in Arizona formed a Goldwater for President Committee, began raising money to purchase buttons and pennants and campaign literature, I begged them to cool it. They wouldn't listen to me.

In Washington the real pros—Senator Thruston B. Morton, who had succeeded Meade Alcorn as chairman of the National Republican Committee; Len Hall, Nixon's campaign manager; and, particularly, my Republican colleagues who were running for reelection—understood my predicament and were generally supportive.

Nixon was busy building his own organization. The whisper of a challenge in the wake of the South Carolina and Arizona actions increased the public's interest in the Republican convention. My fundraising activities on behalf of the Senatorial Campaign Committee drew bigger crowds and increased contributions, but that projected challenge was an illusion. I was a part of it. It made me uncomfortable.

The contest for the Democratic nomination between John F. Kennedy and Lyndon Johnson was claiming most of the attention of the press and TV. The Democrats, in my opinion, have a remarkable talent. They can go through a primary—kicking, gouging, and slugging—then kiss, make up, and unite behind the victor for the general election. Republicans, divided in a primary contest, never seem quite able to get back together. I was determined not to add to the existing divisions within the Republican constituency.

Nixon would have the nomination, there was no doubt about it; but within the party, he enjoyed no more than lukewarm support. As I listened to the Republicans that spring, I concluded this lack of fervor for Ike's heir apparent came about because the party workers were unsure of Nixon's philsophical position. He appeared to be equivocating, anxious to please everyone, determined not to say anything or do anything which might alienate any ideologically united subgrouping within the party.

As chairman of the Senatorial Campaign Committee I went to see Nixon. I told him I thought all our senatorial candidates who were incumbents would be reelected. Then I said, "But you should know that a number of people I've talked with are disappointed with your failure to take a strong stand on some conservative issues—federal spending, a balanced budget, the growing bureaucracy."

Nixon told me I could reassure these doubters. He would demand a reduction in spending and a balanced budget and halt the bureaucratic growth. He said he hadn't mentioned these things because he thought to do so would be taken as a public criticism of the failures of the Eisenhower administration.

We talked for a moment about Senator Kennedy's exploitation of the missile gap. "I could explode that phony in ten minutes," Nixon said, "by displaying our high-altitude reconnaissance photographs and explaining the quality of information we are getting. I can't do that without destroying our sources, and Kennedy, the bastard, knows I can't."

We talked about Nelson Rockefeller. I told Nixon I thought Rockefeller had recruited substantial support among the more liberal Republicans.

Nixon laughed. "Yes, he's real big with the Ripon Society. What the governor really wants is to be on the ticket—to be my Vice President. I won't take him."

We talked about the Platform Committee, and Nixon said he thought the chairman, Chuck Percy, was probably a Rockefeller supporter. "Rockefeller wants to talk to me. I am treating him very politely, but, I promise, I'm not going to visit with him until after the convention."

It is commonly understood that party platforms are written to be ignored and forgotten. Drafters search for God and Motherhood declarations calculated to please everyone and offend no one. After the election, the platform becomes whatever the newly elected President says it is. Like Jell-O shimmering on a dessert plate, there is usually little substance and nothing you can get your teeth into.

In early 1959, Meade Alcorn, the chairman of the Republican National Committee, with the approval and support of President Eisenhower, had formed a committee to do some preliminary work on a party platform, although this was not its stated purpose. The forty-one members on the committee represented every geographical section, a variety of occupations, professions, and particular expertise, and the whole ideological spectrum. Ike had sleected Charles H. Percy, the young, dynamic president of Bell & Howell, to serve as chairman. Because of his work with this committee, Percy had been named chairman of the Platform Committee.

In June the editors of *Newsweek* magazine invited me to write a guest column in response to their general questions: Could the Republicans win in 1960? What would they have to do to win?

The magazine understood I was not a serious contender for the nomination.

The statement I wrote for the magazine called for rededication to the traditional principles of the Republican party. I warned against any posture which might be interpreted as a me-too support for the social welfare programs sponsored by the Democrats.

The Republican Convention opened in Chicago on July 25. I had moved into a two-room suite at the Blackstone Hotel six days earlier in order to present my recommendations to the Platform Committee, where I was scheduled to appear on Wednesday, July 20. I had with me the statement I planned to release Friday or Saturday withdrawing my name from consideration and pledging support to Richard Nixon.

When some of the early arrivals from other states approached my secretary, Mrs. Edna Coever, with a request that I appear before their delegations, we politely refused, saying I was not a candidate and would not be a candidate.

On Saturday morning I had just been introduced to address the Republican Finance Committee when an emissary from Len Hall interrupted. He said Hall, who was Nixon's campaign manager, had to see me immediately on a matter of utmost importance.

I said I would not treat the Finance Committee with such discourtesy—Len Hall would have to wait until I was finished. The messenger then said Mr. Hall wanted me to know that according to the Associated Press, Richard Nixon had gone from Washington, D.C., to New York Friday night for a secret rendezvous with Governor Nelson Rockefeller. The AP story said the two Republicans had discussed the party platform being written in Chicago and possible choices for the vice presidency.

I couldn't believe it was true. If Nixon had gone to New York, it was a direct repudiation of the promise he had made to me.

I apologized to the committee and left the room. Len Hall was staying at the Hilton. He said a member of Nixon's staff had confirmed the AP report. He was as angry as any man I have ever seen. His language was blunt and profane. I didn't blame him. "This won't cost Nixon the nomination," Hall said, "but it might cost him the election."

Had Rockefeller been invited to Washington to visit with Nixon the meeting would have attracted little attention. But Nixon had gone to Rockefeller. It made him the supplicant. The trip would surely be interpreted as an effort by Nixon to strike some sort of bargain with the governor of New York.

I had previously scheduled a press conference at ten o'clock that Saturday morning, intending to read my withdrawal statement. That could wait. The reporters wanted to discuss the Rockefeller-Nixon meeting. Did it mean the formation of a new political partnership? Would Rockefeller be given the Vice President's spot as a payoff?

I called the New York meeting "an American Munich" and said the convention delegates who were supporting Richard Nixon would never accept Rockefeller on the ticket. I did not tell them the Vice President, by his action, had broken his earlier promise to me. Perhaps I should have.

The Platform Committee had been scheduled to complete its work Friday afternoon. Because of the Rockefeller-inspired push to include a plank calling for increased spending on welfare and education and repeal of Section 14b of the Taft-Hartley Act, the committee had been forced to reconvene that Saturday morning. I told the reporters why it had been necessary to hold this extra session and predicted the Rockefeller effort would fail.

In a number of delegations pledged to Richard Nixon efforts were under way to get around that earlier commitment. Albert B. Fay, chairman of the Texas delegation, and Congressman Bruce Alger came to the Blackstone to tell me they intended to caucus their delegates on Monday. They were confident Texas would leave Nixon and vote for me.

Monday night former President Herbert Hoover delivered a thoughtful and inspiring speech. He said:

> Today America is in the midst of a frightening moral slump. . . . Our courts have been hobbled in the use of punishment as a deterrent to crime by procedures. . . . This nation needs a rebirth of a great spiritual force which has been impaired by cynicism and weakened by foreign infections. You can call it nationalism if you will, but there is an American kind of nationalism which is neither isolationism nor aggression and embedded deep within it is compassion for distress, both at home and abroad. It is a kind of nationalism which recognizes changes in the world and requires that we meet them with forward-looking measures.

But the spiritual force of which I speak is also enshrined in one word. That word is "America." We do not use that word merely as a geographical term. At one time, and even now, for millions of Americans that word summoned to mind the whole background of our country.

Mr. Hoover spelled it out. The delegates understood what he was saying. The press ignored him. It was, in show biz terms, a hell of an act to follow.

Among other things, I said, "Now this is no time for small disputes. Well-intentioned men of good motive are engaged in serious debate." I called for party unity. My only words of criticism were directed against our opponents. Nowhere in that statement is there an indication of the frustration and disillusionment and anger which the Rockefeller-Nixon meeting had engendered.

Tuesday the proportions of the revolt against Nixon's nomination could not be ignored. Texas released its delegates from their commitment to Nixon. That amateur band of eager beavers working on my behalf reported I could count on 287 delegate votes. They begged me to let my name be presented to the convention.

On Tuesday evening, July 26, President Eisenhower addressed the convention. He carefully avoided saying anything which might be construed as an endorsement of any possible successor. In one paragraph he condemned "whoever misleads by calculated use of some, but not all, of the facts." He said, "Whoever distorts the truth to serve with selfish ambition, whoever asserts weakness where strength exists—makes a mockery of the democratic process and misrepresents our beloved country in the eyes of a watching world" (a not-too-subtle reference to candidate Kennedy's constant use of the missile gap theme). Ike pointed out that our gross national product had increased 25 percent during the seven and one-half years of his administration and compared this to the eight years of the prior Democratic administration, during which time the GNP had actually declined.

He praised private enterprise, declared that our dependence upon moral law contradicted those who believed "that healthy growth can thus be bought from the funds of the federal treasury." Ike also contrasted the inflation rate, saying prices had increased

48 percent between 1944 and 1952 and only 11 percent between 1952 and 1959.

Since Ike left the White House, the purchasing power of our dollar has decreased by sixty-four cents. The annual rate of inflation under Ike was 1.3 percent. In the second year of the Carter administration it was more than 10 percent.

Ike spoke with pride about the national defense establishment (the Polaris submarine had just passed its final test). He mentioned the intermediate and intercontinental ballistic missiles, saying the Russians had commenced development of these weapons shortly after the close of World War II, but we had failed to start our program until he became President and we were now superior to the Russians. He praised our defense alliances, NATO and SEATO, and declared over and over again that our objective was world peace. He deplored the plight of free men and women everywhere who had fallen under the control of the Soviet oppressor.

Wednesday morning I met with Greg Shorey, Roger Milliken, Albert Fay of Texas, Clarence Manion of Notre Dame, and leaders of the Arizona delegation. Shorey and Milliken were committed. With or without my permission they intended to place my name in nomination. It was a time for blunt talk.

I told them that if we pursued this course and permitted the delegates—287 or all that remained faithful to their promise—to vote for me, it would not affect the outcome. I reminded them of how the Taft delegates had been treated for supporting a loser eight years earlier. I said, "I appreciate your sentiment. Your willingness to put your necks on the line for me is a very humbling experience, but I'm not going to let you do it."

After I left the room, one of my close associates explained it would do our cause no good to take a licking. We might, if we pursued this course, create a real division within the party. The plan he advanced was to have my name placed in nomination. This, we believed, must be done by a member of the Arizona delegation. There would be some seconding speeches; then I would take the podium, withdraw my name, and urge all the delegates supporting me to vote for Richard Nixon.

In my opinion, it was the best of a bad bargain. I thought if we could handle the situation with skill and finesse, we might unite the party. I also cherished the hope the delegates would remark on the difference between my attitude and that of Nelson Rockefeller, who was still pretending to be a serious contender.

I don't think anyone really liked the arrangement. We had selected Governor Paul Fannin of Arizona to make the principal nominating speech. He rebelled at reading the first paragraph of the draft which was given to him because it said, "The action I shall take here tonight is directly contrary to the wishes of a man who has been my friend since childhood. As all of you know, at ten o'clock this morning the man whose name I shall place in nomination specifically recommended against such action. In any other situation I would feel compelled to accept this decision without question, but this is not an ordinary situation. The Arizona delegation, after careful deliberation, was unanimous in its insistence that I carry out this responsibility."

Paul Fannin is one of the few politicians I have been privileged to know who has never equivocated. At the beginning of his career someone said he was too honest to be a good politician. And through all his years in public service he was just that—honest.

His attitude Wednesday was simply this: If Barry doesn't want me to do it, I won't do it. When all the delicate nuances of the situation were carefully explained to him, Fannin agreed the language was appropriate. He understood my true feelings. He recognized that if Arizona passed and permitted South Carolina to put my name in nomination, the delegates wouldn't understand, the TV audience would be puzzled, and the Arizona Republicans would be embarrassed.

Fannin made his speech Wednesday night. In my prejudiced opinion, he was magnificent—no overblown rhetoric, just the facts of the case. The record of that convention says in parentheses: "At the conclusion of Governor Fannin's address, there were cheers and applause and a demonstration lasting approximately eleven minutes."

My supporters had requested an allocation of tickets normally granted to permit nondelegates to come on the floor and participate in a demonstration. We got the tickets Wednesday afternoon. They were for the wrong night. Not a single Young Republican or nondelegate was admitted to the floor. The only people who participated in that demonstration were delegates and alternates.

To claim I was unmoved emotionally would be an outrageous

falsehood. When I saw the state banners parading down that aisle and heard the cheers, I looked toward the booth where Peggy and my daughter, Little Peggy, were seated. They both were in tears, and I was very close to joining them.

The Arizona delegation had asked permission to bring in the Yuma Indian Band to march in the demonstration and had been refused. The convention organ remained silent. But the demonstrators made up for this lack of musical accompaniment.

As the parade went on, I began to realize the numbers were diminishing. Not until much later did I learn the convention ushers had led the Goldwater demonstrators through an exit to an area behind the hall and then attempted to refuse them readmission. When an usher attempted to prevent Steve Shadegg and Bill Turner of Arizona from reentering the hall, they challenged him. He said his orders were to get the demonstrators out of the hall and keep them out.

It may be that Dick Nixon didn't know what his convention managers were doing. But someone told the organist not to play, someone sent us the extra tickets for the wrong night, and someone told the ushers to squelch the demonstration.

When it came to my turn to speak at the convention, this is what I said:

"Thank you. Mr. Chairman, delegates to the convention, and fellow Republicans, I respectfully ask the chairman to withdraw my name from nomination. [Chorus of noes.]

"Please. I release my delegation from their pledge to me, and while I am not a delegate, I would suggest that they give these votes to Richard Nixon.

"Now, Mr. Chairman, with your kind permission and indulgence as a conservative Republican, I would like to make a few statements I think might help in this coming election.

"We are conservatives. This great Republican party is our historic house. This is our home."

I pointed out that no party platform can please every party member. I said that in the past thirty years those with more radical views had found a home in the Democratic party while those with strong historic beliefs were comfortable in the Republican party.

I called attention to the press reports which said that Lyndon Johnson was predicting there would be a split in the Republican party. I asked the delegates to serve notice on the Democratic party's candidate for Vice President that there would be no split. I said we weren't about to turn this country over by default to a party which had lost its belief in the dignity of man, a party which had no faith in our economic system, a party which had come to the belief that the United States was a second-rate power.

I said we had lost elections because conservative Republicans had stayed away from the polls. I said the country was too important for anyone's feelings. In conclusion, I said, "I am a conservative. I am going to devote all my time from now until November to electing Republicans from the top of the ticket to the bottom of the ticket, and I call upon my fellow conservatives to do the same."

CHAPTER 14

Nixon-Lodge—Disaster

In the dictionary the first definition of politics is "the science or art of political government." No suggestion of dishonor attaches to the word, but a politician is defined as "a seeker or holder of public office who is more concerned about winning favor or retaining power than about maintaining principles." When public officials misbehave, we are all prone to say, "Well, that's politics," lumping all officeholders and public employees in the same class.

A great many delegates to the Chicago convention of 1960, perhaps the majority, shared my indignation over the Nixon trip to New York. What truly inspired a frenzy of vituperation was my public support of the Nixon-Lodge ticket.

Dan Smoot, the radio columnist, and Kent and Phoebe Courtney, publishers of the *Independent American,* among others, alleged betrayal. They suggested I must have made a deal with Nixon, been promised some quid pro quo to urge my own followers to work for the national ticket. The result of all this was an aggravating paradox.

The party workers who had been most insistent my name be placed in nomination were now ready to go home and sulk in their tents. Because they had failed to impose their will on the party, they wanted to quit the game.

I deplore the use of labels which has become so prevalent in this century. At best, these qualifiers are meaningless oversimplifications. At worst, they are derogatory and insulting.

I chafe under the dogmatic insistence of some members of the John Birch Society that you must accept 100 percent of their doctrine or be less than worthy. I believe in general their difficulty stems from the references of Robert Welch to Dwight Eisenhower in his book *The Politician*.

About the time *The Politician* was written, Welch had a brother who lived in Phoenix. It's been so long I don't remember his first name, but I do remember he called me and asked if his brother could come and see me about a matter of great importance.

When Robert Welch came, he was carrying a package wrapped in brown paper and tied with string. I had heard of Welch, but I knew nothing of the movement he was attempting to start. He untied the string, removed the brown paper, and handed me a manuscript copy of *The Politician*, which he urged me to read. We had a brief, pleasant conversation; I agreed to look at his book and then give him my opinion.

When I returned the book, I begged him not to print it. I said I couldn't accept his theory that Ike was either a dunce and a dupe or a conscious communist sympathizer. I told him I too was disturbed about the spread of communism worldwide. We had made some disastrous foreign policy decisions, but I thought he would harm his cause if he printed the book.

No man should be judged by a single act. Robert Welch has done much to alert people to the dangers of communism. Most of the John Birchers are patriotic, concerned, law-abiding, hard-working, and productive. There are a few whom I call Robert Welchers, and these are the fanatics who regard everyone who doesn't totally agree with them as communist sympathizers.

There was no reason for me to be pleased with Nixon's behavior. I regarded his selection of Henry Cabot Lodge as a disastrous blunder. Lodge was a highly respected Boston Brahmin, but I couldn't find any evidence of his political strength outside New England. I knew the Kennedys controlled Massachusetts, his home state.

Senator Leverett Saltonstall, a fine Republican and a wonderful gentleman, was one of the incumbent Republican Senators running for reelection in 1960. Saltonstall had a long-established working arrangement with the Kennedy organization in Massachusetts. When Jack Kennedy sought election to the House of Representatives in 1946, Saltonstall, then in his first term in the Senate, was shrewd enough to recognize that Kennedy charm and Kennedy money would make young Jack the winner. He stayed out of that fight. Two years later, when Saltonstall was campaigning for his second term, Kennedy returned the favor. This was not an unusual situation. Similar arrangements between incumbent members of Congress can be found in many states.

During my 1952 campaign in Arizona, Democratic United States Senator Carl Hayden gave only nominal support to my Democratic opponent, Ernest McFarland. When Hayden ran for reelection in 1956, my supporters kept hands off. Now, in 1960, Saltonstall was preoccupied with his own campaign for reelection. Nixon-Lodge were not going to carry Massachusetts against native son John F. Kennedy.

Some party workers will probably regard such an arrangement as distasteful, but it was a practical realistic recognition of relative strength. I intend no criticism of Senator Saltonstall or the Kennedys by reciting these facts. My only purpose is to illuminate one not-often-mentioned aspect of the politics of election.

Lodge would add no particular strength to the ticket in New York State. Governor Rockefeller had been successful by embracing the welfare staters and implementing programs more representative of the ideology of the New Deal-Fair Deal than Republican principles. The governor had made a serious effort to win the nomination for himself in Chicago.

Despite all my misgivings, I was honestly, even passionately, committed to the election of Richard Nixon in 1960 simply because I could not tolerate the alternative. From my point of view, Nixon and Lodge were not the ideal candidates. But Eisenhower and Nixon had not been considered a perfect pairing either. Certainly Kennedy and Johnson were anathema to a great many Democrats.

My friend Jack Williams, who served eight years as governor of Arizona with notable success, is fond of saying, "In this game we have to play with the cards that are dealt to us." For better, or, as it turned out, for worse Richard Nixon and Henry Cabot Lodge had been chosen to carry the Republican banner into that November contest.

Many Democrats were shocked and angry when Kennedy chose

Lyndon Johnson to be his running mate. It was a sword of discontent with two cutting edges. One group, the Camelot Courtiers, treated Johnson with contempt. He was the old politics, flawed by his southern background, his old-line ties.

The Democrats who supported Lyndon as a presidential candidate were suspicious of what they felt sure was a shotgun marriage. There were lamentations from both sides of the Great Divide. Then came a grudging acknowledgment, an embarrassed admiration, for the correctness of this purely political decision. The presence of Lyndon on the ticket would keep the southern troops in line, help carry Texas, satisfy the traditional members of the party who are often inaccurately described as conservative.

It is not difficult for the pragmatist to understand why Kennedy wanted Johnson. The real mystery points in the other direction—why would Lyndon Johnson accept the number two spot?

Long after the election was over, Henry Luce told me that Lyndon had come to his apartment in New York City for dinner the night before he was to go to Los Angeles for the Democratic Convention. Luce said he and his wife, Clare, broached the subject of the vice presidency. Luce told Johnson what his *Time* magazine reporters had told him. "Kennedy is certain to win the nomination for President; the delegates will gather merely to ratify a decision already reached."

According to Luce, Lyndon responded by saying that as the Majority Leader of the United States Senate he exercised more power over the country than any man other than the President. Then he said, "All Vice Presidents are political eunuchs, and I am not, by God, about to let Kennedy cut my balls off." But he did.

The generally accepted explanation for this about-face, and one which Johnson himself offered, is the indisputable fact that the Vice President is just one heartbeat away from the job every Vice President truly wants. In this century, prior to the election of John Kennedy, three Vice Presidents had succeeded to the top job. But Kennedy was only forty-three years old—he was believed to be in excellent health. Lyndon Johnson was a shrewd politician. As such he could clearly comprehend the real reason he was asked to be on the ticket.

The only rational explanation for Lyndon Johnson's turnaround was provided to me by a Johnson insider after Kennedy's death. The Kennedy crowd (my informant said it was Bobby) came to

Johnson in Los Angeles with an invitation to join the ticket. The offer was rejected. Lyndon was told that if he refused the number two spot, and Jack Kennedy could win without him, the new President's first act would be to order a full-scale inquiry into the growth of Lyndon Johnson's personal financial empire, including the monopolistic TV license which had helped make his millions.

The Kennedys commanded an unequaled political intelligence organization. If, as my informant insists, Johnson was pressured into taking the number two spot, I think it quite probable that the facts of the 1948 election fraud were part of that pressure. Almost everyone in the Congress knew the details behind the allegations of fraud in Johnson's defeat of Coke Stevenson for the Democratic nomination to the Senate in 1948. (The additional revelations which surfaced in July 1977 merely confirmed what most of us had known all along.)

My disapproval of the party platform adopted by the Democrats in Los Angeles in 1960 and my disappointment with Lyndon Johnson for accepting the nomination to run with Kennedy prompted me to send Lyndon a letter expressing my feelings on July 15.

Senator Lyndon B. Johnson
State Office Building
Washington, 25, D.C.

Dear Lyndon:

It is the morning after, so to speak, and as I sit here in my study I still have a numb feeling of despair over your actions of yesterday in accepting the candidacy for Vice President. It is difficult to imagine a person like you running in a second spot to a weaker man, but it is even more incredible to try to understand how you are going to try to embrace the socialist platform of your party. I think many people, Lyndon, share my feeling of disappointment.

You were intended for great things, but I don't think you are going to achieve them now.

Sincerely,
Barry Goldwater

I meant everything I said to the delegates in Chicago. I believed then, and still believe, that whatever defects I found in the philosophical position enunciated by Richard Nixon, his policies would prove far more beneficial to the people of the United States than would the policies and codes of political behavior advocated and practiced by Kennedy and Johnson.

Between the closing of the Republican Convention in July and the November election, I campaigned in twenty-six states in support of Nixon-Lodge. In my appeals to voters I pictured the alternative they faced as "intolerable." But I didn't desert my earlier stand on the major issues.

In the popular vote the Kennedy-Johnson margin of victory was 118,850 out of 68,335,642 cast and counted. In percentages, Jack Kennedy won the office of President of the United States by 0.0017 percent of the popular vote.

In the electoral college the Kennedy-Johnson margin was more substantial: 303 to 219. But this was the result of the popular vote in just two states, Illinois and Texas. In Illinois Kennedy's popular vote margin was only 8,858 out of 4,746,834 votes cast and counted—less than two-tenths of 1 percent. In Texas the margin was greater—46,000 out of 2,289,000 votes cast, a difference of about two full percentage points.

On election day I was in Washington, D. C. I had voted absentee in Arizona. About nine o'clock that morning Senator Everett Dirksen called me from Chicago. He said there was widespread fraudulent voting in Cook County and asked me to contact Attorney General Rogers and request that U.S. deputy marshals be sent to certain specific polling places. I agreed to try. Rogers refused to take any action unless specifically ordered to do so by the President of the United States.

I called Dirksen to report the situation. We agreed we both would try to reach Ike. I don't know if the Senator ever spoke with the President. When I finally got through and explained the situation, Ike was outraged, but nothing happened. The President told me much later that by the time he finally got in touch with the Attorney General he was told it was too late to mobilize enough marshals to have any impact at the locations of the suspected illegal voting.

The following morning we received some similar disturbing reports about fraudulent voting in Texas. Within a week energetic reporters in both states were writing stories suggesting the presidential election might have been stolen. The evidence clearly suggests that Kennedy's margin of victory came from the fraudulent votes in Illinois and Texas.

A number of us urged Nixon to demand a full-scale investigation. With a Republican President in the White House, a Republican Attorney General, and Republican-appointed U.S. attorneys, it was reasonable to believe that if the widespread allegations were true, the outcome of the presidential race could be successfully challenged.

Richard Nixon refused to take any action or to authorize anyone to act in his behalf. He said that such a challenge might drag on for months, and in the interim the country would be deprived of any leadership. This, he said, would place us at the mercy of our enemies overseas. Even if the charges were true and could be proved, the enormity of such a reversal would have a disastrous effect. He said that the result would be to disillusion the American electorate, to weaken our constitutional system and that, even if the courts were to declare him a winner, he could never effectively be the President.

In my opinion he was wrong on every reason except the first. In that period of the interregnum, when a nation changes its leaders, there is always an attendant uncertainty. Zbigniew Brzezinski, President Carter's current foreign adviser, at one time passionately advanced the hypothesis that, had the United States moved positively and vigorously in 1953, when Russian leadership was uncertain because of the domestic contest between Khrushchev and Georgi Malenkov, the communists would have been incapable of making any strong response.

As a result of that razor-thin popular vote victory, Kennedy would have a difficult time at best asserting the leadership we needed. If, as a result of a court action filed by Nixon or any other Republican, it should be established that Kennedy had benefited from any fraudulent voting, it would make his task more difficult. If the results were ultimately reversed in both Texas and Illinois, it would result in an electoral college win for Nixon and Lodge of 270 to 252 for Kennedy and Johnson.

The other reasons advanced by Nixon were, in my opinion, specious—noble perhaps, but misguided. The sanctity of the ballot should take first consideration. Our national faith in the electoral process has been severely injured precisely because many Americans believe that in every election there is a great deal of tombstone voting. I still hold to the belief that the Daley machine in

Cook County counted enough illegal ballots to give that state's electoral votes to Kennedy-Johnson when they should have gone to Nixon-Lodge.

The long-established history of vote fraud in Texas cast grave doubts on the reported outcome of the presidential race in that state. The Texas politicians had a technique vastly more productive than just voting tombstones. In the Spanish-American precincts it was common practice to set up a demonstration voting machine outside the regular polls. Many Mexican-Americans who had trouble with the English language were intercepted at this way station, asked to present their qualifications, and then told to use the voting machine. If the vote was against the candidates favored by the operators, they sent the voter away believing his ballot had been cast. If it favored the candidates supported by these slickers, they sent the voter into the regular polling place to cast a vote that would be counted.

In retrospect, it seems to me that had Nixon challenged the admitted fraudulent votes in the West Virginia primary, Kennedy would not have been nominated. Had we gone to court over the ghost vote in North Dakota, public opinion would have been supportive of the challenge to the general election results in Illinois and Texas.

Some of the diehard Nixon critics who had wanted me to lead the charge in Chicago were openly pleased by the Nixon defeat. They argued that had the delegates voted their personal feelings, I would have been the nominee. They claimed the Republicans would have retained the White House. They buttressed their argument with sharp criticism of what they called the ineffective Nixon-Lodge campaign. I couldn't entirely agree we would have been successful, but I did endorse their appraisal of the Nixon-Lodge campaign.

In my Arizona campaigns we developed the strategy of going where the ducks are—that is, making our appeal to voters who, by their past performance or their socioeconomic status, might be expected to respond favorably to the Republican positions. Nixon made something of a fetish of visiting all the states. He made the long flight to Alaska the week before the election and came back with three electoral college votes. Had he spent that time in Illinois, Michigan, and Texas, it might have made the difference.

Nixon's crucial error was his failure to involve Ike in the

campaign. The President wanted Nixon to win. He didn't approve of Jack Kennedy's life-style, Jack Kennedy's policies, or Jack Kennedy's associates.

Ike was the most popular public figure in the nation. As the central architect of a foreign policy which had frustrated communist expansion, Ike could have refuted the Kennedy criticisms. He was eager to do so. Ike told me Nixon had never talked politics with him, had not sought his advice, did not request his participation until the final week or so—when it was too late. I have come to understand and respect Ike's dilemma—he couldn't volunteer. He couldn't force his services on Nixon's campaign group. He had to sit it out and suffer in silence.

In my view, Nixon and Lodge had not given the voters a clear-cut choice. Republican campaigners appeared reluctant to question the legitimacy of the expanding federal establishment. As much as anything else, my disappointment resulted from the prejudiced attitude of the national press. It had, I thought, been taken in by Kennedy's personal charm. Its portraits of Nixon were harsh and unflattering. It made Kennedy Sir Galahad. The televised debates had been a disaster.

I was exhausted mentally and physically from the brutal schedule of my campaign speeches in late September and October 1960. That weariness of body was exceeded by feelings of deep frustration. This attitude of mine was not entirely because the Republicans lost the White House, although that was a part of it. My real concern was for the future of the nation.

The decline of public morality which Herbert Hoover had so eloquently described at the Chicago convention was everywhere apparent. The change in direction the Republicans had promised the voters in 1952 had not been realized. Two major miscalculations in foreign policy could not be easily corrected—the brutal subjugation of the Hungarian patriots by the Russian regulars and the establishment of a communist beachhead in the Western Hemisphere on Castro's Cuba. Our bright hopes for a world at peace were tarnished and stained. The war we refused to win in Korea had resulted only in a shaky cease-fire. The independence and self-confidence of individual Americans had, it seemed, been put to sleep by federal welfare. The states had surrendered much of their sovereignty in return for federal funding. The most fragile of all our legacies, freedom and liberty, were being gleefully bartered away in our eagerness to find the new Utopia.

In 1960 Richard Nixon received 1.3 million fewer votes than had been cast for Ike in 1956. Ike had carried Illinois, Michigan, Texas, and Massachusetts in both 1952 and 1956. Nixon lost all four of these states. The enormousness of the Republican loss with Nixon and Lodge at the head of the ticket becomes even more apparent if we look back to 1948. In that year Truman beat Dewey, but the Republican candidate carried Pennsylvania, Michigan, Connecticut, Delaware, the District of Columbia, Maryland, New Jersey, and New York. Nixon-Lodge lost them all.

Without taking anything away from the Kennedy charm and the Kennedy campaign skill, it is obvious Republican voters were turned off by Nixon in 1960. I believe that disillusionment commenced in Chicago.

CHAPTER 15

Robin Hood!

The inauguration of John F. Kennedy as President of the United States resulted in a dramatic change in American policy both domestic and foreign. Kennedy's inaugural address and his first State of the Union message clearly reflected that we were embarked on a new policy of accommodation, a policy which Khrushchev called "peaceful coexistence."

I had read the December 1960 world communist party statements setting forth their understanding of this new slogan. Rumanian communist spokesman H. Donna declared, "Some try to reduce the notion of peaceful coexistence to the renunciation of war, but peace and peaceful coexistence are not one and the same thing." All the statements were clear. In the eyes of the Soviets the struggle between capitalism and socialism would continue.

Eisenhower and Dulles understood that communism was evil, brutal, inhuman, untrustworthy. They believed the communist projection of man as a producing, consuming animal to be used and discarded was antithetical to all Judeo-Christian understandings which are the foundations upon which the Republic stands.

Alarmed by the failure of the West to understand and prevent communist expansion in Eastern Europe and Asia, American foreign policy from 1953 to 1960 was devoted to the prevention of further communist aggression. Critics of these policies, such as Walter Lippmann, the columnist, and Senator J. William Fulbright, chairman of the Foreign Relations Committee, called it a "cold war" and "brinkmanship." But, until the death of Dulles in 1959, it worked. Domestically, the country prospered. The rate of inflation was under 2 percent, and most Americans who wanted work could find jobs.

While I had complained about increased federal spending and an unbalanced federal budget, revenues exceeded expenditures in two of the eight Eisenhower years. The total deficit in the six unbalanced years was only about $30 billion—the per capita debt slightly less in 1960 than it had been in 1950. For comparison, expenditures in the eight Kennedy-Johnson years went from $81.5 billion to $183 billion. The increase in the public debt was almost $70 billion.

In 1951 and 1952 the Senate Internal Security Subcommittee under the chairmanship of Pat McCarran (D-Nev.), conducted a lengthy investigation into the activites of the Institute of Pacific Relations. The establishment of a communist government in China had destroyed American prestige throughout Asia. The committee concluded that the American policy decisions which helped establish the communist control of China were made by IPR officials who were traitors or were under the influence of traitors whose allegiance lay in Moscow.

IPR was a creation of the Council on Foreign Relations. The CFR is the American branch of a society which originated in England. Internationalist in viewpoint, the CFR, along with the Atlantic Union movement and the Atlantic Council of the United States, believes national boundaries should be obliterated and one-world rule established.

Professor Owen Lattimore, who headed the IPR, when it was so influential in determining American policy in the Far East, was termed a "conscious, articulate instrument of the Soviet international conspiracy." Additionally, the committee named other highly placed members of the IPR—Lauchlin Curry, Alger Hiss, Joseph Barnes, Philip Jessup, and Harry Dexter White—as Soviet sympathizers or perhaps Soviet agents.

John Foster Dulles and his brother, Allen, were early members of the Council on Foreign Relations. When Dulles became Secretary of State, he implemented a policy of resistance to communist expansion, and his old friends at the CFR became his most severe critics.

The CFR argued that communism was changing—that the Russians felt threatened by the superior military power of the West—that its expansionist activities were really defensive. They said that once Russia caught up with the West in industrial and military power, the hostility would be modified. This is the root of the convergence theory supported by J. William Fulbright. Dulles maintained that communism, so long as it remains communism, does not change in any essential respect.

In 1944 the Soviet Union, with 170 million people and 8 million square miles of territory, was the only nation in the world ruled by communism. By 1960 communism had expanded to control about 16 million square miles of territory and more than 1 billion people.

Latvia, Lithuania, and Estonia had been absorbed into the Soviet Union. Poland, Yugoslavia, Czechoslovakia, Bulgaria, Hungary, Rumania, Albania, East Germany, China, Mongolia, Tibet, North Korea, and North Vietnam all had communist rulers.

These nations taken over by communist governments were not incorporated into the Soviet Union proper. We were encouraged to find comfort in the fact that Tito's Yugoslavia pretended some degree of independence. In my view this is the key to our failure to understand the true character of the war being waged against us and all free men.

We have been instructed by history to believe that war is armed conflict—that victorious nations occupy the countries of their defeated adversaries, obliterate former national boundaries, and present to the world a recognizable geographical and political entity. The communist strategy for world domination does not regard immediate territorial annexation or possession essential. The effort of the communists is founded on the knowledge that if they destroy those institutions or conceptual agreements which protect liberty and freedom, overt territorial annexation is not essential to success.

In the early 1950s critics of the Dulles foreign policy seized upon the excessive accusations of Senator McCarthy to brand all those who expressed concern over communist expansion as unrealistic witchhunters. The media carried on an unceasing campaign against the anticommunists.

A review of the history of our relations with the Soviets indicates that those who expressed fear of the communist expansion were more than justified in their beliefs. When the Russians revolted against the czar in 1917, we promptly recognized the new government, believing it would be democratic. After five years of internal bloodshed, the communists, under Joseph Stalin, established the Union of Soviet Socialist Republics in December 1922. Appalled by the brutality of Russia's new masters, we refused to recognize the Stalin government. Eugene Lyons tells us that under Stalin's program to liquidate the kulaks, at least a million peasant families were "torn up by the root, stripped of all their goods, and cast into the tropic or arctic wildernesses." Thousands were executed, and most failed to survive the move. In November 1933 the mass murders and purges apparently forgotten, President Franklin Roosevelt granted full diplomatic recognition to the communist government of Soviet Russia.

In August 1939 Stalin and Hitler signed a ten-year nonaggression pact. Eight days later Hitler invaded Poland, and World War II became inevitable. Before the end of the month Germany and Russia divided the Polish territory.

In 1939 and 1940 and until June 1941 communist propaganda in the United States strongly opposed Britain, France, and the Western powers. This party line made a 180-degree turn when Hitler invaded Russia in 1941.

The United States commenced delivery of war materials and other resources to help the communists fight the Germans. Among other things, we gave the Russians engraving plates, paper, and ink with which to print the occupational currency. During the occupation of Berlin, Russian troops were paid with this paper money, ultimately redeemed by the United States.

At Yalta in February 1945 Franklin Roosevelt embraced Stalin as a partner in the war against the Axis powers. He made a number of significant concessions in return for the promise of Russian support of the Western powers in the war against Japan.

In 1947 Secretary of State George C. Marshall announced an economic program which became known as the Marshall Plan. Cloaked in humanitarian terms, it was sold to Congress as a sophisticated scheme to prevent the spread of communism throughout war-torn Western Europe and, particularly, to prevent any expansion of communist influence in the countries bordering on the Mediterranean.

The communists, who have always been clever enough to avoid direct confrontation with the strengths of the Western world, turned their attention to Latin and South America. The Bogotá uprising of 1948 was planned to disrupt the Ninth Inter-American Congress.

The terrorists hoped to overthrow the constitutional democratic government of Colombia. Before it was over, 136 buildings had been destroyed. A total of $20 million in damages had been inflicted on the Colombian capital. The leftist leader Jorge Eliécer Gaitán was murdered by an assassin, who, in turn, was immediately destroyed by outraged citizens.

Secretary Marshall, Admiral Roscoe Hillenkoetter, Director of the CIA, U.S. Ambassador to Colombia William L. Beaulac—all classified the Bogotá terrorists as communists. According to the Colombian police records, two Cubans—Fidel Castro and Rafael del Pino—were in Bogotá at the time of the riots. On the day Gaitán was shot, April 9, the Cubans had been observed in earnest conversation with Juan Roa Sierra, later identified as Gaitán's killer.

Cuba had suffered under a succession of dictatorial governments beginning in 1933 with the election of Dr. Ramón Grau San Martín as President. In 1940 Fulgencio Batista was elected President. In the elections of 1944 Grau returned to power. In 1948 he was succeeded by Carlos Prío Socarrás.

There had been widespread bribery and corruption under Grau. It was worse under Prío, who is credited with having stolen and transported to the United States $170 million.

In 1952, as the result of a military-supported coup d'état, Batista was again made the head of government. During his earlier term in office his pro-labor stand and his devotion to constitutional processes had made him quite popular with the Cuban electorate.

On July 26, 1953, a force of terrorists under the command of Fidel Castro attacked the Moncada barracks in Santiago. On that Sunday morning, when all was quiet at the Cuban military installation, an estimated eighty guerrillas, wearing Cuban Army uniforms for disguise, attempted to overpower the defenders of the barracks. The terrorists were fought off, but not until they had invaded the infirmary and murdered a number of hospitalized Cuban soldiers.

The Castro brothers and some other survivors surrendered,

were tried, convicted, and sentenced to fifteen years in prison. President Batista, who later on was pictured in the American press as a brutal, oppressive dictator, did not insist on the death penalty. At the trial Fidel Castro testified he "had expected the troops would mutiny and join the insurrection."

The Castro brothers were released after serving only twenty-two months in prison. The whole affair was quickly forgotten, but the movement took its name from the date of the attack—the 26th of July.

At the time it was suggested the Castro brothers were communists. In this period the press was blind to such allegations. It was also a time when the anticolonialists and the spokesmen of the Third World were busy propagandizing the notion that all major powers in the world, with the exception of Soviet Russia, were imperialistic, aggressive, selfish, and wicked.

The Castro brothers fled to Mexico and commenced recruiting an army of terrorists to invade Cuba and seize control of the government. In late November 1956 the Castros and about eighty insurrectionists, including the Argentinian communist Ernesto "Che" Guevara, sailed from Mexico on the yacht *Granma*. The Batista forces intercepted the invaders—all but ten or eleven were killed. The Castros and Che Guevara fled into the mountains of the Sierra Maestra. The whole affair was treated by the American press as one more example of Banana Republic instability. But there was a difference. Castro had an apparently inexhaustible source of money. He was able to recruit dissidents and secure arms.

In April 1957 Herbert L. Matthews, a correspondent for the *New York Times*, managed to interview Castro in his mountain hideout. In three successive front-page articles Matthews presented Castro as a "peasant patriot, a strong anti-communist, a Robin Hood defender of the people." On CBS television Edward R. Murrow cloaked Castro in the garments of a national hero. And in a speech Senator John F. Kennedy likened Castro to the great South American patriot Simón Bolívar.

John Foster Dulles was dying of cancer. Power in the State Department was exercised by second-echelon bureaucrats. These are the career foreign service officers. They are protected in their jobs. Many of them are committed to a "one-world" concept. Most of them believe the only way to avoid an atomic war is to practice a policy of accommodation toward the Russians.

American Ambassador to Cuba Arthur Gardner described Castro as a communist terrorist. He was recalled. Earl E. T. Smith was named to replace him. It is interesting to note that Smith was not permitted to consult with his predecessor. Instead, the State Department sent him to New York to be briefed by the *Times* correspondent Herbert Matthews.

This failure of the State Department to make public Fidel Castro's communist connections is even more difficult to understand when reviewed in conjuction with the official reports from our Ambassador to Mexico, Robert Hill. Hill was aware of Castro's participation in Bogotá. He repeatedly warned his superiors at State of Castro's close connections with known communist Che Guevara. He called attention to the police records of Castro's participation in the aborted Bogotá uprising.

Hill was concerned because of Cuba's proximity to Mexico. In subsequent Senate hearings, Hill testified under oath, "Individuals in the State Department and individuals in the *New York Times* put Castro in power." * One cartoonist pictured the new dictator, Castro, under the caption "I got my job through the *New York Times.*"

On January 1, 1959, at the head of a well-armed military force, Fidel Castro seized power in Cuba. The day before that military takeover Roy Rubottom, the United States Assistant Secretary of State for Latin American Affairs, testified before the Foreign Relations Committee: "There was no evidence of any organized communist element within the Castro movement or that Señor Castro himself was under communist influence."

The United States had refused arms to Batista. We had influenced other suppliers to refuse to sell weapons to the Cuban government.

Not all the American press agreed with Rubottom and Herbert Matthews. In January 1959 the Washington *Evening Star, U.S. News and World Report,* and the Miami (Florida) *News* all declared Castro was a communist and the new government of Cuba a communist dictatorship.

When Castro came to power, John Foster Dulles was dead.

* *Senate Subcommittee of the Committee on the Judiciary, Communist Threat to the United States Through the Caribbean.*

Policy at State was being made by Christian Herter, William Wieland, and Roy Rubottom. Our decision to support Castro may have come about as a conscious, knowledgeable act by the leaders of State. It may have been merely the result of a gross miscalculation. Either way, I am positive Dwight David Eisenhower was never fully informed and was not a participant in that decision.

Professor Walt W. Rostow became Chief of Policy Planning for the State Department under Kennedy. Two former Ambassadors to the USSR, Charles E. Bohlen and George Kennan, held positions of influence within the State Department. They all believed the Soviet Union was changing, mellowing, exhibiting a new willingness to cooperate with the West.

In 1959 Senator Fulbright said he believed, "The public opinion of the world will cause the Russian people to relinquish their control of the once free peoples of Poland, East Germany, Hungary, Czechoslovakia, Latvia, Estonia, Lithuania, and Bulgaria." And in 1960 he said, "I do not believe that the Soviets desire to dominate the world as the Germans did. They have given no evidence they believe they are supermen. Russia, like America, is a nation of many races; and I can see no reason why we cannot get along peaceably."

I was aware of the content of a 1955 report of the Senate Internal Securities Subcommittee. The subcommittee staff studied nearly 1,000 treaties and agreements—both bilateral and multilateral—which the Soviets have entered into not only with the United States but with countries all over the world. The staff found that in the thirty-eight short years since the Soviet Union came into existence its government had broken its word to virtually every country to which it had given a signed promise.

My early years at Staunton Military Academy had kindled an unquenchable interest in military history. This was sustained by my service in World War II and by experience in the Reserves. Now, as a member of the U.S. Senate, I had access to facts about the world situation which were being denied to the public.

On November 14, 1960, I expressed my views on foreign policy in a speech before the War College at Montgomery, Alabama. I described world communism as a conspiracy determined to enslave all the peoples of the world. I said the ultimate objective of American foreign policy must be to help establish a world in which there is the largest possible measure of freedom with justice, peace, and material prosperity.

Referring to the Kennedy campaign claim that the United States had lost prestige in the world, I said, "Prestige is a measure of how other people think of you, well or ill. Contrary to what was implied during the campaign, prestige is not important for its own sake. Only the vain and incurably sentimental among us will lose sleep simply because foreign people are not as impressed by our strength as they ought to be. The thing to lose sleep over is what some people, having concluded that we are weaker than we truly are, are likely to go off and do about it."

I questioned the legitimacy of disarmament proposals and the effectiveness of the United Nations. I did not advocate a belligerent attitude or suggest a foreign policy of intimidation. I believed then, and I now believe, that all mankind instinctively yearns to be free. The failure of the communist system to satisfy man's nature was apparent to me, its temporary success resting on brutal compulsion. I said our responsibility in this hostile world is to defend successfully the concept of human freedom from every assault—ideological, economic, or military.

CHAPTER 16

Operation Pluto

My concern over the new direction in American foreign policy increased in early 1961, when it was made known the Kennedy men in the State Department were attempting to muzzle military spokesmen. Censors were deleting any remarks considered critical of Russians or of Russian communism.

When called upon to explain this action, Undersecretary of State George Ball told the Senate Armed Services Committee that it was inappropriate to have military or State Department spokesmen voice criticism of the Soviets when the President's policy was to establish a new era of accommodation and communication. Ball said the word "victory" has a military and aggressive ring. At about the same time Assistant Secretary of State Harlan Cleveland was saying, "We see new leaders of communism facing with realism the fact that their old dream of a communist one world is an obsolete and perilous delusion."

Seventeen days before John F. Kennedy was inaugurated as the thirty-fifth President of the United States, this government severed diplomatic relations with Cuba. There was nothing else we could do. Castro had dropped his masquerade and flaunted his allegiance to the communist cause. He had ordered the expropriation of all American property in Cuba. The firing-squad executions of political prisoners, the oppressive denial of human rights could no longer be ignored.

In early 1960, with the approval of President Eisenhower, the CIA commenced development of a plan to overthrow Castro and liberate Cuba. Deputy Director General Charles P. Cabell and Richard M. Bissell were in charge of the operation, which was code named Pluto. A force of about 1,400 anti-Castro Cubans was recruited. Training camps were established in Guatemala and Nicaragua. We provided sixteen B-26 bombers to be flown by Cuban pilots. The B-26s had been stripped of tail guns to enable them to carry enough fuel to make the almost 1,500-mile flight from Nicaragua to Cuba and return. Additional aerial support was to be provided by four C-54s and five C-46s. The unarmed transport planes were to carry paratroopers and supplies.

Castro's small air force of fewer than thirty operable aircraft consisted of a collection of World War II surplus models plus one or two Russian jets. The invasion plan, as conceptualized by the CIA and the Joint Chiefs of Staff, called for an attack on the Castro airfields by the sixteen B-26s—the objective to destroy Castro's planes on the ground. On the second day the B-26s were to return and mop up any planes missed in the first attack. On the third day the ground troops were to land under aerial cover, secure the airstrip at Girón, and make it available to the B-26s.

There are very few secrets in Washington, D.C. Most of us knew well in advance about Operation Pluto.

Knowledge of the invasion plan was not limited to insiders. In October 1960 a journal published at Stanford University, the *Hispanic-American Report,* revealed that Cuban freedom fighters were being trained in Guatemala. The Los Angeles *Mirror* and the St. Louis *Dispatch* confirmed the story. On January 10 the *New York Times* printed a front-page article on the upcoming Cuban liberation, featuring a map showing the exact location of the training base.

Although the whole operation had been conceived while Eisenhower was President with the full knowledge and support of Vice President Richard Nixon, Ike put the operation on hold when Kennedy won the November election. He felt the new President should be free to carry it out or, if he thought best, countermand it.

On Saturday, April 15, 1961, I was strapping myself into the cockpit of an F-86 fighter plane at Andrews Air Force Base, preparing to fly to Luke Air Force base in Arizona. As a member of the active Reserve I was expected to fly a certain number of hours each month to maintain my proficiency rating. I was in the middle of the pre-flight checklist when a sergeant climbed up on the wing, thrust his face under the canopy, and told me the President of the United States wanted to see me at the White House.

I changed from my flying suit to civilian clothes and drove to 1600 Pennsylvania Avenue, where a receptionist said the President was expecting me. I was taken immediately to the Oval Office.

The room was empty. I had been there many times when Eisenhower was President, only once or twice since the change of administration. I had never seen the rocking chair which Dr. Janet Travell had recommended as a therapeutic device to ease the President's ailing back. We both were victims of the same medical problem. His difficulty was in the lower spine; mine, considerably higher. On Kennedy's recommendation I too had consulted with Dr. Travell. Now I decided to try the chair she had prescribed for the President.

Over the years of our joint service in the U.S. Senate I had developed a warm personal relationship with John F. Kennedy. He knew I disagreed violently with his political position, just as he automatically opposed everything I advocated. We had crossed verbal swords many times during the McClellan hearings. But on a one-to-one basis, we were friendly adversaries.

It had become apparent to me over our many long private conversations that in many ways Jack Kennedy was the victim of his father's ambition. The White House was a trophy to be won. He reveled in the trappings of the presidency.

When Kennedy entered the room, wearing a dark suit, a small black cigar between his lips, his first words were: "So you want this fucking job, do you?" Then he sat on the corner of his desk and spoke with passion and some bitterness about the Cuban situation.

The President told me he had just been advised the first phase of Operation Pluto had been only moderately successful. He said the eight B-26s flown by Cuban pilots had carried out their surprise attack on three airfields. They had, he said, destroyed only about half of Castro's planes, and three B-26s had been lost.

I said it was my understanding that sixteen planes were to be used by the Cubans. The President said the original plan had been modified. His people in the State Department intended to deny U.S. official support of the invasion. They were afraid that if sixteen bombers were permitted to make the flight, it would be difficult to maintain that denial. The President also told me he thought the original landing site at Trinidad was too conspicuous, and the new plans called for a landing at the Bay of Pigs.

"You know, Barry," the President said, "I made a statement at my press conference on Wednesday promising that no U.S. forces would be used to invade Cuba."

"That was a mistake," I said. "You should not have committed yourself in advance. But as I understand it, all the pilots and all the ground troops are Cuban. Technically our forces will not be involved."

The President said he was beginning to think the whole operation might fail. I asked him what he intended to do.

He replied with a question: "What would you do if you were in my place?"

"I'd do whatever is necessary to make this invasion a success," I told him. "We've got naval forces in the area. Once all of Castro's planes are destroyed on the ground, the brigade can land successfully. Of course, they will need some air cover. We know the extent of anti-Castro feelings among the Cubans. You just get these troops established safely on the island. The people will take care of the rest."

There was a long silence. "What about world opinion? What about my promise at the press conference?" Kennedy asked. "Adlai Stevenson was on the telephone this morning from New York giving us hell. He threatened to stand up in the UN and tell the world we were behind this operation. Schlesinger thinks it's a mistake. Chester Bowles is opposed. Teddy Sorenson has been against it from the day we took office. Hell, Barry, Ike planned it—I didn't."

I told him I knew Ike had planned it. Then I pointed out that after the election Ike had stopped everything, believing the decision should be made by the new administration.

The President admitted this was true. But he said the Republicans had permitted Castro to come to power in the first place, and now we had a communist military regime in our hemisphere.

I told President Kennedy that was precisely why he must go

ahead and guarantee the success of the invasion of Cuba by the anti-Castro freedom fighters. I said the American people didn't give a damn about world opinion, that our friends around the world would applaud him, and that he would be a hero in the eyes of the American voters.

Kennedy walked around behind his desk. "I thank you for coming, Barry," he said. "I knew what you would say. I think you're right. I'm going to do it."

I left the White House rejoicing, not because I had persuaded Jack Kennedy to adopt my views, but because I believed the United States was going to stand firm. Castro would be eliminated, the Cuban people rescued from the tyranny of his communist regime. And after so many defeats, there would be a victory for the free world.

The cloak-and-dagger aspects of Operation Pluto had been devised in an effort to conceal the true role of the U.S. government in the operation. All those in on the planning were fearful of a possible violent reaction from the Soviet Union, the Third World nations, and the Latin and South American countries if the degree of our participation were made public.

To my mind the whole thing was a cheap, undignified subterfuge. From every standpoint—moral, political, humanitarian, economic, and legal—there was ample justification for the liberation of the Cuban people and the destruction of Castro's communist military dictatorship.

It was a plan which should have succeeded. The Cuban people were miserably worse off under Castro than they had been under Batista. American military security was severely threatened by the presence of this communist government so close to our southern shores.

Great nations don't survive as the result of world popularity, nor do they fall before the criticism of so-called world opinion. World opinion didn't destroy Nazi Germany. Allied troops and tanks and aircraft erased that brutal tyranny. World opinion was no match for Soviet tanks in Hungary. A nation which reconizes its paramount self-interest and acts to protect that interest may not be loved in some quarters, but it will be respected.

Operation Pluto ended in bloody defeat. There was no second aerial strike on Sunday, April 16. When the brigade landed, it had no aerial cover. Castro's five remaining planes cut it to pieces.

Did President John F. Kennedy break the promise he made to me that morning in the Oval Office? The answer is both yes and no.

From one of our aircraft carriers standing off Cuba that weekend we did launch our aircraft. The pilots of those war planes were ordered to search out and destroy any remaining aircraft available to Castro's forces.

After the planes were in the air, the order to strike was countermanded in a message from the President of the United States to the admiral in command of the carrier. The American planes were recalled.

My military friends were bitterly critical of the President. They also blamed the admiral. He should, they claimed, have reported it was impossible to get through to the attacking aircraft—"leaned on his orders" is the Navy's language.

Civilian authorities denied our troops a victory in Korea by designating the area north of the Yalu as a sanctuary. That defeat had a disastrous effect on American civilian and military morale.

Our desertion of Cuban patriots was a second demonstration of our faltering national resolution. Call me a hawk if you like. I will respond that in our angry, aggressive world, peace can be preserved only by military power, supported by a people prepared to sacrifice to protect their freedom.

We compromised with that understanding in Korea. The aftereffects of the Bay of Pigs were even more devastating, for we had backed down, given in, deserted the men we had enlisted to carry the actual weapons. The only word adequate to describe our conduct is "betrayal."

CHAPTER 17

Missile Retreat

As a consequence of the Bay of Pigs fiasco, American credibility suffered a damaging blow. In my opinion, we have never recovered from that disaster.

The President's failure to act made a mockery of the brave words in his inaugural address. Khrushchev in the Kremlin, Mao Tse-tung and Chou En-lai in China were undoubtedly greatly encouraged by this demonstrated lack of resolve on the part of the new young President to defend America's self-interest.

Less than four months later, on August 12, the East German communists erected the military wall. They put up a few strands of barbed wire. When we did not react, they commenced replacing the barbed wire with a masonry wall.

I was in West Berlin the night the wire fence was built. When it was discovered the next morning, the commanding general requested permission from the State Department and the White House to destroy the fence. President Kennedy refused to authorize any action.

The fence was the principal topic of conversation when I visited with military and intelligence leaders. They all assured me the Russian move was a testing. They were convinced there would have been no response and no masonry wall had we knocked down the first wire fence.

It was our failure to support the Cuban freedom fighters which ultimately led to the Cuban missile crisis. But before we get to that point, let's see what happened after the brigade was cut to pieces and its survivors captured.

We made a second effort to deceive the world. Castro offered an opportunity to ransom the captured for about $28 million in cash and credit. Still striving to preserve the initial fiction, the U.S. government refused to take any overt action. But President Kennedy appointed Eleanor Roosevelt, widow of the late President; UAW official Walter Reuther; former President Eisenhower's brother, Milton; and Joseph Dodge, who had been Director of the Bureau of the Budget during the Eisenhower administration, to head a citizen's committee to raise the funds necessary to pay the ransom.

Kennedy's Commissioner of Internal Revenue promised that all contributions to the ransom fund would be tax-deductible. This concession made it a governmental action. Any monies pledged to the ransom project would otherwise have gone to the U.S. Treasury. Behind this citizen façade, Richard Goodwin, the President's former speech writer, was active as the liaison officer between governmental agencies and the committee front.

Mrs. Roosevelt and Dr. Eisenhower, as private citizens, were extremely reluctant to engage in negotiations with a foreign government—an action specifically prohibited by the Logan Act. Public opinion, offended by Castro's intransigence, spontaneously resisted the ransom deal, and it collapsed. The Tractors for Freedom Committee dissolved. A second effort, camouflaged as being under the auspices of the American Red Cross, resulted in our giving Castro more than $50 million worth of medicines and other goods to secure the release of the remaining Bay of Pigs prisoners.

In Central Africa U.S. policy had supported the communist Patrice Lumumba in the Belgian Congo and opposed the freedom-loving policies of Moise Tshombe in Katanga. We contributed money and moral support to the UN terrorist activity even when confronted with authentic reports of rape, murder, and pillage.

On September 13, 1961, UN forces made an all-out assault on Elisabethville, Katanga's capital city. The purpose was to force Tshombe and his anticommunist government in the breakaway province to surrender. In New York the UN said the action was defensive. Dr. Conor Cruise O'Brien, who was in command of the operation in the Congo, branded this report false and said the UN assault was a premeditated effort to subjugate Katanga by force in support of the procommunist central government.

In 1961 we supported Cheddi Jagan, the admittedly communist leader of British Guiana, with American foreign aid money and a warm reception at the White House. This dictator's wife, the former Janet Rosenberg of Chicago, had been a communist functionary in the United States and a member of the Young Communist League. We gave money and public support to the dictator Kwame Nkrumah in Ghana, one of the first Soviet satellites in Africa.

Senator Thomas Dodd of Connecticut clearly itemized Nkrumah's communist connections in the United States Senate. He quoted the African dictator's autobiography, which was published in 1957. In that document Nkrumah boasts of his association with American communists when he was a student in the United States, admits that he founded a secret organization in Britain known as the Circle—a terrorist group dedicated to the creation and maintenance of the Union of African Socialist Republics—and declares that the philosophy of Marx and Lenin must be adopted in order to solve African problems. Nkrumah imported a number of American and British communists to serve in his government, including Alan Nunn May, who pleaded guilty to selling Britain's atomic secrets to the Soviet Union. Yet in the face of all this evidence we maintained our benevolent attitude toward the new government of Ghana.

President Kennedy had named my longtime friend and fellow Arizonan William P. Mahoney, Jr., as Ambassador to Ghana. Bill Mahoney and his wife, Alice, are militantly committed to what they perceive to be the cause of social justice. I am sure they never understood or grasped Nkrumah's commitment to communism. Nevertheless, their unwillingness or inability to understand the true objective of the rulers in Ghana contributed to our policy of continued support.

During this period of the late fifties and early sixties shapers of U.S. foreign policy awarded foreign aid money and bestowed our approval on a host of foreign dictators committed to communist doctrine. Juan Bosch in the Dominican Republic, Rómulo Betancourt in Venezuela, Victor Paz Estenssoro in Bolivia, Victor Raúl Haya de la Torre of Peru, Achmed Sukarno in Indonesia—all came to power through nondemocratic revolution. We acquiesced in the expansion of Soviet domination in Eastern Europe and the massacre of the Hungarian freedom fighters.

Commenting on this tragedy, former Soviet agent Oleg Penkovskiy, who had been a member of our intelligence apparatus and was ultimately executed by the Russians as a double agent, said:

> We in Moscow felt as if we were sitting on a powder keg. Everyone on the general staff was against the Khrushchev adventure. It was better to lose Hungary, they said, than lose everything. But what did the West do? Nothing. It was asleep. This gave Khrushchev confidence . . . if the West had slapped Khrushchev down hard, then . . . all of Eastern Europe could be free.*

The Monroe Doctrine, which had effectively protected the nations of the Western Hemisphere against all old-world aggressors for 123 years, was severely injured by our failure to appraise the intentions of Fidel Castro and his revolutionary movement properly. It had been further weakened by our official attitude toward other Latin and South American leaders with communist leanings. It was abrogated and destroyed by John F. Kennedy during the Cuban missile crisis in the fall of 1962.

The Kennedy apologists will argue that a foreign power, Russian communism, first broke that barrier when the United States, under Dwight Eisenhower, permitted Castro to overthrow the dictator Batista. Not so. Castro was then perceived by the world to be a champion of freedom and liberty. The American government promptly recognized his new regime. It was not until much later, when Castro put aside his masquerade, that we had complete confirmation of his attachment to communism and his close ties with the Soviet leaders.

I first learned of the possibility that Russia was installing offensive weapons in Cuba from Republican Senator Kenneth Keating of New York State. The State Department, under command of Kennedy's appointee Chester Bowles, officially pooh-poohed the information. On August 24, 1962, Roger Hilsman, head of Intelligence at State, explained the increase in ship traffic to Cuba

---

* *Penkovskiy Papers*, p. 206, Doubleday, 1965.

by saying the vessels were carrying only electronic gear and construction equipment destined to become a part of Cuba's coastal and air defense system.

Reports from the anti-Castro underground in Cuba told of the arrival of surface-to-air antiaircraft missiles and intermediate-range ballistic missiles. This information was verified by CIA agents operating in Cuba.

Late in August John A. McCone, Director of the CIA, reported to President Kennedy that Mariel, a protected Cuban port, had received eighty-five shiploads of Russian arms. McCone said that all the civilian population had been removed. The docks and off-loading facilities were under tight security. Almost 5,000 Russian technicians were working in Cuba.

President Kennedy was skeptical. He didn't believe the Soviets were ready to risk a confrontation with the United States. There was strong evidence to support this conclusion.

While Khrushchev boasted about his invincible ICBMs, the high-altitude reconnaissance photographs told us Russia was lagging far behind our own missile installations. Our birds were housed in hardened silos, equipped with extremely accurate guidance systems. What few ICBMs the Russians possessed were exposed on temporary launching pads.

At about that time, in a nondocumented speech, I made the offhand statement that we could program our missiles to "hit the men's room in the Kremlin." Spokesmen for the liberal community condemned the statement and challenged me to prove it. Of course, I couldn't without revealing classified information. If I can be forgiven some slight exaggeration because of my admiration for American technology, the statement was basically true.

The "missile gap" which John F. Kennedy exploited so skillfully during the 1960 presidential campaign with his demand to "get America moving again," never existed. Kennedy knew it. He had the information provided by the U-2 reconnaissance flights.

In August 1960, just three months after the U-2 piloted by Gary Francis Powers came down on Russian territory, we launched our first orbiting spy satellite. Ike took a lot of abuse from Khrushchev over the U-2 because as Commander in Chief he equivocated in response to the first Russian reports of the incident. There was no other course open to him. We didn't know whether or not the aircraft had been destroyed and its secrets preserved. We didn't know whether the pilot was alive or dead. Until all the facts were known, any admission of our involvement would have been dangerously premature.

The American public was permitted to think this particular reconnaissance program had to be abandoned. Actually, the usefulness of the U-2 was almost exhausted. Since we could inaugurate our follow-up with the Samos satellite almost immediately, the U-2 downing, while an inconvenience, was not a major interruption in the program. It did not diminish in any way our ability to keep tabs on the Russians.

The obligations of our national defense needs prevented Ike from disclosing the extent of the invaluable information the U-2 program had provided. Had he been able to do so, I am confident the American people would have unanimously applauded this magnificent accomplishment. To tell the world about our new spy satellite was unthinkable. Ike smiled, took the flak, and kept his lips sealed.

But President Kennedy had complete access to this sensitive information. Because he knew of the relative weakness of the Soviets in ICBMs, he could respond with confidence to John McCone's alarming reports about the Soviet missile buildup in Cuba. Kennedy said that under the circumstances the Russians wouldn't dare challenge our missile superiority.

Senator Keating wasn't willing to accept the President's reasoning. He was receiving a steady flow of information from the Cuban underground, much of it verified by our own CIA agents. During this period he delivered a total of ten major speeches in the United States Senate, carefully delineating the probable presence of Russian missiles in Cuba.

President Kennedy knew that Ike totally disapproved of his handling of the Bay of Pigs affair. I had been openly critical of the Tractors for Freedom operation. When Keating showed me some of the evidence he had accumulated, I went to see the President. I told him that if Keating's information was correct, we now had a reason to move on Cuba militarily. We could rid the Western Hemisphere of Castro and remove the menace of those Soviet missiles in Cuba.

I argued that all the great powers would understand why he was required to act. I said that considering our tremendous superiority over the Russians in the field of nuclear weapons,

Khrushchev would not respond militarily.

The President agreed with my evaluation of our relative strength in the nuclear field. He admitted Castro's Cuba had become the base for communist subversion in Latin and South America. He conceded we couldn't tolerate the presence of the Soviet missiles in Cuba. But he dwelt on the ultimate horror of thermonuclear warfare. I came away from that meeting with the impression that no amount of Soviet provocation would ever be sufficient in Kennedy's eyes to justify any action which might lead to the use of atomic weaponry. His attitude toward me was most cordial, even understanding. It was easy for me to recommend a stern course of action, but it was his finger which rested on the red button. He wasn't going to risk having to press it.

Public pressure increased. Senator Keating's speeches, newspaper stories quoting Cuban patriots, the admitted sea traffic finally became too great to be ignored. The administration decided to overyfly Cuba with the U-2.

Heretofore our high-altitude reconnaissance flights had been conducted by pilots operating under the control and command of the CIA. Now Secretary McNamara insisted the mission must be flown by Air Force pilots under his command. Consequently, in early October, Major Rudolph Anderson, Jr., and Major Richard S. Hiser were ordered to familiarize themselves with the U-2 aircraft. On October 14 they made aerial photographs of that portion of Cuba lying west of Havana where it was suspected the installations were being developed.

The resultant photographs revealed missile erectors, transporters, and SAM defensive missiles. These were deployed in an identical manner to similar installations which had been photographed inside the Soviet Union. The evidence could no longer be ignored.

At a White House meeting it was decided to make additional flights. If the Cubans and their Russian technical advisers used the SAM missiles to shoot down a U-2, we would respond with a full military force to destroy all the SAM bases in Cuba in a move of massive retaliation.

On October 22, 1962, President Kennedy addressed the American people to reveal officially the presence of Soviet missiles in Cuba. He called on Premier Khrushchev to halt and eliminate this clandestine, reckless, and provocative threat to world peace. All American military forces were put on alert. Certain Reserves were commanded to report to their stations.

On October 27, Major Rudolph Anderson, Jr., flying a U-2 aircraft, was shot down by a SAM missile over Cuba. President Kennedy countermanded the earlier decision for massive retaliation. The United States made no response.

The national press, lacking any true understanding of the Russian weakness in ICBMs, treated the confrontation with great solemnity. It contributed to the charade. We had come to the brink of nuclear war. President Kennedy was pictured as the resolute, courageous defender—standing up to Khrushchev. The only unanswered questions were: When and where would it start? Would the Russians respond with an attack on Western Europe? Would they send their birds to destroy our cities?

I was on active duty with the Air Force in Florida during the so-called Cuban missile crisis. The aircraft commanders and crews I encountered were begging for action. They said, "Senator, let's get going. We can do the job in an hour and a half." These men were not trigger-happy adventurers. They were professional soldiers, fully aware of the military and political implications. They recognized the threat to our freedom and our safety imposed by the presence of the Russian offensive weapons in Cuba. This was the hard, realistic attitude of our men in uniform. Unfortunately it was not the attitude of our Commander in Chief.

In the days preceding the President's October 22 speech the White House had received reassuring messages from Khrushchev and from the Russian Ambassador, Anatoly Dobrynin. There were, they said, no offensive weapons in Cuba. Caught in this falsehood, Khrushchev did nothing. As a result of the vast sea and air blockade we established, only a single ship was boarded and searched, and that a cargo vessel carrying petroleum. We had originally demanded on-site inspection to satisfy ourselves the missiles were actually being removed. We settled for more aerial reconnaissance.

As a part of the final arrangement the United States agreed to remove the intermediate-range ballistic missiles we had just installed in Turkey and Italy. We guaranteed to protect the integrity of Castro's communist government in Cuba, pledging that "we would mount no assault to disturb Castro and would use our good offices to prevent the launching of any attack from other Latin or South American countries."

Once more the United States had retreated. Our action guaranteed the continued presence of a staging area for the Russian communistic ideological assaults on other countries in the Western Hemisphere and dealt a death blow to the Monroe Doctrine.

One result of the Cuban crisis which has largely escaped the attention of the American public was its ultimate effect on the war in Vietnam. *New York Times* columnist James Reston has written that President Kennedy, hoping to erase the memory of the Bay of Pigs and demonstrate to Khrushchev that he was capable of vigorous action, increased the military budget, sent the Rainbow Division to West Germany to bolster our NATO forces, and intensified the war in Vietnam. Reston says, "Not because the situation on the ground demanded it in Vietnam, but because Kennedy wanted to prove a diplomatic point, not a military point." This construction is further supported by the fact that President Kennedy sent 17,000 marines to Vietnam with orders *not to shoot back.*

Prior to the election of John F. Kennedy the American military presence in Vietnam, Laos, and Cambodia was minimal. The neutralization of Laos, which we approved, was a tragic surrender.

In retrospect, it seems incredible that we could have been drawn into a land war in Asia. History will certainly render a harsh judgment. It is impossible to overstate the destructive impact on American institutions, American self-confidence, and our constitutional government resulting from that twelve-year tragedy.

We do know that the American government under President Kennedy and Secretary of Defense McNamara, with the active support of Ambassador Henry Cabot Lodge, acquiesced in the deposition and murder of Ngo Dinh Diem, President of South Vietnam, and was perhaps the instigator of that coup.*

The American press was preoccupied with the deficiencies of South Vietnam and its leaders and quite tolerant of the brutalities of the invading North Vietnamese. One American writer, Marguerite Higgins, reported accurately on that conflict.†

* See *The Pentagon Papers.*

† Marguerite Higgins, *Our Vietnam Nightmare.*

American public opinion is shaped and nourished by the daily news. The media explained Kennedy's desertion of the brigade as a matter of principle, made him the hero of the Cuban missile crisis.

It is worth noting that the public's almost hysterical, unreasoned attitude toward nuclear war was fattened on the misrepresentations of three works of fiction. *On the Beach*, by Nevil Shute, which came out in 1957 and was made into a successful motion picture, presented an extremely distorted technological assessment. Two novels—*Fail-Safe*, which described the launching of a nuclear attack on Russia through error, and *Seven Days in May*, an account of a military coup by fascist-minded generals—carried a similar message. We were urged to believe the Russians were no threat to world peace. What we should be concerned about, these writers said, was our own national defense forces. These books were acclaimed by all the voices supporting unilateral disarmament.

While I never thought of my earlier concepts of foreign policy and geopolitics as being particularly parochial, I now found that my interest in world politics was increasing. When Eisenhower was President and John Foster Dulles our Secretary of State, the cold war policies they pursued appeared to be effective. As a result of my active status in the Air Force Reserve, I made it a point to keep abreast of our military developments, and this inside knowledge of our true superiority over any potential enemy was reassuring. We had the weapons. The question which began to plague me was: If it came to a question of national survival, would we have the will to use them?

I was still reluctant to view myself as a candidate for the presidency. I could anticipate the chorus demanding Kennedy's reelection in 1964.

I did nothing to hinder the first Draft Goldwater movement which was launched at a Chicago meeting in October 1961, but I didn't encourage the effort. Some observers have attributed my indecision to timidity. To my mind, there were some very practical considerations to be taken into account.

Richard Nixon, as the defeated candidate for President, had very little influence in the Republican party. My personal contacts with the grass roots indicated the party was almost hopelessly divided between Nelson Rockefeller as the leader at one end of the spectrum and Barry Goldwater at the other end. As a result of the favorable press Kennedy received during and after the Cuban missile crisis, the Democrats made substantial gains in the November elections, increasing their strength in both the House and the Senate.

The enchantment of Camelot could not be denied. The press was infatuated with the young man in the White House. What I regarded as dangerous misjudgments in foreign policy was translated by the media into a series of triumphant successes.

Robert S. McNamara and his chorus line of whiz kids at the Pentagon were the objects of unrestrained media praise. In my judgment, McNamara should have been punished for his pursuit of a policy calculated to produce parity with the Russians as a satisfactory replacement for our earlier superiority.

CHAPTER 18

What Might Have Been

After the Bay of Pigs and the Cuban missile crisis, I reluctantly concluded we were losing the world to the communists because of our failure to grasp and understand the true nature of the conflict. Events since then—the defeat in Vietnam, which permitted the communists to take over all of that country, the Russian presence in Angola and Ethiopia, the emergence of communist rule in Pakistan and Afghanistan, the Russian-supported Vietnamese invasion of Cambodia, and, most recently, the recognition of Red China, the abandonment of Taiwan, and the ousting of the Shah of Iran—all have strengthened my earlier opinion.

Appearing before the English-Speaking Union in Kansas City in 1961, Professor Warren Nutter delivered the following descriptive indictment of communism. He said, "Communism is an international conspiracy which has restored slavery to the world." Can there be any doubt in our minds about the truth of this statement when we observe the people of Poland or Czechoslovakia or East Germany or Cuba or mainland China?

At the end of August 1977 we reopened the consulate office in Cuba. One of the first young Cubans to seek our assistance so that he might leave his country described Cuba as a "jail."

Nutter said, "Communism has captured, enslaved, and exploited a billion people against their will and plans to capture the remaining two billion people on earth." Can we find a single example where a free people, free of duress or coercion, has willingly embraced communism?

Nutter said, "Communism has destroyed freedom, liberty, independence, human rights, and dignity wherever possible. It has interfered and intervened times without number in the domestic affairs of free nations. It has established deceit, dishonor, destruction, death, and disaster as recognized, accepted, and necessary instruments of an international policy." In October 1962, when our intelligence disclosed the irrefutable evidence of Russian offensive missiles in Cuba, Nikita Khrushchev and Anatoly Dobrynin were sending messages to President Kennedy declaring they "had sent no missiles to Cuba."

Nutter said, "Communism has starved, murdered, or otherwise destroyed at least one hundred million human beings to advance the false economic and political doctrines repugnant to man.

"Communism has destroyed freedom of religion, of the press, the right to vote, own property, to work where you please, to organize into labor unions, the right to assemble, protest and change government by the will of the people, has destroyed government by consent of the governed, freedom of education, and the right to live in freedom."

There is only one antonym for victory, and that is defeat. In every contest there is a winner and a loser. There can be no such thing as a stalemate. The United States has adopted the pathetic attitude of "we don't want to lose, but we won't try to win." And the communists have never renounced their dedication to ultimate victory.

I cannot explain why there should be any confusion about the meaning and relationship of these words. To my mind they are clear, unequivocal, and definitive. Their meaning has been understood throughout recorded history.

Imagine then my reaction to the words of the chairman of the Senate Foreign Relations Committee, J. William Fulbright, in a speech he gave on the Senate floor on June 29, 1961. Reviewing the struggle with world communism, the Senator said, "We can hope to do little more than mitigate our problems as best we can and learn to live with them."

He called for negotiation, compromise, and increased foreign aid. The total thrust of his argument was that we must, at all costs, avoid any direct confrontation with the Russians. He restated his earlier opinion that any successful American action to overthrow the communist government in Cuba would alienate Latin America, Asia, and Africa. In that speech, which was in a way prophetic, he declared the erection of missile bases by the communists in Cuba would not increase the danger to our national existence.

On July 14, in response to the Fulbright rhetoric, I challenged the chairman to tell us how and why he believed a continuation of the very same policies we had been following since the end of World War II would be successful in the future. I reminded the Senator of the undeniable gains made by the communists since 1945, and I called for an official American commitment to victory in this battle for the allegiance of the minds of men.

On July 24 Senator Fulbright answered my criticism. He ignored my questions concerning the wisdom of pursuing our present costly and ineffective foreign policy. He questioned my use of the word "victory," describing it as "a stirring term with a romantic ring, something that quickens the blood like a clarion call to arms."

He said he did not know what victory means in this age of ideological conflict and nuclear weapons. He advanced the notion that the only alternative to our present policy of compromise and accommodation was nuclear war. This is precisely the propaganda line the communists have been pushing since they exploded their first atomic device.

This war with communism is not of our making. We don't set the ground rules. It is unlike any other war in which we have ever been engaged. Our enemy is committed to the destruction of the United States and the domination of the world. In order to understand the nature of our war with communism, since it is not at the moment a shooting war, it is necessary to understand how this ideological warfare is being waged and won by our enemies.

Communism calls for a completely regulated, dictatorial society with all aspects of life compelled to conform to a master plan. This requires the elimination of all individual freedom, independent thought, personal choice. It is argued that the beneficiaries of this highly efficient superstate society will, once they have learned to appreciate their improved lot, willingly trade off freedom, personal liberty, and personal choice in return for the bounties and protection and quality of the condition newly available.

The exponents of this new society freely admit it is necessary to employ ruthless compulsion—"You can't make an omelet without breaking some eggs." It is estimated that more than 100 million people have been murdered in the effort to establish a new classless world order.

At the end of World War II more than half the human beings inhabiting Planet Earth were ruled by governments which recognized individual liberty and freedom of choice, not all of them to the same degree. In actual practice, without exception, they recognized and were pursuing this concept of individual freedom.

By 1967 that percentage of human beings enjoying some form of freedom had dropped to a little over 30. In 1978, as I write this passage, the number has been further reduced to 17 percent. Only 17 percent of the world population still enjoys political, personal, and intellectual freedom.

The pervasive trend in American government under all our Presidents since Roosevelt has been to enlarge the scope of government at the expense of liberty. The leaders who have taken us in this direction have been at once elitist and egalitarian. They are elitist in the sense that they honestly believe a planned society administered from the top down by a handful of benevolent men possessing superior intellect will eliminate all the hardships now encountered. Their goals are egalitarian: "Render every human being equal to his neighbor in material possessions."

It is this kind of thinking which has produced the superpowerful bureaucracy of federal government. As a class the thinkers we identify as "liberal" have been the leading proponents of problem solving by the creation of new superpowerful government agencies.

We pretend outrage at the brutal compulsion evident in every communist society from Moscow to Hanoi. Nevertheless, some of our leaders have embraced the central tenet of this society, which is control over all human activity, vested in the leaders of the superstate. Supporters of this belief view such planning and control as benign, serving the best interests of the individuals who don't know enough to adopt the proper objectives independently.

Recall how many times critics of our society have chastised Americans for spending more on makeup—creams, lipsticks, emollients, etc.—than we do on cancer research. We are constantly accused of misallocating our social resources—money spent for drink and pleasure, for example, instead of for art and learning. It is certainly true that many Americans are improvident. Their spending habits can be criticized. But to substitute central control for freedom of choice is to trade liberty for slavery.

All my statements on foreign policy emphasize that we must recognize that the only alternative to victory is defeat. Defeat, in this instance, would mean the disappearance of political, religious, intellectual, and economic freedom.

Precisely because of the communist propaganda that any strong opposition to the desires and actions of the communist world leaders would inevitably lead to a nuclear holocaust, I argued it was necessary to increase our response in every theater of this strangest of all wars. I said we should use our economic strengths to hinder and oppose communist expansion. I said we should concentrate on enhancing personal liberty and freedom in the United States. And I said, above all else, "We must retain and increase our military superiority."

Each new day is burdened with uncertainty for the individual and for nations. Greed, envy, the lust for power, and miscalculation have triggered all the wars of history. The few periods of peace the world has enjoyed have been the result of superior military power residing in the possession of a nation or a group of nations controlled by men who are committed in principle to the cause of peace and justice—and are prepared to employ that military power to discourage aggressors.

The *Saturday Review of Literature*, a journal which has never been accused of displaying any sympathy for conservative thought, said, "In Goldwater's foreign policy statement there is nothing of fanaticism. It is a reasoned analysis of the failures of foreign policy under the party he opposes."

I said that unilateral disarmament permitting the enemy to achieve parity with the U.S. weapons systems would enhance, rather than detract from, the possibility of a nuclear war. Knowing what we know of the continuity of communist commitment to world domination, how can it be otherwise? Their ambition is uncompromising; their assault on the institutions of freedom is relentless. They will never feel comfortable or secure so long as freedom exists anywhere on this planet.

The outcome of this struggle is totally predictable. It will end either in defeat or in victory. If we don't win, we will lose. Those candles of faith, those brave testaments to love and honor and truth and the free human spirit so painfully erected over the stretch of time, will be extinguished. The world will grow cold and dark. Why not victory?

All my undertakings in 1961 and 1962 were calculated to strengthen the Republic, encourage the adoption of strong conservative principles, and expose what I perceived to be the errors of the Kennedy administration. I was not seeking the 1964 Republican presidential nomination.

The media could not or would not accept my posture as a noncandidate. In June 1961 *Time* magazine gave very generous coverage to my political career in a five-page spread, including photographs of my family, my home, and my grandfather, and suggested I would be a strong contender in 1964.

It would be totally dishonest not to admit I was aware of and moved by this evidence of growing support of me for my party's presidential nomination. A number of my colleagues in the Senate, including some Democrats, urged me to come out in the open, set up a campaign organization, go after the nomination.

I had been sharply critical of the Kennedy administration. I opposed its domestic policies and called for a congressional investigation into the Bay of Pigs. Even so, my personal relations with the President were warm and friendly. He took it for granted I would be his opponent in 1964 and offered advice.

"Don't announce too soon, Barry," he told me. "The minute you do you will be the target. If you give them eighteen months to shoot you down, they will probably be able to do it."

The President believed as I did that presidential campaigns should be centered on the substantive differences between policies advocated by contending candidates. He was offended by the injection of trivial matters, by the distortions which usually disfigure such contests. Kennedy thought that if we could engage in a serious dialogue—direct the voters' attention to the nation's major problems—and then offer alternative solutions, we would be making a constructive contribution to the public's understanding of the complexities of government.

We talked seriously of campaigning together, appearing before the same audiences. He once reminded me of an article I had written on the general subject of how to be a good opponent in a political contest, making five points. "First of all," I said, "it is fine to oppose, but do not hate. Second, keep your sense of humor. Third, always oppose positively. Fourth, learn all the tricks of campaigning; and fifth, applaud your opponent if he is right."

I knew the Kennedy campaign team would play for keeps. I was aware of the enormous advantage of incumbency. But Jack Kennedy and I had always been able to express our opinions to each other without rancor. I respected all his many fine qualities.

He confessed there was merit in some of my proposals. We both believed the federal government was overgrown, unwieldly, almost unmanageable. Where I blamed the selfishness of certain labor leaders for some of our economic problems, the President said big business was at fault. He wanted a strong national defense capability and believed Secretary McNamara and his whiz kids at the Pentagon were providing it. I thought McNamara was deliberately and systematically reducing our defense posture in pursuit of parity with the Russians.

Kennedy believed his general reduction in taxes would stimulate the economy. I thought it would lead to higher deficits and more inflation and would threaten bankruptcy. Kennedy was right on this. His tax cut did stimulate the economy. Federal tax collection increased even at the lower rate.

To Jack Kennedy politics was a kind of game, like touch football or a sailing contest. Winning was all that mattered. He had no deep-seated overriding political-philosophical convictions to constitute an insurmountable barrier between us. I think he loved this country just as deeply as I do. But while I saw the policies of the Democratic party as threatening and destructive and, therefore, to be violently opposed, he saw them as mechanisms, attractive political gimmicks, devised to achieve political victory.

Organized labor could deliver a lot of votes, therefore, could help win an election—just as a strong offensive tackle could break through the defensive line and open a hole for a ten-yard gain. He was more concerned with being elected President than with being the President. In my opinion, this made him excessively vulnerable to the advice of the men around him. Because, for the most part, they too were motivated by the desire to win the election, he listened to them.

We will never know whether a Kennedy-Goldwater contest could have been conducted on the lines we projected, but it presented an intriguing possibility. I was painfully aware that even under the best of conditions, I held the short end of the stick.

My assessment of the situation also included the real possibility that Jack Kennedy in his second term might be a quite different President. He would no longer be facing the requirement to seek reelection. He might have moved to correct some past mistakes and alter drastically those public policies we agreed required reform.

I suspect that perhaps fifty years from now some scholarly historian will assemble all the data from the archives and conclude that the truly astounding political event of 1964 was not the reelection of the incumbent, Lyndon Johnson. Instead, it was the nomination of Barry Goldwater to head the Republican ticket. In a very real sense that nomination resulted from the efforts of an unlikely, unpaid group of volunteers, spontaneously organized, without any encouragement from me. Surely, if there ever was a true draft, this was it.

I was aware that F. Clifton White had quietly enlisted some very savvy political minds committed to my nomination. Clif never asked my permission because he knew I would say no.

Even though I kept my distance and carefully avoided any conversations or correspondence with the group, I did know they were finding it very difficult to raise any money. All my political instincts warned me against becoming identified with an effort which I thought was doomed to fail.

It is also true that I was deeply engrossed in my efforts to elect Republican Senators. I think now I subconsciously blocked out all the rumors and whispers which, had I been more objective, might have forced me to conclude that, like it or not, there was a growing sentiment within the party for my nomination.

Another factor which may have had a bearing on my personal attitude was a developing friendly relationship with Nelson Rockefeller. I accepted his sudden interest and overtures as a genuine concern for the future of the Republican party. I found reason to admire his politically astute observations. We had one area of complete agreement. Nelson thought that Nixon had waged a miserable campaign in 1960 and that if Nixon were nominated again in 1964, there was no hope for a Republican victory.

In the Senate cloakrooms there were whispers that Goldwater and Rockefeller had formed an alliance. The truth—we didn't meet often. Our contacts were business, rarely social. One time during this period, when I was home, Nelson called my residence. Peggy answered. The voice at the other end said, "Peggy, this is Nelson Rockefeller. Is Barry there?" Peggy replied, "This is Mamie Eisenhower. You must have the wrong number."

During this period Nelson suggested we meet for dinner once a month. He wanted me to bring four or five of my conservative friends. He would invite an equal number of his liberal associates, and we would explore the differences which separated us. In retrospect, I think these meetings were very productive. We were in agreement on the majority of the major issues.

It was during this period that Nelson decided to get a divorce in order to marry Margaretta "Happy" Murphy, whose husband, Dr. James Slater Murphy, a microbiologist, worked for the Rockefeller Institute. The press response to this announced marital change was critical, and some conservatives bitterly condemned the governor.

Nelson resented this. In private, he made some pretty nasty remarks about the conservatives in general. When I heard about it, I called him up and asked him what the hell was the matter.

He said, "You conservatives are picking on me for marrying Happy."

I said, "Not this conservative, Nelson. I've never said a word."

Until 1959 Nelson Rockefeller had benefited from a close association with the very astute and skillful public relations man Frank Jamieson. It is my opinion that Jamieson's death in 1960, as the result of lung cancer, was a crippling blow—one from which the New York governor never fully recovered.

Many of my friends have accused me of being politically naïve, always willing to accept my companions and my competitors at face value. There may be something to that charge. The devious, dark alleys of politics are repugnant to me. The Nelson Rockefeller I saw in 1961 and 1962 appeared much more conservative than his public image.

On November 12, 1962, I was in New York to attend a meeting of the Wings organization, an association of airmen and World

War II pilots. Clif White came to my hotel room to deliver a detailed account of what he and his group had accomplished. I was impressed. He didn't ask me to endorse the effort. He didn't insist on any commitment from me.

One thing seemed clear. Clif White understood convention politics. He knew why and how delegates to national conventions were chosen and what effect the various official Republican organizations had on that choice. He and his group were ready to participate in party caucuses and state conventions; they had enlisted a substantial number of people who were, in reality, the grass-roots strength of the Republican party.

The Associated Press had polled the Republican delegates to the 1960 convention. They reported a strong majority wanted Goldwater as their candidate in 1964. Clif White's study of the makeup of past Republican conventions supported his claim that more than half the delegates who would be selected in 1964 would be repeaters.

When Clif and I met that November, Nixon had been defeated in his race for the governorship of California. In his final press conference he had appeared to renounce any future political ambitions. I was forced to admit the Republican party in 1964 would most likely be faced with the necessity of choosing between Nelson Rockefeller and Barry Goldwater. And for me, the prospect was not pleasant.

I clearly understood the power of Rockefeller's financial backers. He was a bona fide member of the eastern establishment. I had vivid memories of what that group had done to Richard Nixon in 1960 and for John F. Kennedy in that same race.

In 1961 the Alfalfa Club, a fun-loving, hijinks, sophisticated group in Washington, nominated me for the presidency at their annual dinner. Phil Graham, the publisher of the Washington *Post*, made the nominating speech. I offered an extravagant, and I hope humorous, response. I know some parts were funny because Morrie Ryskind helped me write them. In high good humor, I accepted as the Neanderthal man, the ultimate reactionary, the innocent westerner.

In addition to my concern for what I estimated would be the exaggerated, derogatory aspects of such a campaign, should I seek the nomination, I was also genuinely intimidated by the thought of being President. I had seen Dwight Eisenhower lose his struggle with the power centers in Washington. I knew how Jack Kennedy felt about the restrictions and limitations the same group had imposed on him. I was terrified at the thought of four years in the White House confronted by a Democratic-controlled Congress.

As my agonizing indecision prevailed during the opening months of 1963, the one supportive or reassuring aspect was my hope that if it did happen, Jack Kennedy would somehow keep his commitments. We would lift this presidential campaign above the petty, conniving scheming which had flawed every political race in my experience. We would present the American voters with an opportunity to make a reasoned decision based on contending political philosophies rather than on personality.

When that assassin's bullet ended the life of John Fitzgerald Kennedy in Dallas on November 22, 1963, it was for me a great personal loss.

I have long since abandoned all speculation on how a Kennedy-Goldwater campaign might have turned out. Had we been permitted to enjoy the contest we both conceptualized, it would have been different. It might have been beneficially instructive. In a very real sense, the bullet that killed John Kennedy also destroyed whatever possibility there ever was for a Goldwater presidency. In December 1963 my intention was to recognize reality and refuse to be a candidate.

I judged the nation, shocked and grieved by the assassination, would be in no mood to change Presidents. Lyndon Johnson could not be charged with the failures of the Kennedy policies. He had been the true outsider, his contacts with the President more infrequent and more formal than mine. His problems were inherited, not of his own making. I had said in my rules for a good campaign that it was necessary to oppose, but to oppose without hate. All my contacts with Lyndon Johnson had instructed me to believe he would be incapable of opposing without hate.

CHAPTER 19

Goldwater for President

My reluctance to seek the Republican nomination for the office of President in 1964 was, in part, purely personal. My life-style is casual, informal, spontaneous. The possibility of being a prisoner in the White House, my every move attended by the Secret Service, surrounded by a corps of sycophantic advisers, with every move I made, every word I spoke interpreted and analyzed by the national press, was repulsive to me. Even though I had been in the public eye for twelve years, I fiercely resisted the thought of surrendering all my privacy to the job.

There were other considerations. I understood the magnitude of the problems confronting the Republic. I appreciated the stubborn resistance inherent in the bureaucracy. I had seen Ike in an agony of frustration over his inability to move Congress in the direction of the reforms he believed were necessary, a situation made more painful when the Democrats became the majority party in Congress in 1955.

Even though Jack Kennedy was the President of the majority party, he too had been angered and dismayed by the intransigence of the Congress and the bureaucratic overlords. The vast, unwieldy mechanism of the federal government would, I calculated, fiercely resist the reforms I felt were necessary to repair the Republic. I suppose at bottom I was overawed by the presidency. Having no lust for the power of the office, I just could not conceptualize a Barry Goldwater presidency.

There were other factors contributing to my dilemma. I was an outsider, a westerner, from a state with only five votes in the electoral college. As an avid student of our political history I knew the enormity of the odds. I think of myself as a pragmatic politician, one who finds no virtue in leading a lost cause. Yet I could not close my eyes to the fact that circumstances not of my own design had thrust me into a position where if I refused to become a candidate, thousands, perhaps millions of dedicated Americans who had responded to my descriptions of the dangers confronting the Republic would have cause to feel betrayed.

F. Clifton White, William A. Rusher, and John Ashbrook of Ohio launched the Draft Goldwater for President movement at a meeting in Chicago on October 8, 1961. White of Rye, New York, a college professor, deserted the halls of academia to become a political activist. He had earned a position of power and prominence in Young Republican circles.

A Harvard lawyer, Rusher served as an associate counsel for the Internal Securities Subcommittee of the U.S. Senate before joining William F. Buckley, Jr., to publish the conservative newsmagazine *National Review*.

Ashbrook served in the Ohio legislature. He was elected national chairman of the Young Republicans in 1957 and won a seat in the national Congress in 1960.

They all were present at the 1960 convention in Chicago. After the nomination, White served as chairman of Volunteers for Nixon-Lodge in New York. Ashbrook and Rusher worked hard for the Nixon ticket, but like many other Republican loyalists, they were disenchanted by Nixon's trip to New York and by his selection of Henry Cabot Lodge for Vice President.

In early September 1961, at a meeting in New York City, White, Rusher, and Ashbrook decided to instigate the Draft Goldwater movement. The twenty-two men from across the nation whom they invited to meet at the Avenue Motel on South Michigan Avenue in Chicago in October of that year all were practical, experienced political operators. Because I was determined to keep my options open, I ignored this group, but I won't pretend I did not know what was going on.

Time magazine had described me as "the hottest political figure this side of Jack Kennedy." The article noted *The Conscience of a Conservative* had sold 700,000 copies in a little more than a year, that I was the most sought-after speaker in the Republican party, the most effective fund raiser, that my mail was running 800 letters a day. The *Time* reporter had asked me if I intended to seek the presidency and printed my response: "I have no plans for it. I have no staff for it, no program for it, and no ambition for it."

Ostensibly, the Chicago meeting was to launch a Draft Goldwater movement, but I think what the men who came to Chicago really wanted was to provide the nation with a choice—a choice between the liberal and the conservative principles.

Following the meeting, Clif White came to Washington to inform me of what had taken place. He was not asking for my official endorsement or personal authorization. He said they were going to begin at the grass roots, enlist precinct committeemen, county chairmen, and state chairmen, and go after delegates who could be committed to my nomination in 1964.

I told him I knew I could not stop him, but I would not encourage him. In the days following, additional recruits were brought into the Draft Goldwater movement—Peter O'Donnell of Texas; Wirt Yerger, chairman in Mississippi; Tad Smith, state chairman of Texas; Governor Don Nutter of Montana; and Ione Harrington of Indiana.

At the beginning of December 1963 it was my considered opinion that no Republican could prevail against Lyndon Johnson. President as a result of a great national tragedy, he could not be held accountable for the errors of his predecessor. Fate had muted all the issues I might have used in a confrontation with Jack Kennedy. This was my frame of mind on December 8, 1963, when I met with the handful of advisers and supporters who would become the heart and muscle of the Goldwater election team—Bill Baroody, of the American Enterprise Institute; my longtime friend Denison Kitchel; speech writer Karl Hess; industrial relations expert and political philosopher Jay Hall; Dean Burch; Congressman John J. Rhodes; and United States Senators Carl Curtis, of Nebraska, Norris Cotton of New Hampshire, and William Knowland of California.

I opened my heart and my mind. I said, "Our cause is lost."

The other men in that room had a substantial investment in a Goldwater candidacy. Norris Cotton argued that nothing had really changed. He said the great principled issues which divided me from the Democratic President had not been removed by the Kennedy assassination. He said it was my duty to lead the conservative forces. He did not predict victory. He reminded me there was more to life than winning. I thought of something my old coach at Staunton had often said: "We win some, we lose some, and some get rained out; but we always suit up."

Cotton's words endeared him to me. He was saying what in my heart I had recognized all along. Circumstance had made me the leader. I could not in conscience refuse the responsibility no matter how distasteful the prospect, no matter how uncertain the outcome. I had planted the flag on the hilltop; now I must defend that flag.

My critics have remarked, and in retrospect I must agree with them, that my inner circle of advisers had very little experience in the politics of campaigning. Baroody, an intellectual, had devoted his career to dealing in abstracts, pursuing "ideal public policies." Kitchel, my loyal lawyer friend, had never been involved in a campaign. Ed McCabe, who had been around the White House during the Eisenhower years, had a very practical grasp of the problems of administration. Hess was a good writer, a strongly conservative ideologue, but no politician. Dean Burch had been in on the end of my 1958 campaign, but he had not participated in any policy decisions or strategy determinations. Jay Hall had a greater understanding of the practical ways to reach the voters than the others, but he had never been in charge of a campaign. Of course, Knowland, Curtis, and Cotton had won elections in California, Nebraska, and New Hampshire, but many successful candidates come to office without any appreciation of the various elements which forged that victory.

I had been instructed by my successes in 1952 and 1958 to let the manager manage. While I had been consulted and participated in most of the policy decisions of those two campaigns, Shadegg had been in charge, and in a sense, I had followed his orders.

Over the years I have strongly advised candidates running for public office for the first time to select a competent manager and then to do what the manager says. This is because the candidate who is constantly on display has not time to balance all the elements which must go into strategy. Of course, such a relationship requires the candidate to trust his manager's decisions implicitly.

I named Kitchel chairman of the campaign. We may have suffered from errors in judgment rising out of inexperience, but in the long months which followed, there was never any reason to question Kitch's loyalty. He was, and is, my friend, and I must take responsibility for the errors and the shortcomings.

It was an inauspicious beginning. Presidential candidates, whatever their merit, are perceived by their followers to occupy a position comparable to the prince or the emperor of the Middle Ages. Power is measured by closeness to the prince. There is automatically created an ongoing struggle to achieve the number one, preferential position. I think I vaguely understood this in 1963. In an instinctive reaction I turned to those individuals, all from Arizona, who had been my friends and associates. In addition to Kitchel and Burch, I asked Mrs. Emory Johnson of Tucson to head the women's activities and named Richard Kleindienst field director for the Goldwater for President Committee.

Mrs. Johnson, a longtime member of the Republican National Committee, was well known to party politicians. She had been a part of my inner circle in both 1952 and 1958.

Kleindienst, a graduate of Harvard Law School, had served one term in the Arizona legislature. In 1958 he had managed Paul Fannin's successful campaign for reelection to a second term as governor of Arizona. He was, by all odds, the most experienced managerial politician of my inner group.

The Draft Goldwater movement was responsible for my nomination in 1964. The political history of the United States records a multitude of so-called draft movements. Most of them were third-party efforts undertaken with the covert support of the candidate. The organization White, Ashbrook, and Rusher put together was a genuine "draft."

Kitchel and Baroody wanted me to make my announcement in the nation's capital. They argued this location would give us superior access to national television. I balked at this. I said that if I were going to run, I would make the announcement from my home base in Arizona.

I have long held the notion that presidential primaries are political booby traps. They can cripple a candidate's chances for the nomination without truly advancing the cause. It was my personal notion that the way to win the nomination was to run in only a few selected primary states. My western origin caused me to prefer California, and then I thought Illinois, Florida, and perhaps one or two others. This battle plan was vetoed by the Washington group. Bill Loeb, the New Hampshire publisher, was strongly in my corner. Early polls indicated I could walk away with that state's primary. I let myself be persuaded.

December 1963 is a month of unpleasant memories. Not only was I compelled by circumstances to agree to seek the nomination, but I had undergone surgery on my right foot. It was immobilized in a cast, and I was forced to get around on crutches.

We had picked January 3, 1964, in Phoenix, Arizona, as the time for my announcement. I conceded there would be monumental problems of logistics, but my frame of mind was not particularly cooperative. If I had do it, I would do it my own way and on my own ground.

At this meeting I again named Kitchel manager of my presidential campaign; Dick Kleindienst, head of field operations; Mrs. Johnson, chairman of the women's division; and Dean Burch as Kitchel's assistant. The press immediately called my team the Arizona Mafia. There is no rancor in my heart about that misadventure, but I have noted that most successful candidates for president invariably turn to their close associates—the most recent example being Jimmy Carter.

In that announcement statement I said I had decided to become a candidate for the Republican nomination in response to the millions of Americans who wanted a choice. I said I hoped it would be a campaign of principles, not personalities. I promised there would be a direct and decisive confrontation between two antagonistic political philosophies—the welfare state, represented by Lyndon Johnson of the Democrats, and a society of free, independent, responsible individuals, to be represented by the Republicans.

The press took note of the omission of any leaders of the Draft Goldwater movement in the Goldwater presidential campaign group. This was a serious error on my part. I won't cop out by saying I put myself in the hands of the management team and let them make the decisions. I have tremendous respect for Clif White, Peter O'Donnell, Ione Harrington, and all the other members of that Draft Goldwater movement. I felt more comfortable with my longtime Arizona friends.

I was starting off on the wrong foot in more ways than one

when I agreed to enter the New Hampshire primary. It is truly a no-win situation. Locals call it the "beauty contest" since the delegates elected are not bound by law or precedent to vote for the name at the head of the New Hampshire ticket.

I entered New Hamphsire walking on crutches. We had no adequate campaign staff, no advance organization. My longtime senatorial press secretary, Tony Smith, was thrust into the job of press relations. There was no game plan, no rehearsal, no careful screening of what I would say or propose.

The overscheduling was almost unbelievable. Some days I was booked for eighteen hours of appearances before small groups of New Hampshire residents. Hounded by the same national press corps, they never varied their questions. They were antagonists.

It was in New Hampshire that I first said it made sense to me to permit the commander of NATO forces some discretion in the use of tactical nuclear weapons.

I assumed the reporters—at least those who covered Washington—were aware of the fact that this policy had been in effect since the early Eisenhower years. In reporting my statement, a writer made the word "commander" plural and suggested I was willing to let a field captain use a tactical nuclear weapon if he thought it advisable.

Later in the campaign, when I was visiting Ike at Gettysburg, he told me he had only one reservation. Ike said, "Barry, you speak too quick and too loud." I had to agree with him.

When I made my announcement in Phoenix, I discovered we had no national finance committee, and it was not until January 12 that I was able to enlist Daniel C. Gainey of Owatonna, Minnesota, and G. R. Herberger of Scottsdale, Arizona, to undertake raising the money we would need. They did a magnificent job, assisted by Roger Milliken of South Carolina; Stetz Coleman, the southern industrialist; Jeremiah Milbank of Connecticut and New York City; and Henry Salvatori of California.

The New Hampshire primary was further complicated by the fact that my insiders, Senator Norris Cotton and Stuart Lamprey, Speaker of the New Hampshire legislature, were bitter enemies.

It was in New Hampshire that the press labeled me as the candidate who wanted to abolish the Social Security system. In *The Conscience of a Conservative* I had said the Social Security system was actuarially unsound, a pseudoinsurance program totally unfunded, a proposal originally intended to do no more than prevent stark privation, and an actual tax levied against the nation's payrolls but collected and spent outside the government's annual budget.

My concern at that time was based on the fact that I believed the Social Security system was approaching bankruptcy. I wanted to prevent it from collapsing, and I said so, but the headline on the next day's story said: "Goldwater to Destroy Social Security."

The management team—Baroody, Kitchel, Burch, McCabe, Hess, and Kleindienst—regarded Nelson Rockefeller as my only serious opponent. The then governor of New York had gone to college in New Hampshire. He was at home with the people, and he was supported by an excellent advance staff. What I didn't realize then and did not fully recognize until many months later was that all the other Republican party contenders were united in an effort to stop Goldwater.

As primary day drew near, our polls showed my popularity was diminishing, but I was still well ahead of the governor of New York. We were just not prepared at all for the apparance of a new candidate. Robert Mullen, a political organizer; Paul D. Grindle, a professional manager of political campaigns; and David Goldberg organized and launched a write-in campaign for Henry Cabot Lodge, who was not even in this country.

I could not take it seriously. Lodge had been a lackadaisical—some said lazy—candidate for Vice President on the Nixon ticket in 1960. He had accepted appointment as Ambassador to Saigon from John F. Kennedy. The working Republicans recognized this was a crafty move to lay off any blame for failures in Vietnam on Lodge as a representative of the Republicans. Lodge was in Vietnam, but his son, George, endorsed the write-in, conveying the belief the effort had the blessing of his father.

The New Hampshire election was scheduled for March 10. Beginning March 3, the Lodge people saturated New Hampshire's television market with a five-minute program which had been made four years earlier, when Dwight Eisenhower introduced Lodge as the Republican candidate for Vice President on the Nixon ticket.

The film had been skillfully edited. A blast of trumpets was imposed at just the right moment to drown out the word "Vice" in Ike's introduction. I'm sure most viewers of that TV commercial believed Ike was advocating the nomination and election of Henry Cabot Lodge in 1964.

When the votes were counted, I was 12,000 behind write-in candiate Lodge. Nelson Rockefeller ran third; Margaret Chase Smith was number four. The slate of Goldwater delegates headed by Senator Norris Cotton was defeated.

The bad press I got in New Hampshire set the stage for the ultimate image of Goldwater—as a trigger-happy, pugnacious, somewhat uninformed candidate who would destroy Social Security. Incidentally, the writer of the headline which declared I intended to destroy the Social Security system was promptly fired by his employer. I don't know if that misrepresentation of my statement was deliberate or unintentional. Twenty-four hours after the headline appeared, the Rockefeller forces mailed a photo reproduction to every Social Security recipient in New Hampshire. The names and addresses of Social Security recipients are supposed to be confidential. Considering the time required to print a mailing piece and address the envelopes, the Rockefeller campaigners either were marvelously efficient or had advance information that such a headline would be used.

CHAPTER 20

On the Way to the Cow Palace

The process we employ to select the rulers of the Republic is abused and distorted in every campaign. We now have new laws and a Federal Election Commission. The use of taxpayer dollars from the public treasury is justified as a cure for the abusive influence of former big contributors. The reforms we have adopted don't reach to the root of the problem, which is the voters' total dependency on the image of the candidate projected by the media. However much the reporters strive to maintain objectivity, the nature of the news business exalts the flamboyant, places more emphasis on style than on substance. Fear and prejudice command more attention than reason and logic. The headline writer is trained to capture the reader's interest with the dramatic caption. The anchorman on the evening news must oversimplify to hold the viewer's attention.

I was aware of all this when I agreed to become a candidate. I had no illusions. I had no alternatives. I have no regrets.

Fourteen years have passed since I sought and won the Republican nomination for the office of President. Perhaps no one really cares anymore. However, that season of untempered abuse, vindictive falsehood, desertion of civility left its mark on our society and on the world. I have long since overcome the personal pain of defeat.

It would, I am sure, be more prudent to hold my tongue, let the dead past bury its dead. Some of my bitter critics of that period now acknowledge the truth of the positions I supported in 1964. I am indebted to my neighbors in Arizona, who have twice re-elected me to the United States Senate. I cannot keep silent.

The American people, regardless of party affiliation, were sad-dened, shocked, and angered over the assassination of President Kennedy. Lyndon Johnson had been in office only six weeks when the 1964 presidential campaign started. He was regarded with great sympathy. The people instinctively resisted the thought of another change in the presidential office so soon after the tragedy in Dallas.

There is no way of knowing whether Barry Goldwater or any other Republican could have been elected in 1964. Had I run a better campaign, had I been a better candidate, had I not made so many errors, the margin of Lyndon Johnson's victory might have been substantially reduced. Perhaps my greatest error was in not starting sooner. The late entrance was a handicap from which we never recovered.

When I finally recognized I had no honorable alternative, I should have imposed my judgment on the campaign group and stayed out of most of the primaries.

The media, including the *New York Times* and the Washington *Post*, had been reasonably objective in their coverage of my ac-tivities and my statements as a member of the United States Senate. James Reston applauded my statements on foreign policy. Arthur Krock and David Lawrence agreed with many of the positions I had taken. The Los Angeles *Times* was strongly supportive when it requested me to write a column. *Time* magazine treated me with courtesy and fairness.

The conservative philosophy of Senator Barry Goldwater could be tolerated. *The possibility of a conservative Goldwater presi-dency was anathema to the lords of the media.*

Many observers, troubled by the unanimity of action on the part of the eastern press, perceive it to be some sort of sinister conspiracy. It is a curious fact that when Walter Lippmann, the high priest of the liberals' Mount Olympus, pontificated on a particular subject, his conclusions were immediately echoed by dozens of other liberal pundits. Today the individual voices, all sharing a common philosophical viewpoint, play follow-the-leader in order to maintain their membership group.

I should have been prepared to have every word I said twisted, every statement taken out of context. I should have spelled out my proposals in elaborate detail with sufficient specificity to make misinterpretation extremely difficult. But I didn't.

On January 3 I said, "This presidential campaign will be a contest of principle, not personality." It never got to that point. I must assume a share of the blame for that failure.

By the time we reached the November election the press, the TV, and the Johnson strategists had made me the most feared man in America.

I hold the "Stop Goldwater" Republicans responsible for the major distortions of that contest. The Johnson strategists merely exploited the opportunity thus provided.

The commonsense political wisdom of Dick Kleindienst helped correct our original error of excluding the Draft Goldwater people from the Goldwater for President effort. Dick shared his title of field director with Clif White. They divided responsibility. White took charge of the states where the delegates would be selected at state conventions. Kleindienst directed our efforts in the primary states. Both areas were of equal importance. The press, for the most part, ignored the early results in states where delegates were selected by convention and overemphasized the importance of the primary states.

My loss in New Hampshire was headlined as a major defeat, even though the results were not binding on the delegates. The fact that I had acquired fifty-two committed delegates from Oklahoma, North Carolina, Tennessee, and Kansas twenty-two days before the New Hampshire election was all but ignored.

At the end of March Henry Cabot Lodge could make a tenuous claim to fourteen votes in New Hampshire. Rockefeller had three delegates in the Virgin Islands. I had seventy-seven committed votes.

The Illinois primary was held on April 14. I received 62 percent of the popular vote. Forty of the forty-eight delegates elected in congressional districts were Goldwater supporters. We had good reason to believe the ten to be selected at a state convention on May 1 would be chosen from our camp. The press construed my victory in Illinois as a defeat.

We stayed out of the Wisconsin primaries, deferring to the

favorite son, Congressman John Byrnes, who, in reality, was a stand-in—a maneuver by Clif White to keep Rockefeller out of the contest. Byrnes promised our people his delegates would vote for me in San Francisco. By the end of April we had a total of 309 committed delegates.

The Oregon presidential primary law is unique. It requires the secretary of state to put the names of all avowed candidates on the ballot and also to list any potential candidate who has been prominently mentioned in the press as a contender.

An individual who does not want his name on the Oregon primary ballot is required to sign a Shermanesque affidavit declaring that if nominated, he will not run, if elected, he will not serve. George Romney did sign such a declaration. The others refused to do so. Howell Appling, Oregon's secretary of state and one of my supporters, was required by law to put six names on the presidential primary ballot—Richard Nixon, Henry Cabot Lodge, William Scranton, Barry Goldwater, Nelson A. Rockefeller, and Margaret Chase Smith.

In January Kleindienst was of the opinion we should make a strong effort in Oregon. I asked Steve Shadegg to go to Portland and take personal charge. I went to Oregon in February for a Lincoln Day speech and returned on April 6 for three days of personal appearances.

Oregon was a "must win" situation for Nelson Rockefeller. He had an elaborate campaign staff headed by William E. Walsh, who had resigned his position as president to the State Board of Higher Education to devote his full time to securing the Oregon vote for Rockefeller.

In early April I was in New York City; Peggy and I had lunch at Club "21." When we came out of the restaurant, it was such a beautiful day we decided to walk a few blocks before hailing a cab to go back to our hotel. We turned north on Fifth Avenue. As we strolled along, a number of people recognized me. Many of them said, "Hi," or, "Good luck, Barry."

After a block or two I noticed a pleasant-looking man in his mid-thirties about fifteen or twenty paces behind us. I had a strange feeling the man was following us. When we stopped to look in the shopwindows, he stopped. When we started north again, he started north. After about six or seven blocks he caught up to us, smiled, and said, "Senator, you really have a recognition factor in this town."

I said, "I'm glad to hear that, but what is your interest?"

He replied, "Oh, I work for Governor Rockefeller. He wanted to know how people would react seeing you on the street. I'll have to report the people of New York City seem to like you."

The Oregon primary was scheduled for May 15. The California date was June 2. The eighteen delegates to be elected in Oregon would not be bound by law to support the winner of the primary. All eighty-six delegates running in California on a Goldwater slate were committed in writing to support me in the event I won.

In my two succesful senatorial campaigns Steve Shadegg had developed a strategy of "going where the ducks are"—that is, devoting maximum effort in those precincts where we could expect a maximum return. I had only so much time and so much personal energy. There were eighty-six sure "ducks" in California, eighteen doubtful ones in Oregon. I canceled all plans for further campaigning in Oregon. Unfortunately the schedule for personal appearances was already announced. When I didn't come, the Rockefeller people made my failure to appear the central issue. They advertised their candidate as "the man who cared enough to come."

When Shadegg learned from the representatives of the Oregon TV stations that David Goldberg, the man in charge of the Lodge effort, had purchased a substantial number of five-minute time segments, he concluded they were to be used to display that same misleading Eisenhower endorsement shown in New Hampshire. Shadegg sent a telegram to our former President in Palm Springs, asking him either to authorize or to condemn the use of that particular five-minute film.

Ike responded promptly.

Repeatedly I've expressed publicly my high esteem for each of the individuals prominently mentioned as possible nominees for the presidency in 1964. I respect each and oppose none.

The film in question I've never seen, nor have I been contacted in any fashion in respect to its use prior to your communication. If it expresses my high respect for Cabot

Lodge, it is accurate; and I do not object to that esteem being reaffirmed in any place in America. If it suggests that I have given any public indication of a preference for any person over any other in the current contest, then it is a definite misrepresentation. Dwight D. Eisenhower.

When Shadegg made Ike's response public, Goldberg canceled the showing of that misleading five-minute film.

After my switch in plans Shadegg told me he didn't think we could win in Oregon. But he was confident we could knock Scranton out of the race, and that is exactly what we did. Rockefeller ran first with 33 percent of the votes cast; Nixon was second with 28 percent; I came in third with about 18 percent; Scranton's total was 7,000, or 2 percent. He was a poor fourth.

Nelson Rockefeller's victory in Oregon rehabilitated his candidacy. In late 1965 I learned of a maneuver which might have changed the results of the Oregon primary. I recite it now to illuminate what often takes place within the inner circle.

Richard Nixon was a very popular public figure in Oregon. He had carried the state against Kennedy in 1960. His name on the ballot was more of a threat to me than it was to Rockefeller. It was reasonable to believe that Nixon and I would split the voters who consider themselves conservatives, while Rockefeller and Scranton would divide the liberals.

March 5 was the deadline for the filing of an affidavit of withdrawal. On March 1 Sig Unander, one of my supporters, who was friendly with Nixon, approached the former Vice President with a proposition. If Nixon would withdraw from the Oregon primary, Unander was ready to promise that in the event the convention deadlocked and I could not win the nomination, the Oregon delegation would swing over to Nixon.

Nixon was apparently willing to make the deal. But he wanted direct personal assurance from a member of the Oregon delegation that the commitment would be kept.

All this information was relayed to my campaign office in Washington, D.C., with a request that someone telephone Nixon in New York City, give him the name and telephone number of a man who was almost certain to be on the Oregon delegation and would give Nixon the assurances he wanted. Someone on my staff in Washington decided it would be undignified to enter into any such deal. The telephone call was not made. Rockefeller won Oregon with only 33 percent of the votes cast. Nixon and I together got 46 percent. It is reasonable to believe that had Nixon removed his name from the Oregon primary ballot, I would have won that contest.

By the middle of May we were counting more than 500 delegate votes. California was now the crucial battleground. If I could defeat Rockefeller in the Golden State, our total would jump to almost 600. We expected to win unanimous support in the remaining convention states of Washington, Idaho, Montana, and Utah. These votes would ensure victory in San Francisco. If Rockefeller defeated me in the California primary, it would be touch and go at the Cow Palace.

Recognizing the importance of the California primary, Dick Kleindienst moved his base of operations from Washington, D.C., to Los Angeles on May 1. He spent the next fifteen days testing the strength of the Goldwater for President organization. On May 15 Kleindienst told me that if the election were being held that day, we would lose California by at least 200,000 votes. He said our organization was narrow and limited in its concepts. Capable party workers had been excluded. In his opinion, the radio, TV, and newspaper ads of the Goldwater group were no match for the slick media presentations being made on behalf of Rockefeller.

Former U.S. Senator William S. Knowland and Pete Pitchess, the sheriff of Los Angeles County, were in charge of my California volunteers. Kleindienst proposed we bring Dean Burch from Washington to California and put him in charge of the primary effort. He admitted there was a risk. Knowland and Pitchess might interpret this as an indication I had lost confidence in their ability and leadership.

My confidence in Kleindienst's political judgment compelled me to accept his recommendation. I met with Knowland and Pitchess. I laid it on the table without attributing the discouraging news to Kleindienst.

Bill Knowland had been Majority Leader of the U.S. Senate. We were good friends. He was a man of great intelligence, strong philosophical convictions, devoted to the nation's welfare. Without a moment's hesitation, Knowland acknowledged the truth of the situation as I had outlined it. He promised to accept any modification in the organizational structure I thought might increase our chance for victory. Pete Pitchess responded in the same manner. I thought then if personal ego was at stake, and it was, they were too big to let that interfere.

The Rockefeller campaign was being directed by the firm of Spencer-Roberts and Associates, which was generally regarded as the most successful managers in California politics. I had observed the activities of this agency in prior campaigns. It was expert at destroying its client's opponents with skillfully executed, sometimes vicious, negative thrusts.

Howard K. Smith, moderator of the ABC network TV program *Issues and Answers*, invited me to appear for a pretaped interview to be released Sunday afternoon, May 24. In the course of the interview Smith brought up the war in Vietnam. He said he understood I favored interdicting the supply routes from Red China which the communists were using to feed their war machine in South Vietnam. How, he asked, could this be done? I said, "Well, it is not as easy as it sounds because these are not trails that are out in the open. I've been in the rain forests of Burma and South China. You are perfectly safe wandering through them as far as an enemy hurting you. There have been several suggestions made. I don't think we would use any of them, but defoliation of the forest by low-yield atomic devices could well be done. When you remove the foliage, you remove the cover."

I didn't suggest we should use the atomic bomb in South Vietnam. I said there had been several suggestions made. I knew the military had discussed the possibility of using toxic defoliants and extremely harsh chemicals as well as atomic artillery shells extremely low in radiation. I qualified my response by saying, "I don't think we would use any of them."

The network made the program content available to AP and UPI in advance of broadcast. Both wire services released stories suggesting Goldwater advocated the use of nuclear weapons in Vietnam. UPI later retracted its story, but the retraction never caught up with the Sunday-morning headlines. It was a near-fatal blow.

Encouraged by his victory in Oregon, Rockefeller intensified his media campaign in California. Our people estimated he spent more than $3.5 million between May 15 and June 2.

The major thrust of the Spencer-Roberts-directed effort was to picture Nelson Rockefeller as a mainstream Republican enjoying the support of the other contenders—Lodge, Nixon, Romney, and Scranton. The newspaper ads and handouts featured a photograph of Rockefeller with pictures of the other candidates clustered around him. On the opposite part of the page was a photograph of Goldwater. The headline caption asked, "Which do you want? A leader or a loner?"

Bill Knowland telephoned the governor of Michigan to ask if Romney was aware of the advertising message and had approved its content. Romney replied with a telegram declaring, "I am neither supporting nor opposing any candidate."

I sent one of the handouts to Bill Scranton in Harrisburg. His reply came by special delivery letter:

Dear Barry,

I have not been asked by anyone for permission to include my name or picture in this literature. Since I am not a candidate no one represents me in California or anywhere else.

My one overriding interest is for unity within the Republican party. Consequently, I have refused to join "Stop Goldwater," "Stop Rockefeller," or "stop" anybody movements.

I believe that a unified Republican party can score a resounding victory this fall—we cannot do this, however, unless we are unified and strong. With warm, personal regards. Most sincerely.

Bill Scranton

There were almost daily stories in the Los Angeles *Times* reporting alleged acts of vandalism perpetrated by Goldwater supporters on Rockefeller headquarters and Rockefeller campaigners. Sheriff Pete Pitchess assigned his best investigators to these alleged disturbances. They reported there was no truth in any of these charges.

Walter Thayer, president of the New York *Herald Tribune*, persuaded General Eisenhower to sign an article giving a detailed description of the type of man he believed the Republicans should nominate for the presidency. The story was front page in the *Herald Tribune* on May 25. It was possible to interpret the statement to mean Ike was endorsing Nelson Rockefeller.

The *Herald Tribune* waived its copyright and released the story simultaneously to the wire services and to the *New York Times*, which carried the *Herald Tribune* piece on its own front page. To make certain no one missed the point, Roscoe Drummond, syndicated columnist for the *Herald Tribune*, wrote a column claiming Eisenhower's hypothetical description of the ideal Republican candidate was a clear repudiation of Goldwater.

Of course, the reporters wanted to know what I thought about it. I said I endorsed what the former President had said, hoping to take some of the sting out of the piece. Later that day, speaking to a rally at Shasta College, I turned my back on the audience and displayed the feathered shaft of a long arrow. No one missed that point. The crowd roared. The photographers took pictures. Most of the nation's newspaper readers saw the photograph and enjoyed it.

On Monday morning, June 1, General Eisenhower held a press conference in New York. He told reporters, "You people tried to read Goldwater out of the party; I didn't."

One week before that primary, which could have meant the end of the presidential race for me, our pollsters reported Nelson Rockefeller held a commanding lead. Rockefeller had played hard ball in New Hampshire, exploiting the Social Security headline, which he knew was an inaccurate description of my position. Most of the Goldwater team in Los Angeles believed Rockefeller was responsible for the writing of that damaging headline. Walter Thayer of the New York *Herald Tribune* was not publicly identified as a Rockefeller supporter, but since the thrust of that statement by Ike had been helpful to Rockefeller and damaging to me, my team was willing to give Nelson the credit for it.

During that final week in May Rockefeller was scheduled to speak to the students of Loyola University. There is a substantial Catholic vote in California. The Rockefeller publicists were exploiting this appearance as the climax of what they claimed was Rockefeller's successful campaign.

From January to May in the primary convention states there had been no mention of Rockefeller's divorce and remarriage. It was no secret. The whole country was aware that Nelson Rockefeller had divorced Mary Todhunter Clark Rockefeller, his wife of more than thirty years, the mother of his five children, in order to marry Margaretta Fitler Murphy, who had divorced her doctor husband.

The taboos against switching marriage partners were much stronger in 1964 than they are today. The Catholic Church tolerated divorce, but a divorced Catholic who remarried was automatically excommunicated.

James Francis Cardinal McIntyre, bishop of the Diocese of Los Angeles, was a churchman of the old school. The cardinal had been aware of the planned appearance of Nelson Rockefeller at Catholic Loyola, but he had overlooked the implied endorsement of the Rockefeller divorce and remarriage. The Thursday before Rockefeller was scheduled to speak to the undergraduates at Loyola, Cardinal McIntyre countermanded the university's invitation. He explained his action to the press, saying he did not want anyone to get a false impression that the Roman Catholic Church was giving its official blessing to the candidacy of a man who had been divorced and then remarried.

On Thursday, May 28, sixteen Protestant ministers representing the strongest evangelical churches in the state of California met in Los Angeles and issued a statement suggesting that Nelson Rockefeller should withdraw from the race because of his demonstrated inability to handle his own domestic affairs. On May 30 Mrs. Margaretta Fitler Murphy Rockefeller presented her new husband with a son, and on Sunday, May 31, the words of the cardinal and the statement of the sixteen Protestant ministers were echoed in most pulpits throughout the state.

On Tuesday I carried California by more than 58,000 votes. All eighty-six delegates pledged to me were elected. The ball game was over, but the "Stop Goldwater" Republicans tried to play an extra inning in San Francisco.

CHAPTER 21

San Francisco '64

The official records all say Barry Goldwater, Republican candidate for the office of President of the United States in 1964, was defeated by Democrat incumbent Lyndon Baines Johnson. The truth is I lost whatever small chance I ever had to be President in San Francisco at the Republican National Convention.

Lyndon Johnson grabbed the big brass ring in November, but it was my fellow Republicans, Nelson Rockefeller, Henry Cabot Lodge, William Scranton, George Romney, and the other members of the "Stop Goldwater" cabal, who made Lyndon Johnson's victory such a runaway. The press played a strong supporting role, but for the most part it functioned as a carrier of the destructive statements, devastating personal criticism, and outright falsehoods of my fellow Republicans.

By the time the convention opened I had been branded as a fascist, a racist, a trigger-happy warmonger, a nuclear madman, and the candidate who couldn't win. At the time, a number of observers remarked that throughout the campaign and, particularly, in San Francisco my manner was brusque, unfriendly. Perhaps it was. It isn't easy to be cheerful, charitable, and forgiving when comrades from your earlier battles are thrusting their bayonets into your back.

During my first twelve years in the Senate, I frequently questioned some of the policies of the Republican leadership. I never attacked any Republican personally.

Bill Scranton came to Washington as a newly elected member of the House of Representatives from Pennsylvania in 1961. We served in the same 999th Air Force Reserve unit. When he sought my advice about running for governor, I encouraged him to make the race. He in turn urged me to run for President in 1964.

It was Joseph Martin, Jr., and William Nelligan, two Republican supporters of Nelson Rockefeller in California, who first branded me extremist. Martin told the *New York Times* he "resigned his post to keep the Republican party from becoming a branch of the John Birch Society." Martin said, "Goldwater was the only candidate vigorously supported by the Birchers and Rightists lunatic fringe. Inevitably his victory will also be their victory."

In June Bill Scranton was quoted in the New York *Herald Tribune* as saying, "Most of us know that in this troubled world we need an American foreign policy that thinks from the head, not one that shoots from the hip. This is not the hour for us to join those extreme reactionaries who are anything but conservative, those radicals of the right who would launch a system of dime store feudalism that is foreign to these shores and foreign to the American way of thinking. Goldwater can't win."

Columnist Joseph Alsop of the New York *Herald Tribune* stretched the distortion of my answer to Howard K. Smith on the ABC show about as far as it would go. On July 6 he wrote, "Set speeches to large rallies of the already convinced were the Goldwater rule in California. He broke the rule just once. The occasion was the television interview in the course of which the Senator *blithely* suggested nuclear defoliation as one possible way to win the Vietnamese War."

Three days later Walter Lippmann in the New York *Herald Tribune* said, "In foreign affairs Goldwater is ready to confront the Soviet Union and China with a choice between capitulation and war." Henry Cabot Lodge joined the chorus, telling the *New York Times*, "We must never countenance such a thing as a trigger-happy foreign policy which would negate everything we stand for and destroy everything we hope for."

I've never quite understood how it is that Democrats can engage in fierce, sometimes vicious primary contests and then unite behind the winner. Republicans, in what may be a reflection of our party's symbol, never forget and refuse to forgive.

The 1964 Civil Rights Bill came up for a vote on the floor of the Senate in mid-June. I had previously questioned the constitutionality of Titles II and VII—the so-called fair employment practices and public accommodations sections.

Before casting my vote, I told the Senators, "I am unalterably opposed to discrimination of any sort, and I believe that though the problem is fundamentally one of the heart, some law can help, but not law that embodies features like these, provisions which fly in the face of the Constitution, and which require for their effective execution the creation of a police state. . . .

"If my vote is misconstrued, let it be, and let me suffer the consequences. My concern extends beyond any single group in our society. My concern is for the entire nation, for the freedom of all who live in it and for all who were born in it. This is my concern and this is where I stand."

Most of the press branded me segregationist, but not all of them. Columnist David Lawrence called my vote "The courageous act of a man who would rather risk the loss of a presidential nomination or even election than to surrender his convictions to political expediency." Arthur Krock of the *New York Times* agreed, saying, "The Senator set an example of political and moral courage that was the more admirable because of the immediate circumstances."

John S. Knight, president and editor of the Detroit *Free Press*, did not support me, but on June 21 he published an editorial declaring, "I can no longer stand silently by and watch the shabby treatment Goldwater is getting from most of the news media." He said:

> Their deep concern for the GOP's future would be more persuasive if any considerable number of them had ever voted for a Republican nominee—of the syndicated columnists I can think of only a few who are not savagely cutting down Senator Goldwater day after day.
>
> Some of the television commentators discuss Goldwater with evident disdain and contempt. Editorial cartoonists portray him as belonging to the Neanderthal age or as a relic of the nineteenth century. It is the fashion of editorial writers to persuade themselves that Goldwater's followers

are either kooks or Birchers. This simply isn't so. The Goldwater movement represents a mass protest by conservative-minded people against foreign aid, excessive welfare, high taxes, foreign policy, and the concentration of power in the federal government.

The press didn't modify its treatment of me in response to John Knight's editorial, but it gives me comfort to reread it now. The flag I raised in 1964 was one opposed to excessive foreign aid, to excessive welfare, to high taxes, to a foreign policy which was based largely on appeasement and accommodation.

Most Americans labor under the mistaken belief that party conventions are held to permit duly elected party representatives to name the party's nominees for the office of President and Vice President. In a purely mechanical sense this is true. In reality, the choice is made long before the delegates gather.

There have been occasions when a so-called dark horse has been the unexpected winner—Willkie over Dewey in 1940, Eisenhower over Taft in 1952. For the most part, battle lines are drawn much earlier. Delegates are identified by the candidates they support and elected in party caucuses, in county conventions, in state conventions, and on primary ballots, not as individuals authorized to exercise their personal judgment, but as men and women committed to vote for a particular candidate.

The preconvention activities of every candidate are directed at two objectives—to enlist committed delegates and to place his supporters in control of the convention machinery. Taft lost to Ike in 1952 because Eisenhower supporters took control of the Credentials Committee. Franklin Roosevelt was able to overwhelm the two-term tradition and win nomination in 1940 because his forces controlled the convention machinery. In 1960 Nixon's people had been in charge in Chicago, and Kennedy forces were in control in Los Angeles.

My old friend Senator Thurston B. Morton of Kentucky was the permanent chairman in San Francisco. We had agreed to the selection of Mark Hatfield as the keynoter, and Senator Carl Curtis was my floor leader.

The National Committee had wisely chosen Congressman Mel Laird of Wisconsin to be chairman of the Platform Committee. Laird is conservative, but no one has ever accused him of being a right-winger. At times he and I have disagreed over matters of policy. Because I had a majority of committed delegates to the convention, we also had a majority on the Platform Committee.

My first task in San Francisco was to appear before this group of Republicans who were writing the platform on which I confidently expected to campaign for the office of President. The men and women on that committee understood my position on the great issues, and in my short remarks to them I said, "I will not presume for a moment to tell you what should go into this platform in terms of specific planks or programs. You are Republicans. You know our Republican record. You know where we stand in Congress. You know the program we've created and fought for. You know the ones we have resisted. You know where we have disagreed on this or that detail, but most important, you know the great basic principles on which we agree.

"Let those meaningful principles guide your minds and hearts and reject the temptation to make this party's platform a bandstand for any factional cause. You must seek a document that will unite us on principle and not divide us.

"We don't come to this time and this place merely to dot i's and cross t's. We have come here to cross the great bridge from weary, futile, and fatuous leadership in the national administration, to strong, active and hopeful leadership and you must take the first step."

When I said those words, I had in mind the critical situation at the Constitutional Convention in Philadelphia. After weeks of haggling it appeared the delegates would be unable to reach an agreement. In that hour of crisis George Washington said, "If to please the people, we offer what we ourselves disapprove, how can we afterwards defend our work? Let us raise a standard to which the wise and the honest can repair. The event is in the hands of God."

I can find no better words to express my innermost feelings about the issues to be decided in San Francisco. I knew we had made mistakes. I had provided my enemies with numerous opportunities to attack me by failing to be rigidly specific in all my recommendations. I honestly felt the party members should write the platform. I truly believed that if the American voters could be provided an opportunity to understand the real difference between what we would do as Republicans and what the other party offered, our cause would prevail.

The platform drafted under the supervision of Mel Laird was generally satisfactory to me, but I had not controlled its writing. As *Time* magazine pointed out, it was a platform on which I could run, but for that matter, so could almost any other Republican.

In no other nation on earth will you find anything comparable to that quadrennial ritual, the U.S. presidential election. It is a spectacle unsurpassed. Those uninformed, indifferent citizens emerge from their cocoons of apathy prodded by their fears of what one candidate may do to them and by their hope of what another candidate may do for them. Highly paid public opinion pollsters attract a great audience from those who want to read the end of the book immediately after being introduced to the cast of characters.

On Sunday evening, July 12, at forty-seven minutes past six I received a document which forecast with uncanny accuracy the shape the 1964 presidential campaign would take. It was a four-page letter. The salutation was: "Dear Senator," nothing more. The signature was typed "Sincerely yours, William W. Scranton." It said:

> As we move rapidly towards the climax of this conven-
> tion the Republican party faces a continuing struggle on
> two counts.
> The first involves, of course, selection of a candidate.
> Here the issue is extremely clear. It is simply this; will
> the convention choose a candidate overwhelmingly favored
> by the Republican voters, or will it choose you?

I knew I wasn't overwhelmingly favored by Rockefeller, Lodge, Romney, Scranton, or Margaret Chase Smith, but after seven months of campaigning I could count on the vote of at least 800 delegates.

> Your organization does not even argue the merits of the
> question. They admit that you are a minority candidate, but
> they feel they have bought, beaten and compromised enough
> delegate support to make the result a foregone conclusion.
> With open contempt for the dignity, integrity and com-
> mon sense of the convention, your managers say in effect
> that the delegates are little more than a flock of chickens

whose necks will be wrung at will.

I have doublechecked the arithmetic of my staff, and I am convinced that a true count at this minute puts your first ballot strength at only some 620 votes.

Along with my other deficiencies, it was being alleged that I had not mastered simple addition.

Our count differs from that of your managers because we have calculated an important element which you are incapable of comprehending. That is the element of respect for the men and women who make up the delegations to this convention.

We are not taking them for granted. We are not insulting their intelligence or their integrity. We are not counting noses, we're counting hearts.

We're not issuing orders, we're providing a rallying point for responsibility in the Republican party.

You will be stopped on the first ballot because a sufficient number of your nominal supporters have already indicated to us that they will not vote for you.

They are not breaking commitments to you; you have broken commitments to them.

In this introduction I had been called a minority candidate, charged with buying, beating and compromising delegates, for whom I had no respect. But this was only the introduction. What followed became the basis of LBJ's campaign against me.

The letter continued:

You have too often casually prescribed nuclear war as a solution to a troubled world.

I read that sentence twice. Never once in all my statements or my writings on foreign policy had I ever advocated nuclear war as a solution to a troubled world. I have never believed the security interests of the United States required us to destroy communist Russia. Its doctrines are antithetical to human nature as I understand it and must ultimately be brought down by the weight of its own errors. I did believe, and still believe, we should resist the enslavement of free nations by the communist expansionists. This charge wasn't being leveled by some pacifist, left-wing radical; this total distortion of my search for peace was coming from a fellow Republican.

You have too often allowed the radical extremists to use you.

Where? When? Who? How? I asked myself.

You have too often stood for irresponsibility in the serious question of racial holocaust.

I had voted for every civil rights measure except for the one in June, and my objections to that piece of legislation were on very solid constitutional ground.

You have too often read Taft and Eisenhower and Lincoln out of the Republican party.

At that point I had to wonder if Bill Scranton had taken leave of his senses.

And that brings me to the second count on which the Republican party is fighting for its soul.
In the last few days the ill-advised effort to make us stand for Goldwaterism instead of Republicanism has set off ripples of public opinion across the nation.

Was the damned fool questioning the integrity of Mel Laird and the delegates on the Platform Committee?

All of us in San Francisco are so close to the hour-by-hour story unfolding here, that there is a danger we may overlook the overall impression being created in the minds of the American people.
Goldwaterism has come to stand for nuclear irresponsibility.
Goldwaterism has come to stand for keeping the name of Eisenhower out of the platform.
Goldwaterism has come to stand for being afraid to forthrightly condemn right-wing extremists.

Goldwaterism has come to stand for refusing to stand for law and order and maintaining racial peace.

In short, Goldwaterism has come to stand for a whole crazy quilt collection of absurd and dangerous positions that would be soundly repudiated by the American people in November.

I put the letter down. The rest of it was an effort to persuade me to engage in a debate with Bill Scranton on Wednesday evening before the full convention. I told Kitch and Barboody, who were reading Xerox copies of the Scranton letter, that if I had done any of the things Scranton charged me with doing, that if I held any of the beliefs he attributed to me, I wouldn't vote for myself, and Peggy wouldn't vote for me either.

My first thought was to send the letter back to Scranton with a note suggesting that someone had typed his signature to a letter it would have been impossible for him to write. There was really nothing new. The governor of Pennsylvania had merely collected all the charges my Republican opponents had been making since January. Surely he didn't think I would debate with him in front of the convention.

We decided to release copies of the Scranton communication to every delegate. I gave a copy to the press with a simple statement saying I couldn't believe my old friend Bill Scranton had written such a letter or intended the language to be so violent. I was sure of one thing: Scranton's brutal, defamatory remarks about the character of the delegates would not win him any votes.

Until that moment William Scranton was high on my list of possible vice presidential choices. He came from a highly industrialized eastern state, and I knew he would be extremely acceptable to the liberal wing of our party. Kennedy had co-opted the southern Democrats by selecting Lyndon Johnson. The notion had much to recommend it.

In the sometimes devious, always uncertain world of politics there is one immutable rule universally observed by all practitioners: There must be a reason for every political move.

We found out later that Scranton had not written the letter himself. It had been drafted by a member of his staff. It wasn't personally signed because he hadn't seen it before it was delivered to me. All this heightened my curiosity about a possible motive.

Had I been elected in 1964, it would have closed the door to the presidential ambitions of Rockefeller, Romney, Nixon, and Scranton, assuming that as the incumbent I could have been re-elected in 1968. These other contenders would have been too old to make the run in 1972. Had I, in fact, chosen Bill Scranton to be my Vice President and had the ticket been victorious, Scranton would have become the heir apparent. In my mind the only satisfactory answer to this riddle is that Scranton was used by one of the other contenders, who above all else wanted to make certain that William W. Scranton was not on the ticket in 1964.

After the convention Bill Scranton campaigned for me with considerable vigor and industry. Considering what he said about me in that letter, I could never understand this turnaround. It is not difficult to understand why so many citizens believe most politicians to be self-serving hypocrites.

On Wednesday evening of that week eight candidates were presented at the convention—William Scranton, Nelson Rockefeller, Henry Cabot Lodge, George Romney, Hiram Fong, Walter Judd, Margaret Chase Smith, and Barry Goldwater. Senator Everett Dirksen of Illinois asked the Republicans to make me their candidate.

On the first ballot I received more votes than any candidate in either party had ever achieved on the first ballot of a contested convention where the roll call was permitted to continue to conclusion without allowing any state to change its votes: 883 out of 1,308—more than twice as many as the combined first-ballot votes of all other candidates.

In a room adjoining our suite at the Fairmont a field representative from the Opinion Research polling organization in Princeton, New Jersey, had set up his flip charts and was prepared to report the results of his organization's latest polling sample. Respondents had been interviewed the week before the convention opened.

We had enjoyed a quiet dinner in the suite. I had been working on my acceptance speech with the help of Karl Hess and Harry Jaffa. As the results of that first vote were being reported to the convention, we all went into the other room to view the results of a more important poll. On the night I was nominated in San Francisco this highly professional sampling of public opinion revealed that almost 80 percent of the voters had made up their minds to vote for Johnson. Only a little more than 20 percent were for Goldwater.

The reasons given by the voters for not wanting me to be their president were in general a recital of all the charges my Republican opponents had made during the primary and convention campaign. I was an extremist. I was a hawk who would get us into war. I would abolish Social Security. I was anticivil rights. I was opposed to farm subsidies. I disapproved of such government ventures as the TVA. I was antilabor.

Only a few of those polled were outright supporters of Lyndon Johnson. They preferred the President because they were afraid of me.

I knew the convention events that week had done nothing to lessen my public image as an extremist. At the Platform Committee hearings, Senator Hugh Scott from Pennsylvania had attempted to amend the platform by adding this paragraph:

> The Republican Party fully respects the contribution of responsible criticism and defends the right of dissent in the democratic process, but we repudiate the efforts of irresponsible, extremist groups, such as the Communists, the Ku Klux Klan, the John Birch Society and others to discredit our party by their efforts to infiltrate positions of responsibility in the party or that attach themselves to its candidates.

In support of that amendment Nelson Rockefeller made a passionate five-minute speech, during the course of which he said, "Precisely one year ago today, on July 14, 1963, I warned that the Republican party is in real danger of subversion by a radical, well financed, highly organized—a minority, wholly alien to the sound and honest conservatism that has firmly based the Republican party in the best of its centuries' traditions . . . the methods of these extremists elements I have experienced at first hand. Their tactics have ranged from cancellation by coercion of a speaking engagement before a college, to outright threats of personal violence."

Rockefeller went on to say, "I can personally testify to their existence, and so can countless others who have also experienced anonymous midnight and early-morning telephone calls, unsigned and threatening letters, smear and hate literature, strong-arm and goon tactics, bomb threats and bombings, infiltration and takeover of established political organizations by Communist and Nazi methods—these extremists feed on fear, hate and terror. They have no program for America, no program for the Republican party, no program to keep the peace and bring freedom to the world."

Is it any wonder the voters were learning to fear a Goldwater presidency? My supporters were compared to Communists and Nazis, to the Ku Klux Klan. Hugh Scott, a member of the United States Senate, and Nelson Rockefeller, the governor of New York, had said these things. The Communists and the Nazis have been convicted before the world for their use of murder and blackmail and gross falsehood. No American citizen of my acquaintance has any sympathy for the brutal terrorism of the Ku Klux Klan. To my mind the excesses committed by Hugh Scott and Nelson Rockefeller in branding the patriotic members of the John Birch Society as comparable to the Commies, the Nazis, and the Ku Klux Klanners was a moral sin deliberately and calculatedly committed. It violated every precept of decency and charity and in effect was an assassination as evil as any act ever committed by the Communists, the Nazis, or the Ku Kluxers.

At the conclusion of that first roll call William Scranton was recognized for the purpose of urging the convention to make the nomination unanimous. He tried to be gracious. He pledged his support to my election in November. He tried to compare his remarks to my withdrawal statement delivered in the 1960 convention, but it was a halfhearted effort. He spoke of principle having been lost. He implied that might had triumphed over right.

That phrase I used at almost the end of my acceptance speech was presented by the press to the public as almost my total acceptance speech. I said, "We Republicans seek a government that attends to its inherent responsibilities of maintaining a stable monetary and fiscal climate, encouraging a free and a competitive economy and enforcing law and order."

I said, "Balance, diversity, creativity—these are the elements of the Republican equation." I quoted Abraham Lincoln's comments of 1858, when he described the Republican party as being "composed of strange, discordant and even hostile elements."

I said, "Anyone who joins in all sincerity we welcome. Those who do not care for our cause we don't expect to enter our ranks in any case. And let our Republicanism so focused and so dedicated not be made fuzzy and futile by unthinking and stupid labels. I would remind you that extremism in the defense of liberty is no vice and let me remind you also that moderation in the pursuit of justice is no virtue."

I think of myself as a simple, uncomplicated man. Duty, honor, country hold for me the meaning given them by General Douglas MacArthur. It's not a part of my nature to equivocate. I detest extremism in the presently accepted derogatory connotation of that word. The dictionary gives a number of definitions for extreme—"of a character or kind farthest removed from the ordinary or average—the utmost of highest degree." That single sentence summed up my approach to the presidency. For I intended to do my utmost in the defense of liberty and to pursue justice in a manner far removed from the average. Perhaps I should have quoted the true author of that statement verbatim.

Harry Jaffa, a learned professor of history and politics, brought the phrase to my attention in a draft of a statement to be made to the Platform Committee. I had heard it earlier in a letter from the writer Taylor Caldwell, for whom I have great admiration.

The words were first used by Marcus Tullius Cicero in connection with his defense of Rome against the evil and violent patrician Lucius Sergius Catiline. The precise quotation is: "I must remind you, Lords, Senators, that extreme patriotism in the defense of freedom is no crime and let me respectfully remind you that pusillanimity in the pursuit of justice is no virtue in a Roman."

The morning after my nomination President Eisenhower asked me to come over to the Fairmont Hotel to explain what I meant by the phrase I had used. When I arrived Ike said he had read all the uncomplimentary remarks in the press and was worried. I replied, "Mr. President, when you landed your troops in Normandy, it was an exceedingly extreme action taken because you were committed to the defense of freedom."

Ike's face broke into that inimitable grin. "I guess you're right, Goldwater. I never thought of it that way."

CHAPTER 22

The Campaign

The newspaper reports and television commentators covering the San Francisco convention provided the nation with a bleak, almost frightening picture of a ruthless Goldwater machine crushing opponents, denying anyone who disagreed with us the right to speak, and somehow dishonoring the process by which parties select their presidential nominee. The Democratic party's convention in Atlantic City, New Jersey, was, in fact, a coronation, not a convention. Lyndon Johnson orchestrated the entire performance. There was some clumsily contrived suspense over the identity of Johnson's choice for Vice President. But after he had publicly dumped Bobby Kennedy, all the insiders knew it would be Hubert Humphrey. The Johnson men wouldn't even allow the showing of a filmed tribute to John F. Kennedy until after the nominations were concluded.

I didn't read a single dispatch from that gathering bewailing any lack of democratic process. There were no complaints about the cross-examination Hubert Humphrey had to endure to prove his willingness to be subservient in every way to the President.

On Wednesday, August 26, the third day of the Democratic National Convention, Johnson summoned Hubert Humphrey to the White House along with Senator Tom Dodd of Connecticut.

Johnson was using Dodd as a decoy. He had already made up his mind to name Humphrey Vice President. But at the White House he lectured Hubert on the need for loyalty, the requirement that the Vice President be absolutely subservient to the President's desires.

Several years later I asked Hubert Humphrey why he had accepted this humiliation at the hands of a man who knew less about government than he did, who had never been bound by principle, and whose tactics as Majority Leader had engendered more fear than respect. In those years, when Lyndon wanted something, he would stand face to face and put his hand on a member's shoulder. He would exploit flattery and friendship, remind you of former favors, and then if you didn't come around, he would be explicit about what your failure to cooperate might cost your state.

We called the friendly approach, when he just put a hand on your shoulder, the Half-Johnson. When he put his arm clear around you and thrust his face close to yours to make his threats, we called it the Full-Johnson.

Hubert told me he hadn't been at all offended by that widely publicized White House interview. "You and I have been around long enough, Barry, to know an uncooperative Vice President could cut the man in the White House to ribbons. When the palace guard around Kennedy displayed such contempt for Lyndon, he contemplated doing what he knew he could do to embarrass the White House.

"We just went over the rules. I told him I knew the limitations and would observe them. We were in deep trouble in Vietnam. There were riots in the cities. He was doing his best to cool the civil rights question. As I read him that day, deep down inside he was scared. He wasn't worried about beating you. His problem was how to run the country."

I liked Hubert Humphrey. I couldn't agree with him on political questions, but I liked him.

To my mind, Hubert's appraisal of Lyndon Johnson was an accurate one. I told my old colleague of my secret meeting with the President shortly after the Democratic Convention.

Before the start of the general election campaign I called the President to ask if we could meet privately and confidentially. I told him I wished to discuss a matter of vital concern to both of us. I think Johnson was a little shocked by my direct approach, but he graciously set a time and a place. I didn't tell anyone what I planned to do. The walls have ears in this power center of the free world. Secrets are not easy to keep.

I said, "Mr. President, we know the rules and the ropes. We are divided by party and political philosophy. We disagree on almost every substantive issue, but I think we are united in our love of country."

President Johnson put one hand on my shoulder and said, "You know damned well, Barry, that the nation is first in my thinking."

I said, "I believe that, and that is why I am here." I was getting the Half-Johnson. For a minute I thought I would get the Full-Johnson.

"The war in Vietnam," I said, "is a national burden. The people are already divided. The legitimacy of our presence is being questioned. The conduct of the war is being criticized. My views on this matter are clear and, I think, well known. I asked to see you because I do not believe it is in the best interest of the United States to make the Vietnam War or its conduct a political issue in this campaign. I have come to promise I will not do so."

The President seemed greatly relieved. He spoke with considerable passion about the problems of the war, the difficulties of fighting so far from home, the conflicting reports in the press and from his intelligence sources. Then he thanked me for my offer.

I told him I felt the same way about the civil rights question. I said if it became a political issue, it could polarize the country. I told him I would not attack his position. I hoped he would refrain from challenging mine.

Lyndon Johnson was a southerner, but he didn't approve of segregation any more than I did. I got the impression he thought the Congress had moved too fast, trying to correct in one decade the wrongs of 100 years.

We shook hands. I kept my promises, and Lyndon Johnson kept his. The Vietnamese War and the civil rights problems were never major issues in the 1964 presidential campaign. Other voices raised them from time to time, but they were never part of my campaign speeches. My detractors in the press pretended to believe I would certainly appeal to the red-neck southern vote. I didn't.

The LBJ campaigners did a thorough job of exploiting and emphasizing all the charges my fellow Republicans had made about me. I don't recall a single statement from the President or the White House which could be regarded as in violation of that private agreement.

Perhaps I was quixotic. Dissatisfaction over the Korean War had been a principal factor in Eisenhower's victory in 1952. Johnson was vulnerable on Vietnam. Had the American voters known the truth about the Kennedy White House involvement in the murder of Ngo Dinh Diem, they might well have turned against his successor in office. Through my military contacts I had a very clear picture of what had taken place. The Diem regime was corrupt by our standards. Those close to the President were rewarded with wealth and power. But Diem was an authentic hero to the South Vietnamese. He had fought against the French, refused to collaborate with Ho Chi Minh, in fact, turned down an appointment to a position of power in the North Vietnamese communist government.

The American press, led by David Halberstam of the *New York Times*, focused on the horrifying self-immolation of certain Buddhist priests. Marguerite Higgins, in her accounts, suggests there was communist programming behind these actions. According to her, the reported midnight raid on the pagodas which resulted in the arrest of 1,400 people, mostly monks, never took place.

Secretary of Defense Robert McNamara, and to a lesser degree General Maxwell Taylor, had lost confidence in Diem. American agents contacted Diem's enemies in the South Vietnamese military with a promise the U.S. would not be unhappy if Diem were ousted as a result of a military coup.

Our military commander in Saigon, General Paul D. Harkins, was opposed to the maneuver. Ambassador Henry Cabot Lodge supported it.

Shortly before Diem's enemies made their move, Diem contacted Lodge to inquire about the attitude of the United States. Lodge said he would do anything he could to insure the safety of Diem and his family. The rebellious generals executed Diem, his wife, and his brother.

After the assassination of President Kennedy, Lyndon Johnson retained McNamara as Secretary of Defense and Dean Rusk as Secretary of State. Beginning in January 1964 two aggressive programs against the North Vietnamese, fostered by the U.S. government, were put into operation. One of these was known as the 34-A operation. We made flights over North Vietnam with our U-2s. We kidnapped North Vietnamese for intelligence interrogations. We made commando raids from the sea and parachuted psychological warfare teams into the North.

The second military thrust was launched from Laos. T-28 fighter bombers bearing the marking of the Laotian Air Force made regular bombing raids. Twenty-five to forty aircraft were involved. U.S. Air Force and Navy jets gathered the photographic intelligence on which the T-28 raids were based.

We can now believe the reported Tonkin Gulf incident was probably an answer to the 34-A operations and the T-28 bombing raids. I have used the term "reported incident" deliberately. The manner in which that alleged attack on the destroyers *Maddox* and *C. Turner Joy* was revealed to the American public, coupled with the Johnson administration's request for the so-called Tonkin Gulf Resolution, led a number of knowledgeable observers to question if there had indeed been an attack by North Vietnamese torpedo boats on American ships. As the war progressed, that suspicion grew.

My position on the Vietnam War was clearly understood. I said we should either end the war as quickly as possible—using our superior power to force the North Vietnamese to recognize the independence of South Vietnam and end their hostile acts—or pull out and come home.

From a military standpoint it was absolute folly to involve American troops in a ground war in Southeast Asia. We had the air power and the sea power to make a continuation of the war impossible for North Vietnam.

Lyndon Johnson, with his covert actions, was, in fact, attempting to carry out my suggestion that we use our air and sea power, but his thrusts were tentative. If the President had used our available air and sea power, the war would have ended in 1965. The truth was concealed from the American people until *The Pentagon Papers* were published much later.

By early September it became apparent I would never recover from the image of Goldwater which had been projected to the American voters by my Republican challengers in the primary period. In our public opinion samplings I was never more than 30 to Lyndon Johnson's 70 percent. I am sure his pollster, Oliver

Quaile, was reporting the same thing to the White House.

I went to Florida to speak about the quality of life, our loss of freedom, and the growing violence disfiguring American society. The reporters ignored what I said and wrote that I should have discussed Social Security and my plans to abolish it.

My position was clear. I said I wanted to make Social Security solvent, to improve it. The first thing wrong with Social Security is the fact that it is compulsory. Secondly, it is not actuarially sound; it promises more benefits to more people than the income or premiums collected will provide. By no stretch of the imagination can it be called an insurance program.

Supporters of Social Security speak of the trust fund when, in fact, there is no trust fund. It is a bookkeeping deception. The actual monies collected under the Social Security tax law go into the general Treasury of the United States. This has been true since the inception of the program, and the monies have been spent each year. The so-called trust fund is no more than a promissory note from the government of the United States to the bookkeepers of the Social Security system to honor their demand on the Treasury of the United States.

In Tennessee my speech was lost or ignored or deliberately overlooked by the press, which again dredged up a statement I had once made saying we should sell TVA to private interests for a dollar and get the government out of business. In the Midwest I tried valiantly to make it clear to the farmers that when they accepted government subsidies, they must be prepared to accept government control.

To most of the public I was the man of war, and Lyndon Johnson the man of peace. All this because I had said then, and still believe, that the surest road to peace is through military strength.

Never once in any of my writings or any of my speeches have I ever advocated the use of our military power to destroy communist Russia. I did say, and I have said time and time again, that if America maintains a superior defense capability, Russian communism must eventually fall of its own inherent evil assumptions.

Most of the press pretended to believe the Johnson-Goldwater contest was devoid of any substantive issues. That assumption is false.

In 1964 I addressed myself to the quality of life in the United States, centering my remarks on the need to preserve individual freedom. I warned that a continuation of existing policies must inevitably lead to expanding bureaucratic control over the people's lives. I said that continued unbalanced budgets would bring on more inflation and that one day the sheer weight of the national debt would destroy our economy.

I argued that government was necessary to protect the people from our enemies overseas, to restrain the greedy and the lawless, and to provide a civil framework for the growth of commerce and industry. I said that everything else which needed to be done could be better done by the people themselves without governmental interference.

In 1976 Jimmy Carter picked up many of my complaints. I truly believe he won that election because the people are sick and tired of federal control, federal taxes, inflation, and the lessening of individual freedom. It is tragic that once he was elected, Jimmy Carter promptly forgot his campaign promises.

The New York advertising firm of Doyle Dane Bernbach was responsible for the two television commercials which I still remember with considerable horror.

Let me quote the description printed by the *New York Times* on September 15, 1964:

> A little girl licking an ice cream cone appeared on millions of television screens all over America. [A woman's voice] told her that people used to explode atomic bombs in the air and that the radioactive fallout made children die. The voice then told of a treaty preventing all but underground nuclear tests and how a man who wants to be President of the United States voted against it.

"His name is Barry Goldwater," she said, "so if he is elected, they might start testing all over again." A crescendo of Geiger counter clicks almost drowned out the last word; then came the male announcer's tag line: "Vote for President Johnson on November third. The stakes are too high for you to stay home."

This was the first commandment of the Johnson forces: Goldwater is a nuclear warmonger. And the second was like unto it. Again I quote the *New York Times:*

A little girl with wind tossed hair was shown in a sunny field picking daisies. As she plucks the petals of one daisy, she counts. On the sound track, coming in stronger and stronger, a male voice counts backwards. When the girl reaches 10 the man's voice, in the doom-filled cadences of the countdown, reaches zero. The screen is rent with an atomic explosion. "These are the stakes," says the voice of Lyndon Baines Johnson. "To make a world in which all of God's children can live, or go into the dark. We must either love each other, or we must die." The doom-voice returns, urging viewers to vote for President Johnson on November 3: "The stakes are too high for you to stay home."

There is no profit in speculation. Perhaps I would have found it impossible to implement the reforms I had in mind. Empirical judgment suggests we would be living in a vastly different world had I won that election.

I was committed to bringing the war in Vietnam to a quick ending—victory or withdrawal. I was committed to reducing federal expenditures. In 1963 the budget was just under $100 billion. Today it is more than $500 billion. I was committed to reducing the public debt. Since 1964 it has grown from $300 billion to almost $800 billion.

I hold the Congresses responsible for the bloated bureaucracy and much of the excessive spending. I would have resisted both with all the power of the White House.

CHAPTER 23

Wheeler-Dealer in the White House

Running for President was something like trying to stand up in a hammock. We knew from the polls a victory was not in our lane. While the loss was large, my twelve-year crusade for the noble cause of freedom did not end on that November Tuesday in 1964.

The lofty, rational presentation of contending political beliefs I had envisioned degenerated into a campaign of epithets and gross falsehoods. I think I could have accepted the defeat of the individual Barry Goldwater with humor and good grace. It was the apparent repudiation of all the beliefs and understandings I cherished—which had guided me in public life—that I found so hard to accept.

My dear Peggy, who had never wanted me to enter politics, might have said, "I told you so." But she never did. My children came to me with warmth and understanding. They didn't seek explanations or make excuses. My friends, those who had marched with me, those who had worked behind the scenes, helped me understand.

I gather, from discussions with my grandchildren, the public schools don't put much emphasis on poetry these days. In November and December 1964 the words of Kipling which I had memorized at my mother's insistence came back to comfort me:

> *If you can bear to hear the truth you've spoken*
> *Twisted by knaves to make a trap for fools,*
> *Or watch the things you gave your life to, broken,*
> *And stoop and build 'em up with worn-out tools.*

I had refused to play it safe, to be a candidate for reelection to the Senate while running for the office of President. It would have been legal to do so. Lyndon Johnson had been reelected to the Senate the year he was elected Vice President. In January 1965 I became ex-Senator Barry Goldwater, but I didn't intend to retain that status.

One unanticipated result of my defeat was the development of a much closer relationship with General Eisenhower. Most of the chroniclers of that campaign suggest Ike was not enthusiastic over my candidacy. I don't think he was at first. I excused his lukewarm attitude as a natural response to the divisions within the party. A number of Ike's closest associates had done their best to paint me a trigger-happy, unreasonable spokesman for the far-right splinter groups.

Early in the campaign I spent a day with Ike at Gettysburg to make a TV film for use in the campaign. The most charitable thing I can say about the film is that it wasn't effective. But in the course of that day's conversation it seemed to me that for the first time the former President grasped a clear picture of what I believed to be the major issues of the campaign and where, in response to my principles, I stood on these issues.

After the election Ike proposed the formation of a Republican policy group. He wanted an ad hoc committee to keep tabs on the Johnson administration and provide support for our leaders in Congress. He told me he intended to invite Tom Dewey, Senator Everett Dirksen, Richard Nixon, Representative Charles Halleck, the former national chairman of the party, Len Hall, Thruston B. Morton, and one or two others. Ike said he particularly wanted me to join the group.

I was pleased to serve. I was discovering that a defeated presidential candidate becomes an irrelevant nonentity in the minds of most party leaders. Former Presidents are often ignored after they leave the White House. A defeated presidential candidate is the lowest man on the political totem pole.

Newly elected President Lyndon Johnson was anxious to unite the country behind his conduct of the Vietnam War and his proposed Great Society social program. He invited our Republican policy group to the White House a number of times during the first six months of 1965.

At one of these meetings I had an opportunity to speak privately with the President. I urged him to replace Robert McNamara as Secretary of Defense. I brought up the matter of the disastrous A-111 plane and restated my belief that McNamara was deliberately pursuing a policy of parity with the Russians. I said we were losing our advantage.

Lyndon listened intently. A time or two he nodded his head in agreement, but when I finished, he said, "Barry, I just can't do that."

The expression on the President's face, the inflections he used elevated the conversation far above a routine offering of advice and a refusal to accept it. The President offered no defense of McNamara. He did not contradict my criticism. Again it seemed to me an indication of an uncertainty, a lack of confidence. I began to suspect that for all his bravado, his aggressiveness, his seeming ability to make a quick decision, Lyndon Johnson could not measure up in his own mind to the responsibilities of the presidency. As Majority Leader of the U.S. Senate he had found the ability to get things done sufficient reward. As President he wanted desperately to be admired and loved by all the people and was afraid to make decisions. It is my opinion that in his private mind Lyndon Johnson was always comparing himself to Jack Kennedy and coming off second best.

As Commander in Chief he had clear authority to conduct the operations in Vietnam any way he thought would be most effective. Because I had been to Vietnam many times, the President frequently brought up this subject when we were together during this period.

I remember one day, when the dispatches from the front had been extremely depressing, he brought out a sheaf of maps and began to lecture me on the difficulties of the war. I said, "Mr. President, put the damned maps away. I've been there. I have been there five times. I know the terrain. I know the people. I know the resources we have. I have spoken with our commanders. Until you take off their hobbles, there is no way we can win."

At that period, the spring of 1965, American pilots were forbidden to fire on enemy airplanes until the enemy fired on them first. If one of our fliers recognized a new SAM base either under construction or completed, he could not fire on it unless the SAM base fired on him. All allowable targets were relatively unimportant, and there was an absolute prohibition against doing anything about a "target of opportunity." This is Air Force language for the circumstances pilots encounter on almost every flight. They see an ammunition convoy which has not been reported or enemy troop movements unknown to intelligence as opportunities to inflict severe damage on the enemy, and the McNamara policy prohibited this.

During one of my visits to Vietnam the North Vietnamese MiGs were inflicting heavy casualties on some of our ground units and on the naval patrol vessels. Some of the pilots decided to "lean on their orders" and ignore McNamara's restrictions. In the first twenty-four-hour period they destroyed nine MiGs. Then the Pentagon stopped their activities.

I told Johnson our no-win policy was directly responsible for the loss of thousands of American lives. I said if he stopped the war, he would be a hero. He could use our power to win a victory. He could tell the people of Vietnam it was not worth the casualties and bring our fighting troops home. He told me either course was unacceptable.

I replied saying defeat or victory would be better than what McNamara and his civilian advisers were doing now. This mismanaged, dragged-out unnecessary waste of American lives inflicted more harm on the people of the United States than any other event of the twentieth century. That war and its aftermath have had a profound impact on our cultural, economic, financial, and governmental understandings. The truth of that tragedy has been deliberately concealed and distorted by the government officials involved, including Presidents Kennedy and Johnson, by the American press, by our communist enemies.

Eisenhower was President when the French were driven from Southeast Asia by the communist forces commanded by Ho Chi Minh and supported by Russia and Red China. We did not sign the Geneva Conference of 1954 because there was no provision for the eventual reunification of the two Vietnams.

In response to pleas for help from the noncommunist South Vietnamese government, the United States, under Eisenhower, sent about 600 military advisers to South Vietnam. This was the extent of our participation when John F. Kennedy became President.

Kennedy increased the American military presence to about 17,000 troops. This increase in force was more of a diplomatic move than a military move.

Walt Whitman Rostow, a resident intellectual at the Kennedy White House and deputy special assistant to the President for National Security Affairs, was the principal architect of the Kennedy-McNamara military policy in South Vietnam. Rostow believed that we could, by covert action and threats of massive bombing, intimidate the North Vietnamese and force them to abandon their guerrilla war against the south.

Marguerite Higgins, in her book *Our Vietnam Nightmare*, describes the murder of Diem and reports asking Roger Hilsman, "How does it feel to have blood on your hands?" His quoted reply: "Oh, come on now, Maggie, revolutions are rough, people get hurt."

Our primary mistake in this ghastly misadventure was the administration's refusal to declare a state of war officially. Had we done so, had we legitimatized our presence in South Vietnam, had we left the conduct of the war in the hands of the military, the world would be a far different place today. Because it was an undeclared war, the public felt no need to sacrifice. There were no restrictions on the press in the battle zones, and the "we don't want to lose, but we won't try to win" attitude destroyed troop morale and produced public frustration.

Civilians at State and Defense consistently overruled decisions of the Joint Chiefs. In September 1964 at a White House strategy meeting it was decided to stage massive air strikes on North Vietnam. This decision was kept secret in order to permit Johnson to present himself to the voters as "the candidate of peace."

It was Lyndon Johnson who in April 1965 decided to use American ground troops for an offensive against North Vietnam. Here again the decision was not based on tactical considerations. The administration anticipated a collapse of the South Vietnamese government and hoped to strengthen political control in the South as a result of this new offensive.

Before the war ended, we had almost 700,000 American troops in Vietnam.

In protest to the illegitimacy of our presence in Southeast Asia idealistic young people joined the campus revolts. The draft dodgers and the deserters became heroes. The angry, disillusioned American public forced Lyndon Johnson to abandon his hopes for a second term as President of the United States.

The years from 1965 through 1968 were four of the most satisfying years I have known as an adult. There was time to become reacquainted with my family, to return to those outdoor spaces in Arizona which have always held a special place in my heart. In those four years the correctness of the positions I had taken became gradually apparent to a greater number of my fellow citizens. President Johnson persuaded the Congress to pass most of the social welfare legislation originally proposed by Kennedy. The Great Society programs gave an avalanche of federal funds to a variety of new agencies designed to help the poor, the black, and the illiterate.

Despite all this new federal money, there were riots in almost every major city across the nation. Black leaders Johnson had tried to help turned against him. On the college campuses the antiwar movement developed into a powerful anti-Johnson force.

Inflation, the direct result of excessive federal spending and borrowing, became a real problem by 1966. But it was nowhere near as great as it is now. In that year the Federal Reserve Board raised the discount rate from 4 to 4½ percent, and there was loud protest. In 1978–79 the discount rate is roughly double that.

In 1978 President Carter tried to enlist the voluntary cooperation of businessmen and trade unionists to keep wages and prices down. In 1966 Lyndon Johnson did the same thing. It didn't work then. It won't work now because wages and prices are not the root cause of inflation. Federal spending is.

By the fall of 1966 I was making my plans to run for reelection to the Senate from Arizona in 1968. I was also becoming convinced Lyndon Johnson would be a one-term President. I was not sufficiently clairvoyant to predict he would refuse to be a candidate. But there was such strong evidence of dissatisfaction in the Democratic party with the failing Johnson policies, I predicted he would be defeated for the nomination in 1968.

It was against this backdrop that Richard Nixon began to emerge from his self-imposed retirement. The extent of the vicious overkill Lyndon Johnson had used in his campaign against me was now generally recognized. The candidate who had claimed to be the man of peace had escalated the war without winning it.

His "guns and butter" policy was depressing the economy. There is a delightful irony to be found in the truth that, instead of destroying the Republican party, as my enemies contended, my presidential campaign and my campaign volunteer workers may have been responsible for the election of a Republican President in 1968.

CHAPTER 24

The Comeback of Richard Nixon

In 1968 Richard Nixon became the fifth man in the history of the Republic to be elected President of the United States after having lost an earlier contest for that office. Following Lyndon Johnson's overwhelming victory in 1964, the political pundits were busily writing obituaries of the Republican party.

By the end of 1966 President Johnson was in deep trouble with his party and with the country. The Republican presidential nomination for 1968, once thought worthless, became suddenly attractive. Michigan's governor, George Romney, and Governor Nelson Rockefeller of New York were the most visible contenders. Rockefeller continuously denied he had any presidential ambitions, but the press took his protestations with a grain of salt. During these two years Richard Nixon had been traveling the country, helping raise funds for Republican candidates, speaking to Republican gatherings, and vigorously stifling any suggestion that he might again seek the White House.

Under the leadership of Chairman Ray Bliss the Republican National Committee undertook a grass-roots, nuts-and-bolts rebuilding campaign. Bliss told everyone over and over again the 1968 presidential nomination would not be worth a damn unless the party could elect some Republicans in 1966—a statement I endorsed at every opportunity.

The effective political operators in the party were holdovers from 1964—state chairmen, National Committee members, county chairmen. These forces actually procured the nomination of Richard Nixon and then were responsible for his successful election campaign. The initial steps started independently, but almost simultaneously. In mid-March 1966 Fred LaRue of Mississippi, John Grenier of Alabama, William Middendorf of Connecticut, Sherman Unger of Illinois, and Fred Agnich and Peter O'Donnell of Texas attended a dinner party in Washington, D.C.

All of them had been principals in my campaign. Believing there was a possibility of electing a Republican in 1968, they were anxious to find a potential candidate and start the long, tedious buildup. They all were experienced, knowledgeable veterans of convention politics. The man they wanted to support was Richard Nixon. They regarded George Romney as an amiable but clumsy politician, and they were bitterly opposed to Nelson Rockefeller's brand of Republicanism.

At almost the same time Richard Kleindienst, who with F. Clifton White had been in command of our delegate search in 1964, sent Nixon a detailed plan of action calculated to win the 1968 nomination. Kleindienst went beyond the convention to develop strategies for the general election.

Peter O'Donnell and his group, with the approval of Richard Nixon, formed a volunteer Nixon for President organization. Gaylord Parkinson, retiring Republican party chairman of California, was hired to head this effort. Kleindienst became Nixon's personal representative in the search for delegate strength.

The history of that campaign belongs in some other book. I was busy with my own race in Arizona for reelection to the Senate. I had told Nixon I would support him. I intended to keep that promise. But in the early months of 1968 a number of disturbing situations developed.

There was one Nixon committee headquartered in Washington, D.C., and another one in New York City. The volunteer group initiated by O'Donnell was shouldered out of the way by certain insiders who were closer to the possible candidate. O'Donnell resigned because it appeared to him Nixon was determined to be a loner, would run his own campaign, didn't want and wouldn't take friendly advice. The errors of 1960 would be repeated. I am convinced that if Peter O'Donnell had told the press his true reasons for bowing out, Nixon would not have won the nomination.

It was Dick Kleindienst who suggested that John Mitchell be named campaign chairman. Kleindienst says his only reason for doing this is that Dick Nixon wouldn't trust anyone else. Kleindienst admitted to me that John Mitchell knew nothing of politics, had never been involved in a campaign for elective office, and was in many ways extremely naïve. But since he was the only man whom Nixon trusted, there was no other choice.

Governor Ronald Reagan of California had refused to be an announced candidate or to enter any of the primaries. But his team, headed by Clif White, had developed an elaborate plan to make Reagan the nominee after an anticipated deadlock at the Republican Convention in Miami.

I had assumed that as the party's nominee in 1964 I would have a role in Miami. Nixon's men, Len Garment, John Sears, and Bill Timmons, who were handling the convention arrangements, suggested that I might want to come to Miami after the nominations and the balloting and then introduce the candidate to the nation. I knew both Rockefeller and Romney were apprehensive about the effect I might have on the delegates if I spoke before the votes were counted.

After numerous changes, it was finally decided that I would come to Miami, deliver the opening address on Monday night, and then fly home on Tuesday. When I arrived, I found the Nixon forces were nervous. They were not at all sure they had enough delegates to nominate their candidate on the first ballot.

I made the speech, but my name wasn't listed in the official Republican magazine published in advance of the convention. In San Francisco, when I won the nomination, some of the delegates—those who had hoped for another candidate—were less than enthusiastic. In Miami, when I spoke about the need for party unity, the response was overwhelming. I don't recall anything like it in my entire political career. NBC's David Brinkley described it as "the most spontaneous, emotional, enthusiastic Republican response of the entire convention."

When I returned to my hotel, there was a note please to call Nixon. I did. He then asked me, as a personal favor, to remain in Miami and meet with the delegates on Tuesday and Wednesday. A survey of those who attended as delegates to the Republican Convention in 1968 made by an independent research group after the convention revealed that 20.7 percent of the delegates said they were influenced to vote for Nixon as a result of their meetings with me those two days.

If I had it to do over again, to make the choice between the policies and programs of my friend Hubert Humphrey and the promises and policies of Richard Nixon, I would still support Nixon. But knowing what we now know is a bitter taste in my mouth, a feeling that somehow we should have had a better choice.

I like Ted Agnew, but when Nixon selected him for Vice President, I was totally surprised. I am now convinced that Nixon had given no thought to his vice presidential running mate. All his efforts had been concentrated on winning the nomination. If it can be said that I was not prepared to make all the decisions thrust upon a nominee after San Francisco, I think it is equally correct to say that in some regards Nixon was even less prepared.

The Nixon insiders immediately isolated most of the knowledgeable political operators who had helped win the nomination. Kleindienst, for example, was sent to Washington to keep a watchful eye on Ray Bliss, who the Nixon group feared would upset the campaign.

Nixon was his own strategist—Mitchell little more than a pleasant figurehead. But that campaign was conducted, in general, along the lines set forth by Dick Kleindienst in the memo he had written two years earlier.

As I watched the Nixon slippage, realizing that Humphrey was gaining almost every day, my concern increased. During this period Nixon called me personally almost every week. Every time I suggested he should exploit the mismanagement of the Vietnam War.

In Salt Lake City the Democratic candidate, Hubert Humphrey, had called for an unconditional halt to the bombing of North Vietnam. There was reason to believe that Lyndon Johnson might take such an action to strengthen his Vice President's chances.

Nixon was determined not to say anything or do anything which would give the press a reason to attack him as a hawk. He believed standing in the middle between the militant George Wallace and the doveish Hubert Humphrey was the place to be. During this period the press had repeatedly attacked Ted Agnew. The reporters almost made an international incident out of the "Fat Jap" statement.

I learned from Bob Mardian, who had been on the airplane at the time, the true circumstances were these. A Japanese reporter for the Baltimore *Sun*, whom Agnew had known for many years, had reached the airplane ahead of the vice presidential candidate's party and fallen asleep with his head lolling out in the aisle. Agnew carefully lifted the sleeping man back into a safer position without waking him. Then he said to someone, "The Fat Jap is sure a sound sleeper, isn't he?"

The press called this a racial smear. Mardian says Agnew told him the reporter had started out being antagonistic when Agnew was elected governor. Over the years they had become good friends. The reporter referred to Agnew as the "Dumb Greek" openly, to his face, always with good humor, and Agnew called the reporter the "Fat Jap."

Hubert Humphrey almost caught up with front-runner Nixon, but almost doesn't count. Nixon won. As a Republican I was extremely pleased. I believed the experience he had gained as Ike's VP and the lessons he had learned from his defeat in 1960 would move him to take immediate charge of the federal establishment. Perhaps I expected too much.

On January 9, eleven days before he was to leave the White House, Lyndon Johnson asked me to drop by for a private farewell drink. My memories of that meeting are something I will always cherish. Johnson was friendly, humble, nostalgic. He talked about his failures and about his accomplishments. He said he should have taken my advice and fired Robert McNamara. We sipped bourbon as he reflected on the Vietnam War. His comments about the lieutenants he had trusted for advice were not vindictive. There was an overtone of sadness and a sense of resignation. For all his faults, despite all his driving, at times brutal treatment of both friend and foe, on that afternoon he helped me understand the awesome responsibilities of the office.

Lyndon Johnson shared my passionate love for this nation and for its people and for its institutions. He was not bitter. He was puzzled. He had tried and failed. To him the reasons for that failure were an impenetrable mystery. His Great Society programs were not working. He knew it. He couldn't understand why.

Somehow all the money and all the programs and all the personal effort he had devoted to trying to help the poor and the needy and the blacks had been ineffective.

During the campaign he had made a number of harsh personal criticisms of Richard Nixon. Now that it was all over he expressed some sympathy for his successor. He said he would like to be helpful if he could. Then he reminded me we were meeting on Nixon's fifty-sixth birthday. He said the President-elect was in Connecticut at the home of a daughter, and he thought it would be nice if I would call and congratulate Nixon. He said, "Barry, you might sympathize with him a little, too. This job is a killer."

I suspect that most of my readers who will recall the bitterness of the 1968 campaign and the intemperate remarks and personal criticism Lyndon Johnson made of candidate Richard Nixon will find all this difficult to believe. To some it may seem hypocritical that we who had been so divided by our political philosophy and our partisan ties could hold such a conversation.

I have never held any hatred in my heart for those who opposed me. I didn't come to the White House that day just because Lyndon Johnson, the President, had invited me. He didn't ask me just because I was a member of the United States Senate. We were both battle-stained warriors with a shared experience and facing the complexities of trying to make the government of this Republic responsible to the people.

I wasn't particularly personally fond of Lyndon Johnson. I don't think he had any great affection for me. But the President, any President, is surrounded by fawning sycophants, and I think in these final hours of his presidency Lyndon Johnson was facing reality.

When I returned to the apartment, I did call the President-elect. He was pleased. I told him I had just left the White House and Lyndon Johnson had suggested I call, and that, too, pleased Richard Nixon.

CHAPTER 25

The Wall Around Nixon

In January 1969 I took my oath of office as a member of the United States Senate for the third time. I was sixty years old. The voters of Arizona had given me a larger plurality than in either of my two other successful elections. Former Governor Paul Fannin, who had been elected to my old seat the year I ran for the presidency, had now served four years. Although I had been in the Senate from 1952 to 1964, the rules made me the junior Senator. But the Republicans elected for the first time in 1968 treated me with great respect, and in that freshman class they called me the professor.

The Republican ticket of Richard Nixon and Ted Agnew had carried thirty-two states and defeated Hubert Humphrey and Edwin Muskie by an electoral college vote of 302 to 236. In the popular vote the difference was razor-thin. George C. Wallace and General Curtis LeMay got 13.5 percent of the popular vote. The difference between Nixon-Agnew and Humphrey-Muskie was less than three-tenths of 1 percent.

Richard Nixon became the thirty-seventh President of the United States with the lowest percentage of popular votes received by a winner since 1912, when Bull Moose candidate Theodore

Roosevelt siphoned off enough support to let Woodrow Wilson win with only 41.9 percent of the popular vote. But close counts only in horseshoes and hand grenades.

There was a Republican in the White House. We had gained sixteen seats in the Senate. The Democrats still held the majority, but now the margin was only fifty-eight to our forty-two, and we could count on support from some of the southern Senators.

In the House of Representatives Republicans had gained seventeen seats. The Democrats had 243, but we had a strong working minority of 192.

Even more impressive and gratifying to me was the fact that the voters had elected thirty-one Republican governors—the greatest number of Republican chief state executives since the Harding landslide of 1920. And all this took place just four years after the pundits had written that my defeat at the hands of Lyndon Johnson signaled the end of the Republican party as a viable, political instrument.

Once the ballots are counted and the headlines printed, the attention of most citizens swings back to their own daily concerns. Those who voted for the winners were confident things would get better. Those who were with the losers were hoping things wouldn't get worse. It is only the politicians who are engrossed in a study of the returns.

It seemed to me the Nixon campaign had lost direction in the final weeks. The major issues—the conduct of the Vietnam War and the costly failure of the Great Society social programs—were muted. The contest had become one more of personality than of principle.

I think this very narrow victory had a profound effect on Richard Nixon. While 41.1 million Americans voted for either Humphrey, Wallace, or LeMay, only 31.7 million voted for the Republican ticket. Nixon was in truth very much a minority winner. In my opinion it was this knowledge which kept him from exercising the power of the presidency aggressively. Certainly it was a major factor four years later in the determination of CRP (Committee to Re-Elect the President) to cover every base, overwhelm the opposition.

As things turned out in 1972, Nixon could have waged a stay-at-home, front-porch campaign and defeated George McGovern. It was the memory of the closeness of the election of 1968 which was responsible for the excesses of 1972—the plumbers, Watergate, and all the rest.

Because so many of my personal friends and 1964 supporters had been a part of the Nixon campaign effort, I assumed the White House would solicit my suggestions and recommendations. In Miami at the convention Nixon had gone out of his way to express appreciation for what he graciously called the "determining influence" of my meetings with the delegates after that Monday night speech.

The John F. Kennedy inauguration had been a gala extravaganza. To my mind the Nixon inauguration was an obscene Roman holiday. We were at war. The state of the economy was questionable. Despite high taxes, we were running a federal deficit. The declared winner of that November contest was certainly not the majority choice of the American people.

"And coming events cast their shadows before." *

In keeping with modern tradition Nixon had scheduled elaborate balls at all the big hotels in Washington. Governor Ronald Reagan of California had been asked to host the reception at the Sheraton, where Peggy and I were living while our apartment was being redecorated.

The announced plan called for the President to come to each hotel, visit the box of the host, be escorted by the host to the microphone, and be introduced to the party faithful, who had paid a bundle for their tickets. At the Sheraton the Nixon party entered from the side opposite the Reagan box. The President was ushered to the stage and introduced by Art Linkletter, who had entered with the party. After his brief remarks and a period of handshaking with the crowd, Nixon and his party were ushered out the same way they entered. There was no recognition of Governor Reagan's position as host for the ball. The President didn't visit the governor's box or speak to him.

At the time I dismissed this unnecessary discourtesy as unintentional—a foul-up on the part of those who were handling the President's visitations. I was sure Art Linkletter had been an in-

* From "Lochiel's Warning" by Thomas Campbell.

nocent participant, and I didn't think the President was responsible. In retrospect I have come to believe this was the first evidence of the unforgiving, exclusionary policies of the inner palace guard—those who were ultimately responsible for Nixon's downfall.

My first face-to-face meeting with the new President after his inauguration was on January 18 at the Alfalfa Club dinner. We were waiting in an anteroom for the head table to be assembled. I told Nixon I thought he was moving too slowly. Out of some 3,000 available executive appointments he had made only about 80. I warned him the Kennedy-Johnson holdovers would frustrate any effort he made to take charge of the administrative machinery.

Nixon said he understood the problem and intended to do something about it. He said his first and most pressing concern had been the selection of his Cabinet. This should have been a tip-off. I am convinced most successful candidates for the presidency have their minds made up on this subject immediately after the votes are counted, if they haven't done so in advance of election day. The President said that he would like to visit with me privately in the near future and that Bryce Harlow would make the arrangements.

Cabinet members are highly visible. It is the undersecretaries and the assistant secretaries, the chairmen and the members of various boards and commissions who, too frequently, are responsible for policy determination.

Dwight Eisenhower had been a political neophyte when he was elected President. Nixon, the savvy, experienced politician, had suffered with the rest of us when Ike failed to take decisive command of the executive branch. We all had criticized Eisenhower's delegation of this responsibility to his subordinate, Sherman Adams.

On Wednesday evening, March 5, I went to the White House for my first private visit with the President since his election. We met in the living room on the second floor. Bryce Harlow, who had made the arrangements, was the only other person present.

I was unprepared for the warmth of Nixon's greeting. On similar previous occasions it had been difficult for him to drop his reserved, formal attitude. Now he inquired about Peggy's health. He expressed interest and satisfaction that my son, Barry, Jr., was running for Congressman Ed Reinecke's vacated seat in

California. Then he asked, "Where do you see the problems, Barry?"

I said I thought he should try to get rid of the holdover employees from the Kennedy-Johnson administration, particularly those in the State Department who were responsible for our no-win policy in Vietnam. I told the President I had a paper on this subject prepared by General Richardson. The President told me Lyndon Johnson had urged him to get rid of Robert McNamara and the McNamara clique in the Defense Department and to "never trust the Russians."

In what some observers believe to have been an effort to influence the outcome of the 1968 election Lyndon Johnson had ordered a halt to the bombing of North Vietnam. We were engaging in peace talks with the North Vietnamese in Paris. I asked President Nixon how long he intended to continue the bombing halt. The reports I'd seen indicated the Paris talks were going nowhere. The North Vietnamese had increased their guerrilla activity, destroying villages and murdering civilians.

Nixon said he intended to give the peace effort at least six months. He didn't think the American public would stand for an all-out military assault on North Vietnam. He said he was in a no-win situation. He told me that Secretary of Defense Laird, who had just returned from Saigon, was hopeful we could soon commence withdrawal of American troops and substitute South Vietnamese replacements. If this didn't work, if no progress were made in Paris, he would then, perhaps, have to order a resumption of bombing.

I told him I disagreed with the delay, but he was the Commander in Chief. I hoped the plan would work.

The 1968 Republican party platform promised to reduce the inflation rate—then running about 4 percent—and to end waste in government. Most successful Republican candidates were opposed to the proliferation of government at all levels. As a candidate Nixon had promised peace in Vietnam but not surrender. He had promised to make government more efficient but had stayed away from any sharp criticism of either the size or the spending of the federal government.

I had been before the voters in Arizona. I knew what they wanted—lower taxes, less federal spending, and a reduction in federal interference. When I tried to convey this to President

Nixon, I got the impression he thought that Arizona was atypical and that I was too blunt and too positive in my opinions.

When their party wins the White House, Senators and Congressmen are expected to recommend competent, qualified party members for important posts in the new administration. I had recommended the appointment of Lieutenant General William Quinn, U.S. Army retired, to be Ambassador to Greece. Quinn had served in Greece. He was well known and well liked by both the military and the political leaders. I thought he would be ideal for the job. Herb Klein and Fred LaRue of the White House staff discussed this recommendation with me. I was left with the impression General Quinn would be considered.

On the day before Easter Peter Flanigan, who was also on the White House staff, called to tell me Quinn could not be considered at all because John Mitchell had promised the job to a friend in Chicago. Naturally I was disappointed. What troubled me most was that neither LaRue nor Klein had mentioned this obstacle in our earlier conversations. I made some inquiries. I discovered that apparently the left hand at the White House—that is, LaRue and Klein—had not been told what the right hand was doing. There was, I discovered, an inner, inner guard. Two men, John Ehrlichman and Bob Haldeman, and to a somewhat lesser degree John Mitchell, were exercising presidential authority without any consultation with the other members of the White House staff.

I knew both Haldeman and Ehrlichman. They were in my judgment administrative types with little sensitivity for political reality. They had never been identified with the Republican party. They had not been visible in the President's campaign. It bothered me to discover the controlling positions they were holding in the Nixon White House.

On April 26 Admiral Lewis Strauss came to my office by appointment. Strauss had served as a member of the U.S. Atomic Energy Commission from 1946 to 1950, as special assistant to President Eisenhower on atomic energy matters, and as Chairman of the AEC from 1953 to 1958. He was Secretary of Commerce in 1958 and 1959. Certainly Strauss was a qualified expert on the whole atomic question.

We had lunch. The admiral told me that in June 1968 Richard Nixon had asked his help in two specific areas. One, he wanted Strauss to persuade General Eisenhower to endorse the Nixon candidacy. Nixon said it was an urgent matter because he believed the President was in very poor health and he was afraid Ike might die before he got around to making a supportive statement. Strauss, who was very close to Eisenhower, did secure the former President's strong endorsement. Nixon expressed his great gratitude to Strauss in a personal letter, which the admiral showed me.

The second matter was much more serious. Nixon had been given information indicating the possibility that during Lyndon Johnson's administration the Atomic Energy Commission had allowed a sizable quantity of fissionable material to disappear. Nixon was fearful that if he became President and the shortage was discovered, it might be blamed on him.

Through his connections and friends on the commission Admiral Strauss had learned there was indeed a shortage—not grams or pounds but perhaps as much as half a ton or more. The admiral, not having any official position or the power of subpoena, or authority to take statements under oath, had been extremely careful to verify all the allegations. He had then written a detailed report naming his sources of information. He provided approximate dates and concluded that, in his opinion, the matter was of vital importance to our national security.

The admiral said he had come to see me because Nixon had not acknowledged receipt of the report, had made no attempt to contact Strauss, and as far as the admiral could see, no action was being planned. He asked if I thought it would be possible for me to prod the administration into taking the proper course in order to investigate thoroughly this disappearance and perhaps to recover the material.

I told the admiral I had seen President Nixon privately only once since his inauguration. Because I had been branded an atomic warrior in 1964, any inquiries I might make on this subject would probably be counterproductive. I suggested he talk to Mel Laird at Defense or Henry Kissinger, the President's National Security Adviser. Strauss understood and sympathized with my position.

I reviewed the matters I had discussed with the President at that single meeting. Strauss then told me he had been at the White House for a high-level strategy session on September 4, 1961. He said Secretary of Defense Robert McNamara had at that meeting recommended to President Kennedy the dispatch of 16,000 ground troops—marines—to South Vietnam.

Strauss said that Undersecretary of State George Ball had strongly opposed the move. Strauss said Ball predicted that if we acted on McNamara's suggestion, we would have at least 300,000 American troops in Vietnam within two years.

The admiral said that Secretary of State Dean Rusk had disagreed with George Ball. General Maxwell Taylor had supported McNamara, and Kennedy had followed the advice of his Defense Secretary. Ultimately Taylor and McNamara ordered the troops into combat. This was the true beginning of the tragic Vietnam War.

CHAPTER 26

Excuses, Excuses

When Richard Nixon took office as President, he was immediately confronted with a variety of difficulties—certainly not of his own making. The war in Vietnam was going badly. The student protesters who had played a major role in forcing Lyndon Johnson to abandon his dream of a second term were feeling their oats. The mood of the country was a sort of expectant cynicism. It wanted the new President to cure the nation's ills, but it was not at all sure he could or would bring about the changes he had promised during his campaign.

This attitude was prevalent in the Congress. The Democratic majority wasn't prepared to cooperate fully with the new leader, but it was not totally antagonistic either.

The moratorium on bombing in Vietnam which Johnson had proclaimed in November had not improved the climate in Paris. The peace talks were bogged down in petty haggling. To make matters worse, tensions had developed between Secretary of Defense Mel Laird, Secretary of State Bill Rogers, and National Security Adviser Henry Kissinger. I don't think the President was aware of this until it was almost too late to do anything about it.

Dwight D. Eisenhower died on March 28, 1969. I saw the President at the funeral. I knew Nixon had been to see Ike a few weeks before his death. He told me they had a good talk. He said Ike approved of the planned withdrawal of troops from Vietnam and had lectured him on the folly of not using the full military power of the United States to end the war.

I remember that during my visits with the former President in 1965 he had frequently spoken about the lifesaving virtue of superior force. "When it is a battalion against a battalion or a company against a company,' he had said, "the troops with the greatest determination can usually win, but the cost in casualties will be extremely high. When the attacking force outnumbers the enemy two or three to one, the objective is taken quickly, casualties are light. That is the way to win."

I wondered if Ike had been as passionate an advocate of force in his conversation with President Nixon. If so, perhaps we might now expect a change in the President's attitude. Despite all the kind things Nixon had said that day at the memorial service, I had learned through our years of association that it was very difficult for Richard Nixon to forgive his critics. It was part of his nature to cherish a grudge.

During his first year in office Richard Nixon sanctioned and supported a number of covert military operations in Vietnam. The bombing raids on Cambodia to destroy Vietcong strongpoints and supply lines commenced in March. The public did not know about them until May. When the North Koreans shot down our Navy plane on routine patrol in April, Nixon considered direct military retaliation. The memory of the capture of the *Pueblo* was still vivid in the public mind. When his military advisers objected to a direct response on the sound ground that we didn't have enough resources to risk a war in two separate theaters, Nixon decided to increase the pressure in North Vietnam. But he kept his subsequent actions a secret.

Meanwhile, Henry Kissinger was having frequent secret meetings with the North Vietnamese. I am personally fond of Henry Kissinger. I think he was an effective Secretary of State. But he believed in highly personalized, ultrasecret diplomacy. He saw himself as the personal manipulator of events. He sought to play off the fears and aspirations of one world leader or faction against another. Where John Foster Dulles had made American policy a matter of public knowledge, Kissinger went to great lengths to prevent the public from receiving any information about his activities. Much of the time his security efforts were successful; but there were inevitable leaks, and when the leaks occurred, Nixon was furious.

By midsummer 1970 the school integration program in the South directed by Robert Mardian under the aegis of the Attorney General's office had the southern Senators and Congressmen deeply disturbed. Mardian had been gentle and tactful. He had also been very firm. The southern red-necks vented their anger on their Representatives in Washington.

On August 6 Harry Dent, the President's southern political manager, arranged a meeting at the White House. When Dent asked me to attend, I explained I was not a southerner, that a plank in the Republican party platform supported desegregation. The President was merely enforcing the law. Nevertheless, Dent insisted that I come.

When I arrived at Dent's office at the White House about four-thirty that afternoon, I found he had assembled Congressmen Sam Devine of Ohio and Les Arends of Illinois and Senators Bob Dole of Kansas, John Tower of Texas, Strom Thurmond of South Carolina, Ed Gurney of Florida, and Attorney General Mitchell. Devine, Arends, and Dole were certainly not southerners. I felt more comfortable.

The southerners were extremely upset. They said the northern bureaucrats in the Nixon administration were deliberately causing trouble. They aimed much of their criticism at John Mitchell.

At five o'clock we moved into the Oval Office. Vice President Agnew and Bryce Harlow were with the President.

Nixon told us he understood that some of the Republicans in the Senate and the House were unhappy with his administration. "If we are doing something wrong," he said, "I want to know about it so that we can remedy the situation."

Senator Thurmond told the President there was no justification for revoking the tax-exempt status of private schools in the South. He said this was being done by Nixon's Internal Revenue Service, that if it didn't stop, it would destroy the quality of education in the South and produce a true rebellion.

Nixon claimed he had known nothing of the IRS tax ruling until he had seen it in the press. "We've got some gung ho son of a bitch over there who doesn't give a damn for the political

realities or the problems of this administration. I'm going to cut
his throat."

That gave me an opening. I said, "Mr. President, you have a
lot of those gung ho, reform-the-world, damn-the-general-public
liberal holdovers in every department. We pass a law in the Congress," I said, "and they write the regulations. They don't give
a tinker's damn about the intent of the Congress. We are being
choked to death by the decisions of a group of bureaucrats who
were never elected."

I told him that in my opinion only John Volpe, Mel Laird, and
John Mitchell out of all his Cabinet members had really taken
command of their departments. Nixon said he knew about the
problem, but it was very difficult to get rid of these people.

I told the President he could do it if he worked at it. "You
may not be able to fire all of them," I said, "but you can certainly
transfer them and take away their present authority."

Then I told him of the Roth investigation and the rat program
fiasco. Congressman William Roth, a young member from Delaware, had spent two years trying to determine how many public
assistance programs were available in the federal establishment.
He found out there were 1,300 programs administered by a variety
of agencies. They operated separately. There was no communication between them, and they were unknown to many of the
people they were established to help.

The House of Representatives had endured an emotional debate
over the appropriation of funds for rat control in major cities. This
was in response to a newspaper story about some children who
were bitten by rats in New York City. After all the furor died
away, it was discovered there were eight rat control programs
operating in various governmental departments at the time.

I told the President I had made a speech on this subject in July
and promised to send him a copy if he promised to read it. I said,
"This federal government has grown so big and so powerful and
has so much money no one in Washington begins to understand
all the governmental activities."

Nixon said he would be glad to read what I had to say; then
he chided me for not keeping in closer contact with the White
House. "You haven't been here since last August," he said.

I told him that was true. I said my house in Newport was only fifteen miles or so from his summer house in San Clemente, but the damned Coast Guard wouldn't let me get within three miles of him.

The President laughed and suggested I give him a telephone call and he would get me a pass. I replied that if I was in Newport and he was in San Clemente, I had to call the White House in Washington to have the call connected to the summer White House in San Clemente—about 6,000 miles of long-distance wire—and I thought that was a ridiculous expense.

When the meeting broke up, the southerners felt they had won their battle. At least they thought they had an assurance from the President the southern schools would be given more time to comply with federal regulations. I came away believing Richard Nixon, who had served fourteen years in Washington—four as a member of the House of Representatives, two as a member of the Senate, and eight as Vice President—was unaware of what the unrestrained bureaucracy was doing to the nation.

Nixon's problems at home were complicated by the increasingly violent activities of the so-called peace groups. Professional agitators exploiting the public's dissatisfaction and puzzlement over events in Vietnam were recruiting activist groups on most college campuses and in all the larger cities. The young people they enlisted were taught to hate American traditions, to despise middle-class moral values, to question the free-enterprise economic system, and to criticize viciously all those who held positions of authority in the government.

For the most part these followers were highly emotional, confused youngsters. In the name of peace they set fire to university buildings. They bombed banks, blew up libraries, burned books, and assassinated innocent civilians. In the first full year of the Nixon presidency there were 2,000 so-called peace demonstrations, resulting in 500 serious injuries and 8 deaths. To prove their devotion to love and peace and the gentle virtues, these young anarchists were responsible for almost 250 fires.

In what seemed to me a tragic reversal of traditional value judgments, the newspapers and the television lionized the perpetrators of this destructive action. Draft dodgers became heroes. When the Stanford library at Palo Alto was burned and when the laboratory at the University of Wisconsin was blown up, the press expressed some indignation for what they considered "individual excessive acts," but the movement which spawned this anarchy was never condemned.

A number of observers have declared that during this period the general public never clearly understood why we were in Vietnam. If that be true, and I suspect it is in a general way, surely the press and the television are to be faulted. If it is their responsibility to report objectively the events of each passing day, why didn't they illuminate our entry into and participation in that conflict between the communists of the North and the freedom-loving people of the South?

Once again I think the answer is to be found in the failure of three Presidents—Kennedy, Johnson, and Nixon—to deal frankly and openly with the press and with the people. The unwarranted secrecy and covert actions provoked the angry response.

When President Eisenhower sent 500 or 600 military advisers to South Vietnam, he did so openly. When Kennedy sent the 17,000 marines to Vietnam with orders not to shoot back if shot at, he was bluffing. Johnson secretly escalated the war in 1964. Nixon kept the bombing of Cambodia a secret. When the press and the public discovered what had been going on, they were both resentful and critical.

I am not so naïve as to believe that all of a nation's military and diplomatic maneuvers can be conducted in full public view. But repeated deceptions erode public confidence. When it develops that the major reason for the secrecy is the fear of failure coupled with the desire to avoid blame, our willingness to forgive and understand diminishes rapidly.

My reference here is exclusively to military operations. The delivery of weapons and other material to our friends cannot be kept secret for long.

Our intelligence apparatus, on the other hand—the CIA and the FBI—have been emasculated as a result of congressional demand. Both these agencies have been undeservedly abused by the press and by the officers of government. It should be noted the acts for which they have been criticized were all the result of some White House order. Presidents have compromised both the CIA and the FBI by ordering the agencies to perform certain assignments not within the purview of their regular operation.

The Freedom of Information Act, which now permits our nation's enemies to examine government files concerning their operations, is an abomination. The whole law enforcement establishment from the FBI to the lowliest constable has suffered. Police departments depend on their informants. The government's intelligence units depend on reliable informants. To destroy confidentiality and rip away the anonymity traditionally provided informants is sheer stupidity.

No one has been more vocal in defense of the individual's constitutional rights than I have. I believe just as strongly that the government and its intelligence agencies have a constitutional right to defend us against those who intend to destroy the government.

I regard J. Edgar Hoover as a national hero. I believe most of the chiefs of the CIA have been dedicated, talented individuals. The errors they have been charged with should be attributed to the President who chose that course of action, not to the agent.

My first criticism of the Nixon presidency, which I voiced to the President personally at every available opportunity, centered on his political failure to take steps necessary to change the character of his administrative appointees. In one rare moment of utter candor the President confessed to me he was appalled by the excuses offered by many of his Cabinet officers for the retention of holdover Kennedy-Johnson bureaucratic administrators. He said he was told that to remove the men would destroy morale in the department or provoke an avalanche of criticism in the press or leave the agency without an officer who could relate to the past and maintain continuity. He vowed that if he were reelected, this wouldn't happen the second time around.

My second criticism was over the failure of the Nixon administration to trust the American public. On one occasion during this period I was called to a meeting at the White House. A number of the President's congressional supporters had been assembled to devise a strategy to ensure passage of a bill authorizing the development and deployment of an antiballistic missile (ABM) system.

After about an hour of concentrating on ways to persuade the Congress to support this defensive necessity I begged the President to go on television. I said he should tell the American people the truth about the terrifying buildup of Soviet military capability. I argued that if the people were given the facts—permitted to understand how the Soviets had outdistanced us in both offensive and defensive weapons—they would give overwhelming support to the ABM legislation. I said the public wanted a superior defense capability and would support research and development of whatever else might be needed to reestablish a parity of military power between the United States and Russia.

I suggested that if the President didn't want to be the bearer of these bad tidings, all he had to do was to lift the classification on certain information already in the possession of a great many members of Congress. I said we would do the job for him. A number of other Senators—Peter Dominick of Colorado, John Tower of Texas, Strom Thurmond of South Carolina, Cliff Hansen of Wyoming, and Ed Gurney of Florida—who were at the meeting agreed with me.

Nixon shook his head, said the timing wouldn't be right. Then he brought in Henry Kissinger, and we had about an hour's lecture on foreign policy.

In defense of the adamant position adopted by the President I should explain that any comparison of relative military strength is complicated by a variety of technical factors. It is argued that our ICBMs have more accurate guidance systems than those of the Russians. At the same time it is conceded the Russians possess a greater throw weight. We were then considered to be a sea power, whereas the Russians were a continental land power. Unfortunately this is no longer true. Their naval strength exceeds ours. To make it more difficult, most of the data used to evaluate the effectiveness of our new weapons are entirely theoretical. We have never actually launched an ICBM from a silo at a target. The relative effectiveness of being able to assign multiple warheads carried by a single missile to different targets can be debated. Indeed, the merits of an antiballistic defense can be questioned.

Those responsible for America's defenses stoutly deny and resist every claim of Russian superiority. But even those who, because of the positions they occupy, must defend our current capability will admit the superiority we enjoyed during the Eisenhower administration has been dissipated.

Everett McKinley Dirksen died on September 7, 1969. I shall never forget standing on the rooftop garden of the Adams Hotel in Phoenix one night in 1951, when Ev Dirksen urged me to become a candidate for the U.S. Senate.

He was, even then, a political giant—a leader in the Congress.

His encouragement prompted my decision. When I came to the Senate in 1953, Ev Dirksen served as my wise counselor, my most constructive critic. He was my loyal friend.

Considered by some the most powerful Republican in the Senate, in our times together he was always humble, reasonable, and more concerned with the future prosperity of the nation than he was with the personal fortunes of Ev Dirksen. A dramatic speaker with a magnificent voice and a mastery of technique, he could charm an audience, instruct it, and inflame it.

Dirksen was a bridge from the past to the present. His mind was occupied with the future. Born in 1896, he served from private to first lieutenant in World War I. After returning home to Illinois, he worked his way through law school and finally won admission to the bar in 1926. He was elected to the U.S. House of Representatives in 1932 and served seven terms in the House. Threatened with blindness, he did not seek reelection in 1948. In 1950 he ran for and was elected to the Senate from Illinois.

Ev Dirksen's sixteen years in the House, his experiences in World War I and during the turbulent, hectic years that followed had given him a deep and fundamental understanding of the character of American politics and the American electorate. In his later years he made some dramatic recordings which were extremely popular and, I think, earned him quite a lot of money. His record of service to the American Republic entitles him to the respect and gratitude of every degree of citizen.

It was Ev Dirksen who nominated me for the Presidency in San Francisco in 1964. His death left a void in my life. I treasure the memories of my association with this great American.

It has been said that republics degenerate into democracies and democracies into anarchy and we move from anarchy to tyranny. In 1970 the antiwar groups became frenzied and violent. Their language was unrestrained. They called for a plebiscite to end the war. This feeling is reflected in the acts of Congress designed to limit the President's authority as Commander in Chief.

The violence reached a climax in San Jose, California, one week before the 1970 November elections. A mob of 2,000 protesters threw stones and eggs at the President of the United States. They broke the windows in one of the cars in his motorcade. They smashed the glass in the press bus, injuring a number of people.

Again the press failed categorically and unanimously to condemn the violence.

What followed a day or so later is important if we are going to understand all the excesses of the Nixon supporters in 1972—i.e., Watergate, the plumbers, the break-ins, the phone taps, etc. The President decided to respond to the San Jose violence in a speech scheduled for delivery in Phoenix, Arizona. The rally was held in an airplane hangar at Sky Harbor, Arizona, on November 1.

Nixon used some very strong language to condemn the terrorists activities. He called those responsible "violent thugs" and the "super hypocrites of our time."

The President had decided beforehand to use a film or videotape of this speech for rebroadcast to the nation on election eve. His staff knew of this decision and had been instructed to make the proper arrangements.

Incredible as it may seem, the arrangements for the filming were made with a local Arizona provider who lacked the equipment or the technical know-how to do the job right. I was on the platform with the President. The acoustics in the hangar were miserable. The President's speech, which he had envisioned as a major response to the lawlessness of the peace groups, was actually recorded in black and white.

When the program was offered for broadcast on election eve, some stations declined to run it because of its technical inferiority. Nixon was furious. In comparison to Senator Ed Muskie's election eve broadcast in support of Democratic candidates, the President sounded shrill, vengeful, and unsure of himself.

I tried and failed to find out who was directly responsible. When it came time to prepare for the 1972 presidential campaign, the Committee to Re-elect the President was overstaffed with television producers and technical experts.

On May 2, 1971, during the great peace march on Washington, D.C., I had a personal encounter with the extremists when about fifty of them forced their way into my reception room to enact a war scene. They screamed obscenities and sprayed red paint on some of the walls and furnishings. The police were called to remove them.

I issued a press release announcing I was closing my office until order could be restored. I wasn't going to expose my staff to the hazards of travel through a city controlled by a mob.

The following morning the D.C. police ordered the protesters out of Potomac Park and began arresting those who resisted. The detainees were taken to the RFK Stadium, photographed, finger-printed, and released on $10 bail.

Nixon, who was in San Clemente, issued a statement declaring the protest would not alter his conduct of the war and condemned the violence. The background of this move is interesting. John Mitchell had assigned Richard Kleindienst to develop security plans. There was talk the President would be asked to call out the Army or the National Guard.

Chief Jerry Wilson of the D.C. Police Department had dinner with Kleindienst the night before the scheduled demonstrations. He said his department could cope with any disturbance and argued that if the President called out the Guard or the Army, it would only further inflame the passions of the mob, and the President would be their target.

"If you let me handle this," he told Kleindienst, "they can get mad as hell at the chief of police, but they can't blame the Nixon administration."

Wilson's men used only enough force to subdue the violent among the agitators. He was nevertheless bitterly condemned by a broad segment of the American press.

On the morning of the arrests I had an eight o'clock appoint-ment at Georgetown University Hospital. I was to commence therapy on my left shoulder, which had been in a cast as an aftermath of an operation to remove a painful calcified bone spur.

After the treatment I walked through the university grounds toward my apartment. Perhaps forty or fifty of the would-be dem-onstrators had taken refuge here. I stopped to visit with them. I was appalled by their lack of understanding of the true issues. They didn't know why we were in Vietnam or what the Congress could do about it or what the President could do about it. They were unaware of the troop removals. By this time, as I remember it, Nixon had brought home almost 75,000 of our military men. And they didn't really care. They had come to raise hell with no thought to the consequences.

CHAPTER 27

No Comment, No Criticism Nixon Administration—Part II

Indecision and a willingness to temporize—to postpone the hard decisions—were the characteristics of Richard Nixon's first term as President. We who were his friends in Congress were puzzled and frustrated. Since the beginning of the cold war America's defensive strategy had called for maintaining a military capability superior to that of the Soviet Union. Nixon rejected "superiority" in favor of what he called "sufficiency." We now know this was done to create a favorable climate for negotiations with the Russians and the Red Chinese. He didn't tell us so at the time.

In 1967 President Johnson had proposed the development of an antiballistic missile system, capable of destroying enemy missiles in the air. Richard Nixon scaled down the Johnson request. We were told that despite this reduction in scope, the development of such a weapons system would be a powerful lever to force the Russians to agree to a limitation on the developing armaments race.

During this period my visits with the President were cordial but infrequent. He knew I was opposed to the limitations he placed on our military operations in Vietnam. I thought it was immoral to ask American troops to fight and die in a war they were forbidden to win.

In the spring of 1970 the President ordered the destruction of the Vietcong sanctuaries in Cambodia. I was encouraged. I thought it meant a change in policy. We would now use our superior power to force the Vietnamese to the peace table.

This same lack of firm resolution was apparent in the President's dealings with Congress. When we took up legislation to authorize construction of the supersonic transport, I was told Nixon wanted the bill passed. The leaders of the opposition—Senators George McGovern of South Dakota and William Proxmire of Wisconsin—employed outrageous demagoguery and outright falsehood. As the leader of the group in the Senate favoring the SST I said my respected colleagues were employing the "big lie technique." I permitted the *New York Times* to quote me. I released a carefully prepared article itemizing the potential benefits—both civilian and military—which would flow to the United States if we supported this technological breakthrough.

During this period I received no support from the White House. No one called to offer help or to ask how the battle was going. I am convinced that had the President provided supportive, expert opinion, construction of the SST would have been authorized.

When the Ninety-first Congress had been organized in January 1969, I supported the move to elect Howard Baker of Tennessee Minority Leader in place of Hugh Scott of Pennsylvania. Baker lost by five votes. Before the Ninety-second convened in January 1971, it was known Baker wanted to try again. Nixon's man, Bryce Harlow, told me the President wanted Scott reelected. He asked me to visit with Scott and offer him encouragement.

During my years in the Senate I had never been able to feel comfortable with Hugh Scott's ideological orientation. On big spending, big government proposals, Hugh Scott always came down on the side of the eastern liberals. Nevertheless, in response to the presidential request, I called on Scott. We counted Republican noses. I promised my support.

On the night before the Republican caucus at which the Senate leadership would be selected in 1971, Vice President Agnew called to tell me the President wanted Scott dumped and was soliciting my vote and my support for Howard Baker.

I told the Vice President I was shocked. I said, "Whatever the reasons for the President's altered position, the move is politically stupid."

Agnew said Nixon, looking forward to 1972, was fearful Scott, in the position of Minority Leader, might use his influence to favor some opposing candidate for the nomination. I told Agnew it was much too late to make the switch. Besides, Nixon had promised to follow my recommendation and name Bob Dole chairman of the Republican National Committee. Dole is a staunch conservative. He would control the party machinery. Even if Scott deserted the President, he would be unable to influence the convention.

In May, President Nixon asked me to represent his government at the World Air Show in Paris. I jumped at the chance. It would permit me to fly in the French-British Concorde and the Russian TU-144. As the official representative of the U.S. government I could take Peggy with me. It would be a pleasant break for her.

What I discovered in Paris was extremely disturbing. Leaders in world aviation had concluded that because of the U.S. refusal to go ahead with the SST, we were ready to relinquish our premier position in aircraft technology.

My examination of the Russian supersonic plane forced me to revise my earlier thinking about Soviet technology. The leading edge of the TU-144 was made of titanium. This metal absorbs and dissipates heat much faster than aluminum, permitting higher operating speeds. The Concorde had a leading edge of aluminum. The Russian aircraft was equipped with a pure fan-jet engine. The Concorde had afterburners. The pure jet is cleaner and more powerful.

The instrumentation in the Russian cockpit I was permitted to examine was primitive by our standards. I wondered what they might have hidden beneath the floor—if they were doing this deliberately to keep the rest of the world in the dark. It was an incongruity I couldn't explain to myself.

On the Concorde the cabin was filled with highly sophisticated instruments, but the afterburners failed to ignite. We were able to achieve only a speed of Mach 1.

The Russians told us they had been unable to detect any injury to the environment as a result of their exhaustive flight tests at supersonic speeds. I recalled with some bitterness the exaggerated claims I had heard on the Senate floor about the dire environmental damages such flights would bring.

On June 17 I went to the White House to spend an hour with

the President and to deliver my written report about the Paris display. On June 13 the *New York Times* had commenced publishing the Pentagon Papers—top secret documents dealing with the Vietnam War. The material had been stolen from classified files by former Pentagon employee Daniel Ellsberg. Nixon condemned the *Times*. He called Ellsberg a traitor and complained of the constant leaks from State and Defense.

We then discussed the 1972 presidential contest. Nixon said his narrow victory in 1968 had prevented him from carrying out many of his campaign promises. He believed it was essential to win by an overwhelming plurality in 1972. I agreed that a smashing victory would be good for him and good for the country, particularly if we could increase our Republican membership in the Congress.

The President switched the discussion to Red China. He said he wanted to improve our relations with the mainland Chinese. He planned to do this without granting full diplomatic recognition. His underlying motive was to exploit the natural animosities between Red Russia and Red China. He said he was confident the United Nations would not admit Red China to membership. He professed admiration for Taiwan and said he would never do anything to injure that relationship.

Nixon thought the domestic economy would continue to improve—there would be more jobs, unemployment would decrease. He was worried somewhat about inflation, which was then hovering around a 6 percent level. But he vowed his administration would never resort to wage and price controls. He said he thought the Congress had voted standby authority in a deliberate effort to pass the buck and embarrass him. He was not going to be caught in that trap. On August 15, 1971, President Richard Nixon went on the television to announce the imposition of standby wage and price controls on a temporary basis.

When President Nixon decided to pursue détente with Red China and Russia, he drastically altered existing American foreign policy. When he first mentioned this subject to me at the White House meeting in June, he had been somewhat vague, using very general terms. I had agreed that any lessening of tension between the great powers would improve the chance for peace. But, I reminded him, we had seen no indication the Russians were prepared to abandon their expansionist policies. I said the Red Chinese had encouraged and supported North Vietnam, and without the matériel coming through China, our troubles in Vietnam would come to a screeching halt.

Nixon had admitted all this was true. He didn't tell me who was promoting this new approach, but I knew that certain members of the State Department, the Council on Foreign Relations, and some of our former Ambassadors to Russia, including Averell Harriman, argued Russian belligerence was defensive. They maintained the Russians felt threatened by the superior military power of the United States and had, in effect, been forced by us to develop their own huge weapons system. The President had given me no indication that he was already making overtures to China and to Russia as the first step in creating détente.

Since this word has become so much a part of our language and is closely linked with world peace, it would be useful to examine its precise meaning. It comes to us from the French, and the dictionary says, "A relaxing, especially of international tension; see: detent." So détente really means detent, and this is defined as "A mechanism for temporarily keeping one part in a certain position relative to that of another, released by application of force to one of the parties."

Détente, then, is not peace. It is a situation where international equilibrium is maintained by playing off one power against another or a combination of powers against a single power and thus preventing the outbreak of hostilities.

This is essentially what U.S. foreign policy had been attempting to accomplish since the end of World War II. We had relied on a single deterrent—American military superiority—to restrain the aggressive ambitions of Soviet Russia. The Russians and the Red Chinese, unwilling to confront the United States directly, had resorted to the employment of client states and "liberation movements"—so-called indigenous uprisings.

On July 15, 1971, I was flying a T-39 from Washington to the West Coast. We refueled at Tinker Air Force Base, Oklahoma. Shortly after takeoff, the Dallas-Fort Worth center called the aircraft to inform me Andrews Air Force Base in Washington was trying to reach me. I was told to tune my radio to a particular frequency.

The operator at Andrews acknowledged my call. He said that Dr. Kissinger wanted to talk to me and that he would patch me through to the White House. Waiting for the hookup to be completed, I thought the nation must be facing a major crisis.

When the patch was made, Dr. Kissinger said he wanted to get in touch with me because by the time I landed in California the President would have announced he was going to Peking. Kissinger wanted me to promise to keep my mouth shut until he had an opportunity to brief me. He said the President would be speaking to the nation on television. "We believe this move will be in the interest of world peace, and we beg you not to criticize until we can bring you up to date and give you all the reasons we believe this trip is necessary."

I knew the White House had the communications capability of reaching almost anyone, anywhere on earth. Such a thing had never happened to me before. I promised Dr. Kissinger that if the reporters contacted me, I would make no comment.

I wasn't completely surprised. We had gone through the period of Ping-Pong diplomacy. The rift between Red China and Russia was clearly established. But to my mind their differences were over the purity of Marxist doctrine as it was being followed in China and in Russia. Both were committed to the destruction of the capitalist system and the United States of America. I couldn't believe any border disputes or "within-the-family squabbles" would overwhelm their mutual commitment to this same objective.

On Thursday, August 5, I breakfasted with Dr. Kissinger in his office at the White House. He thanked me for my silence. He said the announcement of Nixon's projected visit to China was having a profound effect on Moscow. He had never seen the Russian ambassador so exercised. The day after the President's televised statement the Soviets had invited both Nixon and Kissinger to visit Russia. There were indications Hanoi might now be ready to release the U.S. prisoners of war they were holding. Kissinger predicted that if the meetings in Peking made real progress, we could expect an early and satisfactory end to the war in Vietnam.

I expressed my concern that this move might destroy our relationship with Taiwan. Kissinger assured me this was not going to happen. He then discussed what he considered the inevitable reemergence of Japan as a world military power. We should encourage this. The economic advances made in Japan after World War II with our assistance, Kissinger said, would guarantee Japanese alignment with the Western powers.

We then talked about the political situation. Kissinger lamented what he described as a lack of vigor on the part of conservative Republicans in Congress in defense of the President.

I bluntly told him conservative Republicans were disappointed in Nixon. I said it appeared to us the administration was drifting left.

Kissinger denied this. He said the *New York Times* and the Washington *Post* were being very kind to the President, showing the public a new Nixon. "And," he said, "the President wants to cultivate this new climate."

I said Nixon had been elected because of the prevailing conservative mood in the country—if he lost his conservative base, it would be disastrous. Kissinger agreed with me.

This glimpse of Dr. Henry Kissinger, the private man, was revealing. He appeared to be extremely knowledgeable and very pragmatic in his approach to world problems. He seemed to understand and appreciate my viewpoint. We agreed to meet at least once a month.

On October 25 the United Nations voted to expel Taiwan and to admit the People's Republic of China. The vote was 76 to 35 with 17 abstentions. The United States made no strong objections. I was disturbed and disappointed.

When I had breakfast with Dr. Kissinger for the third time late in November, he told me intelligence had discovered nearly 4,000 new military trucks in marshaling yards near Hanoi. He said the President intended to order the trucks destroyed as soon as Congress adjourned. He didn't think the President's announced visit to China had been the deciding factor in the admission of Red China to the UN. He had not expected the expulsion of Taiwan. If things didn't go well in Peking, we would immediately increase the military pressure on North Vietnam.

This visit was interrupted by a message that President Nixon would like to see us both in the Oval Office immediately. Bob Haldeman was with the President when we entered.

Nixon said he was pleased to know that I was meeting with Dr. Kissinger regularly. The date for his trip to China would soon be announced. We had the Russians worried, and that was good.

Bob Haldeman was critical of the conservatives for not giving the President more support in the Congress and around the country.

I suggested one way to accomplish this would be for the President to keep in closer contact with his supporters in the Congress. Then I renewed an earlier proposal. I urged the President to go on TV and give the people all the facts about the Soviet military buildup. I said, "A great many Americans now believe we are inferior to the Russians." I also asked Haldeman to provide every member of Congress with an accurate itemization of our defense vis-à-vis the Russians. I said, if the charge of inferiority was untrue, as both the President and Defense Secretary Mel Laird were claiming, we should let the facts answer the critics.

The matter of the truck concentration near Hanoi came up. The President said he was delaying action because he didn't want to give the antiwar members in Congress a chance to veto the plan. He thought they might attach an amendment to one of the bills he wanted passed prohibiting the air strike.

When Congress did adjourn, I went to South Vietnam. I visited all our major military installations. I spoke with our commanders. There had been, I learned, an aerial attack on certain limited targets in the vicinity of Hanoi. No great concentration of military vehicles had been destroyed. The officers who carried out the raid told me damage had been minimal.

A day or so before I was to leave Washington for Vietnam, the Vice President asked me to come and see him.

I like Ted Agnew. We had visited on a number of previous occasions. His message of invitation carried a sense of urgency.

Agnew thought the "palace guard"—Ehrlichman and Haldeman—wanted him off the ticket in 1972. He was contemplating making an early announcement of withdrawal.

I urged him not to do this. I said Republicans throughout the country had more confidence in him than they had in Nixon.

Agnew said he didn't know President Nixon any better after three years as Vice President than he did when he was asked to come on the ticket. He was not asked to participate in White House decisions. Much of what he knew about government operations came to him secondhand. He had not known about the overtures toward China until Nixon made his televised announcement.

I reminded him Jack Kennedy had isolated Lyndon Johnson. Hubert Humphrey always felt he was being left out in the cold.

Agnew agreed this was a part of the job. But, he said, in Miami

Nixon had commented on his own frustrating years as Vice President and vowed things would be different.

"I have been their hatchet man," Agnew said. "You know what the reporters did to me after the Des Moines speech."

I did know. On November 3, 1970, President Nixon made a nationwide televised address on the subject of the war in Vietnam. The networks' instant analyzers cut the President's speech to ribbons. Nixon sent Agnew to Des Moines, Iowa, to deliver the administration's rebuttal. The speech was prepared by Pat Buchanan of the White House staff, with some editing by Vic Gold, who had worked for me in 1964 and was now Agnew's press secretary. At Des Moines, Agnew condemned the press, particularly the three TV networks. He said, "An unelected elite—no more than a dozen commentators and executive producers—control the news." He charged these men with deciding what 40 or 50 million Americans will learn of the day's events in the nation and the world.

Agnew's blunt words aroused the ire of the national media. Reluctant to challenge the President directly, they made Ted Agnew their number one target. There had been a second and anticipated fallout—a sharp rise in Agnew's personal popularity with Republicans throughout the nation. Some of the men closest to Nixon were infuriated by this. The Vice President was supposed to play a supporting role, never take center stage.

Agnew believed John Ehrlichman was the one responsible for isolating him from the White House and the President. To prove his theory, he described events just prior to and following the Des Moines speech.

The annual Washington Gridiron Dinner is a no-holds-barred affair. The roasting of public figures by the reporters is supposed to be offered with good humor, but the attacks can be bitter, scurrilous, and oftentimes gross exaggerations of the truth.

Ehrlichman had told Agnew that President Nixon wanted him to attend the Gridiron Dinner scheduled shortly after the Des Moines speech. "They wanted me to be the sacrificial lamb," Agnew said. "I knew I would be the target of a lot of criticism. I didn't want to go. I told Ehrlichman that if the President wanted me to go to the Gridiron Dinner, the President would have to ask me personally."

About a week later Nixon did call Agnew from Camp David.

They had a long conversation. The Gridiron Dinner was not mentioned. Agnew concluded he wouldn't be required to attend. On the morning of the day the dinner was to take place, the Vice President received a handwritten note from Nixon telling him he was to represent the administration at the Gridiron affair.

All of this may seem very petty, and in truth it was; but it strengthened my growing impression the President was permitting himself to be isolated. If Agnew's discontent became public knowledge, it not only would rock the boat, it might sink the ship.

CHAPTER 28

The China Trip

As Congress reconvened in January 1972, we were entering the twelfth year of the war in Vietnam. More than 40,000 Americans had died in a war the civilian policy makers had forbidden the military to win. Nixon had been President for three years. He had reduced the American troop strength in Vietnam from a high of 543,000 to less than 70,000, but there had been no real progress at the peace table in Paris.

On Wednesday morning, January 26, President Nixon summoned the Republican leadership to attend a special, confidential briefing on the progress of the war. We were told the negotiations in Paris were going nowhere. Hanoi appeared to be confident it could turn the people against the President. Nixon said every time a Fulbright or a Church or a Kennedy criticized our position in Vietnam the Paris negotiators took advantage of it.

We learned that Henry Kissinger had made thirteen visits to Paris to meet with Hanoi's negotiators. All his trips had been carried out in secret. The news media had been completely fooled.

Nixon said Hanoi was still demanding we pull out of Vietnam and turn the country over to the Communists. This he would not do. But he said the opposition in Congress to the war was making things very difficult. It was preventing him from taking any positive steps in either Paris or Vietnam. He said the war powers legislation passed by the Congress had dangerously restricted his ability as Commander in Chief to move toward a satisfactory solution of the conflict.

I felt compelled to point out to the President that when Senator Clark of Iowa and Senator Church of Idaho had first proposed this legislation, only Secretary Rogers and I had testified against it. I said then I thought the legislation unconstitutional. "From what you have told us this morning, Mr. President," I said, "it is apparent these restrictions on the authority of the Commander in Chief have been of great benefit to our enemies." The President replied, saying he hoped that someday a more knowledgeable Congress would correct this error.

I was asked to report on my recent trip to Vietnam. I said that in my view the troop withdrawals had not lessened our ability to defeat the North Vietnamese. We had sufficient ground strength to protect our bases, and I thought an all-out bombing of the north, coupled with the closing of the harbor of Haiphong, would force Hanoi to accept a reasonable settlement. The President was unwilling to do this in advance of his trip to Peking.

On February 17 I went back to the White House to hear the President, Secretary Rogers, and Dr. Kissinger tell us what they hoped to achieve in China. The presidential party was scheduled to depart Andrews Air Force Base at ten-thirty that morning.

Secretary Rogers spoke at length on the importance of the Pacific perimeter to American policy objectives. He said world peace would depend to a large extent on the development of cordial commercial and diplomatic relations between the nations of the Pacific—a proposition I had long accepted as fact.

Rogers reported our allies in this theater—South Korea, the Philippines, Molucca, Thailand, Japan, Australia, and Taiwan—had reacted adversely to the announcement of the President's trip when it was made in July. He maintained that since that date our diplomatic representatives had persuaded leaders of these nations to accept the mission as an effort to further peace and establish goodwill. Rogers said we hoped to open trade with China on much the same basis as we now traded with Russia. He stated categorically we would not establish diplomatic relations with the People's Republic of China now or in the future.

When Nixon spoke, he repeated this pledge. He said there was no agenda; the representatives of the United States had nothing more specific in mind than to open the door to establish a dialogue. And he said that despite the action of the United Nations, we would continue to support the right of the people of Taiwan to remain independent of the mainland.

In my view, most of us at that briefing believed the President's visit might benefit the cause of peace. I could see no harm in talking with our enemies so long as the President and his party recognized the Red Chinese as enemies of both peace and freedom.

There was extensive media coverage of the President's visit. On February 28 the People's Republic of China and the United States of America issued a joint communiqué. The White House called to ask me to comment favorably. This I refused to do. I did say I would withhold comment until the President returned and we could learn the full details.

On February 29 I went again to the White House. President Nixon talked for almost thirty minutes describing his impressions of Chou En-lai and Mao Tse-tung. The only other American present at their private meeting was Dr. Henry Kissinger. Nixon quickly explained that excluding the American Secretary of State Rogers did not in any way downgrade the importance of the Secretary's official position. It was, he said, all in keeping with Chinese protocol, in which the Secretary of State occupies the seventh position in the hierarchical structure. Afterward those of us who had been aware of the power struggle between Nixon's Secretary of State and his National Security Chief concluded Kissinger had won.

The language in the official communiqué, which caused me grave concern, expressed mainland China's adamant insistence that Taiwan is a part of China, declaring:

> The government of the People's Republic of China is the sole legal government of China. Taiwan is a province of China which has long been returned to the motherland. The liberation of Taiwan is China's internal affair in which no other country has the right to interfere and all U.S. forces and military installations must be withdrawn from Taiwan.

In the U.S. part of the communiqué we said:

> The United States acknowledges that all Chinese on either side of the Taiwan Strait maintain there is but one

China and that Taiwan is a part of China. *The United States government does not challenge this position.* It reaffirms its interest in the peaceful settlement of the Taiwan question by the Chinese themselves. With this prospect in mind it affirms the ultimate objective of the withdrawal of all U.S. forces and military installations from Taiwan. In the meantime, it will progressively reduce its forces and military installations on Taiwan as the tension in the area diminishes.

A number of American newspapers had interpreted this part of the communiqué as an indication the Nixon administration was prepared to abandon Taiwan in an effort to improve relations with the mainland. The President angrily denounced this construction. He told us he had released a statement to the press in Shanghai declaring we would maintain and respect all our treaties with Taiwan.

Nixon said Mao and Chou clearly understood all this and had not insisted we change our policy. Then he emphasized what he thought were the four important areas of agreement in principle with the Red Chinese. He complained the press had overlooked or failed to understand these most important parts of the joint communiqué, wherein the two sides had agreed on the following:

1. Progress toward the normalization of relations between China and the United States is in the interest of all countries.
2. Both wish to reduce the danger of international military conflict.
3. Neither should seek hegemony in the Asia Pacific region and each is opposed to efforts by any other country or group of countries to establish such hegemony.
4. Neither is prepared to negotiate on behalf of any third party or to enter into agreements or understandings with the other directed at other states.

The President told us preparations of the communiqué had required hours of negotiation by Dr. Kissinger. He said the Chinese quibbled endlessly over almost every word and sentence.

Dr. Kissinger commented that he thought the leaders of China would have the same problem with the communiqué in their country as the leaders of the United States were having here. Then he looked at me and said, "I can see Chou En-lai with his Chinese Goldwaters having the same trouble the President is having with Barry right now."

I couldn't give full faith and credit to the claim that the Red Chinese were sincere in their renunciation of a desire to dominate the Asia Pacific area. True, they were not yet a world power. They might not become one until the twenty-first century. But we knew Red China had built a road across northern Thailand to the Burmese border. We had reason to believe Red Chinese agents were active in India, in the Philippines, in most of Southeast Asia. They had supported and supplied the subversive effort to take over Malaysia—an enterprise which had been frustrated by the British.

At that White House briefing Nixon told us the Red Chinese leaders paid very close attention to what was being said on the floor of the House and the Senate of the United States. He said they interpreted some of the remarks of the members of Congress who were opposed to the Vietnam War as an indication of a "weakening of America's will."

Secretary Rogers spoke briefly about the Red Chinese contention that Taiwan was a part of China. He reminded us Nationalist China held the same view and had never abandoned hope of returning to the mainland to reestablish a Chinese republic.

It was perhaps the longest and most detailed briefing I had ever experienced at the White House. The suggestion was made that the President should go on television to clarify the communiqué. Nixon opposed this and was supported by Rogers and Kissinger. The President said one of the purposes of the briefing was to enable those of us who were in attendance to make clarification if any clarification were necessary.

When I returned to my office, I dictated a lengthy memorandum covering as completely as I could everything which had been said that morning. I also explored the options open to me. Should I criticize and question the language of the communiqué? Was I duty-bound to support the President? I have learned, when confronted with a dilemma such as I faced that day, it is useful to put my thoughts down on paper.

The report I wrote to myself covered more than ten typed pages. My first inclination was to refuse comment. "If I am pressed, I will have to say I support the President and the language of the communiqué. If I speak favorably, my conservative friends will accuse me of having abandoned Nationalist China. This is not true, and I must not let anyone gain that impression." My memo to the Alpha File concludes with these words: "To sum it up, if I cannot believe my President, then I have lost all my faith in men and friends and in my leadership."

In the light of subsequent events I may have reached a wrong decision. Whatever the true intentions of Richard Nixon in respect to Taiwan, the China communiqué became the basis for President Carter's recognition of the Red Chinese government. Its existence provided Carter with an excuse to withdraw recognition of Nationalist China and abrogate our mutual defense treaty.

At the time both Nixon and Kissinger assured me this would never happen. In December 1978, when Carter made his surprise announcement recognizing Red China and repudiating our defense treaty with Taiwan, both Nixon and Kissinger supported the Carter decision.

CHAPTER 29

No Substitute for Victory

Reelection politics figured prominently in every discussion I had with the President between 1969 and midsummer 1972. If Nixon didn't bring up the subject, one of his associates would. The political impact of Nixon's China trip was considered by the White House as important as the diplomatic results.

CRP—the Committee to Re-elect the President—was an exclusive White House operation. There was very little consultation with the Republican members of Congress or the Republican National Committee. I understood and sympathized with the reasons for this. Nixon was determined to avoid the errors committed in 1968. His desire to win big in 1972 was almost an obsession. Although he was in no way responsible for the Vietnam War, he had become the target of the antiwar movement. The potential challengers of the Democratic party—Senators Henry Jackson of Washington, Edmund Muskie of Maine, and George McGovern of South Dakota—adopted diverse strategies in their pursuit of the nomination. Hubert Humphrey of Minnesota was eager to try again, but his announced availability produced no more than a lukewarm response from McGovern activists who had taken charge of the Democratic party machinery. Their strength was the intensity of the antiwar feeling. But in addition to stopping the war, they were committed to a restructure of the American society and our economic system.

Much has been written to suggest that Haldeman and Ehrlichman were responsible for the excesses committed by CRP. It is true they staffed the committee with their personal representatives.

I am sure the White House hoped the public would accept the Committee to Re-elect the President as a campaign group operating under the authority of the President but separated from the White House. It is difficult for me to believe President Nixon was not fully aware of every decision, every activity, every move by CRP. In 1960 and again in 1968 candidate Nixon had been his own campaign manager, more than the other presidential candidates of my acquaintance.

This appraisal is supported by my knowledge of one of the President's very early activities in connection with his reelection. In early fall 1971, the President authorized Dick Kleindienst to approach my longtime associate Steve Shadegg. The President wanted Shadegg to take charge of the delegate hunt—to contact the delegates to the 1972 Republican Nominating Convention as they were selected and secure their commitment to vote for Nixon.

Shadegg told Kleindienst the suggestion was preposterous, totally unnecessary. He said convention delegates would never deny the nomination for a second term to a Republican incumbent President.

The first allegations of impropriety on the part of the Nixon administration were made in March 1972 by Washington newspaper columnist Jack Anderson, who claimed that the International Telephone and Telegraph Corporation had contributed $50,000 to the Republican party in return for favorable settlement of an antitrust suit. The allegations were based on a memorandum Anderson said was written by Dita Beard, an ITT lobbyist.

The Republican National Committee had selected San Diego, California, as the site of the 1972 convention. My friend Richard Herman of Nebraska was in charge of the arrangements. In order to host the convention, the city had agreed to construct a number of temporary facilities to augment the limited space available in permanent installations.

ITT had indeed made a contribution, but the money was given to the city of San Diego to help defray the extra costs for the convention, not to the Republican National Committee. The antitrust settlement in question had actually forced ITT to divest itself of some valuable profit-making insurance companies and Avis Rent-A-Car. The businesses ITT had been forced to sell represented about $1 billion in annual sales. The contribution had been urged by the Sheraton Division of ITT, which was about to open a new hotel in San Diego. It wanted its new inn to enjoy the prestige and publicity which would flow from its serving as the Nixon presidential campaign headquarters during the convention.

Attorney General Richard Kleindienst, who had just been confirmed by the Senate, replacing John Mitchell, now nominal head of CRP, called for a new hearing. He said he wanted to "defend his honor."

I don't know whether Richard Nixon had anything to do with this decision or not. Kleindienst is a stubborn Dutchman. He had done nothing wrong. In his anger he wanted a podium so he could lash back at his accuser. It was a tactical blunder.

The liberals on the Senate committee, especially Teddy Kennedy, Birch Bayh, and John Tunney, cleverly exploited this opportunity. They gave national publicity to any witness who wanted to attack the Nixon administration. Kleindienst was accustomed to operating in a court of law. This was a Senate committee hearing, a kangaroo court, with the supposedly impartial investigators conducting the prosecution.

John Mitchell's former law firm, of which Richard Nixon had been a member, had once represented a subsidiary of ITT. Mitchell, quite properly, had disqualified himself from the Justice Department case.

Kleindienst had forced a good settlement, or at least one which punished ITT severely. At the hearings it came out that President Nixon had called Kleindienst once to tell him not to pursue the ITT suit any further. Kleindienst refused and complained to Mitchell about the President's interference. Ultimately the Justice Department officials in charge of prosecuting the case decided the proposed appeal was without merit. Settlement was accepted.

The press and the TV ignored the magnitude of the penalties imposed on ITT and dwelt upon the alleged impropriety of the President and the Dita Beard ITT memo. Richard Herman, who had never been very enthusiastic about San Diego, concluded it would be impossible to provide necessary security and moved the convention to Miami Beach.

John Mitchell was exhausted by the ITT hearings. He was having domestic problems. Nixon accepted Mitchell's resignation as chairman of CRP and appointed White House troubleshooter Clark MacGregor to serve in his place. When the first stories of the break-in at the Watergate on June 17 appeared in the press, John Mitchell denied there was any connection between CRP and the burglary. The White House, through press secretary Ron Ziegler, called it a third-rate attempt.

I couldn't believe Nixon or Mitchell or any experienced political operator would have sanctioned such an unproductive, unnecessary move. The perpetrators had been excruciatingly clumsy. Even when James W. McCord, Jr., who had been arrested at the Watergate, was identified as an employee of CRP, I still accepted the White House disclaimer. I should have been more suspicious.

In July the President called me to the White House to discuss his plans for the campaign. By this time it was apparent the Democrats would nominate George McGovern. I told Nixon all he had to do was stay in the White House, be presidential, and pursue an honorable peace in Vietnam. He said his committee would be in touch with me about my role at the convention.

Earlier in the year I had informed National Party Chairman Bob Dole that I wasn't planning to go to the convention or take any part in it unless I was personally asked to do so by the White House. Less than ten days before the convention was scheduled to open, the White House did call to ask me to make one of the opening speeches. They suggested I should pay tribute to the members of Congress who had passed away since the 1968 convention and promised to send over a list of the deceased.

I remarked to my secretary, Judy Eisenhower, that necrology was the proper slot for an old has-been. When the list was delivered, I discovered there were more Democrats than Republicans, with a total of about forty. And I could imagine the reaction of the delegates to a speech dwelling on that number of departed Congressmen.

I called the White House to say I wouldn't make such a speech. I was told to pick my own subject, that I would be on the program at eight-thirty Monday evening, the opening night.

We started work on the text of the message I wanted to deliver. A day or so later Bill Timmons of the White House staff called to tell me it had been decided I would speak on Tuesday, not

Monday. I told Bill I had planned to leave Miami Tuesday morning. It was Monday night or nothing. He then asked for an advance copy of my remarks. I promised to send him one as soon as I had finished writing the speech.

On the Friday before the convention was scheduled to open, I had to fly to Nellis Air Force Base in Nevada, from there to Edwards in California, and back to Palm Springs to meet commitments made earlier. I flew back to Washington Sunday morning. Pat Buchanan of the White House staff called to ask me to change two or three words in the text. I had no objection. But my staff had discovered there was nothing in the Republican convention program to indicate my appearance. There had been no press releases from convention headquarters or from the White House. It was difficult to imagine why.

We flew down to Miami Monday afternoon. It was then I discovered the President was scheduled to arrive Tuesday evening at about the time Timmons had wanted me to make my speech. It was apparent they wanted to change the time of my appearance because Nixon's arrival would claim the full attention of the press and the television people. There would be little coverage of whatever went on at the convention.

We checked in at the Hotel Algiers. Fred LaRue, who had worked on my campaign in 1964 and was now assigned to CRP, came over to ask me to make major changes in the text. LaRue wanted me to cut out any reference to the deserters and draft dodgers and to former Attorney General Ramsey Clark.

This conversation took place in the bathroom while I was being made up for the lights and cameras at the convention. I told LaRue I wouldn't change the speech. I said if he insisted, I would just go back to Washington.

I delivered my prepared remarks in their entirety. CBS commentator Walter Cronkite noted my reference to the draft dodgers and Ramsey Clark produced the greatest audience response. He also said my appearance had been unexpected and unannounced.

I don't recall seeing the President again until after the election, but in September and October I made a dozen appearances on behalf of the national ticket. On November 22 I went to Camp David in response to a special invitation from the President. I flew out from Andrews in one of the White House helicopters. It was snowing and cold. After a short wait in one of the small guest cabins I was driven to the main lodge.

The President's manservant, Manuel, an old friend of mine, greeted me warmly and ushered me into a very comfortable room. There was a roaring open fire. The President was alone. We sat down facing each other across a small coffee table. White House photographer Ollie Watkins came in to make some pictures.

When we were alone, Nixon opened the discussion by telling me Nelson Rockefeller had come to see him. He didn't want the people to get the impression he was talking only with the liberals, so he had asked me to come up. Would I mind if his staff sent out the publicity and the pictures?

Nixon asked me what I thought he ought to do now. He had a mandate from the people—47 million votes to 29 million for McGovern; 520 votes in the electoral college to 17 for McGovern, the biggest electoral college win since Franklin Roosevelt defeated Alfred Landon in 1936.

Nixon said now the election was out of the way he intended to concentrate on solving the country's problems. He was going to reduce the cost and size of the federal government. He wanted the states to have more authority. And he was going to force the North Vietnamese to the peace table.

I told him I thought he had the greatest opportunity of any President elected in my lifetime. I reminded him of what I had said earlier, that if he didn't take hold of the government by May 1973, he would never make it. I told him this didn't mean firing everybody or anybody. We both knew civil service tenure was a problem. But I said he could transfer those in third- and fourth-line policy positions who opposed him. I said that if we went to Mike Mansfield, I believed we could enlist the support of the Democrats to make the upper-echelon government employees subject to presidential appointment and removal. Nixon said he intended to retain Bill Rogers as Secretary of State for a while, even though he had concluded Rogers didn't have the guts to get rid of people.

Nixon talked about John Connally of Texas. He said the former Democratic governor was about to switch registration. Once this was done he intended to give Connally an important post in the administration. He indicated he thought John Connally would make an excellent Republican candidate for President in 1976. Nixon told me he had offered Nelson Rockefeller the appointment as Secretary of Defense and the governor had refused.

My notes for the Alpha File on this meeting run thirteen pages. We covered the Pentagon. I pointed out we had four tactical air forces—Army, Navy, Air Force, and Marine: four services doing the job one could do. I said this produced competition in procurement and resulted in considerable waste because each air arm insisted on having its own specialized aircraft to duplicate what some other air arm was doing.

Nixon mentioned the waste in the three intelligence-gathering services—the FBI, the CIA, and the USIA. The President told me he was going to appoint CIA Chief Dick Helms Ambassador to Iran and name James R. Schlesinger, then Chairman of the Atomic Energy Commission, as his replacement.

We discussed the communications systems maintained by the Army, the Navy, and the Air Force. I pointed out that at one time the three service groups had used compatible frequencies. This was no longer so. I deplored the duplication. It seemed to me the system might operate to prevent proper cooperation between the military branches in time of crisis.

In the course of our conversation, which lasted more than an hour, I told the President I was inclined toward not running for reelection to the Senate. Nixon said if I did retire, I should think about taking a diplomatic post. We talked about Mexico. The President said, "It is yours if you want it for two years." I came away from Camp David convinced the second Nixon administration would be vastly different from the first.

On December 18 the President ordered heavy bombing of North Vietnam and the mining of Haiphong Harbor. After twelve days of this heavy aerial bombardment the North Vietnamese informed the President they were ready for peace and petitioned for a reopening of the Paris talks. Twenty-seven days later representatives of North and South Vietnam, the United States, and the Vietcong signed the treaty ending the longest war in U.S. history.

It is important to remember that by this time U.S. troop strength in South Vietnam had been reduced to a total of less than 50,000. Respected military men had opposed Secretary McNamara's decision to increase our ground strength in Vietnam. In military circles it had long been an accepted article of faith that to engage in a ground war in Asia would be suicidal for the West. For six years under Johnson and almost four years under Nixon we had refused to employ our superior air and naval forces. We had fought a no-win war.

In the twelve years of that conflict U.S. casualties totaled 260,024. More than 56,000 Americans died. Apologists for our earlier strategic policies can argue the North Vietnamese were as exhausted and war-weary as we were in December 1972.

When the U.S. policy makers decided to take advantage of our superior military capabilities, they brought the war to an end in approximately twelve days. It might have taken twelve weeks had we waged an all-out air and naval offensive earlier. It wouldn't have taken twelve years. There is small comfort for me in the recognition that those of us who urged an all-out drive to win the war were proved right.

In the aftermath of Vietnam we are confronted with a number of questions. It can be argued there was no compelling reason for our intervention in the first place, although the correctness of the domino theory is now established.

One conclusion is inescapable: Limited war is a brutal, reckless sacrifice of lives and treasures. Once hostilities commence there is no substitute for victory.

CHAPTER 30

The Beginning of the End

When some twenty-first-century Edward Gibbon writes the history of the decline and the fall of the American Republic, the year 1973 will emerge as the significantly critical period. If the lessons to be learned from this tragedy are ignored, 1973 may mark the beginning of the end of the constitutional Republic. What promised to be a period of great progress ended traumatically with the resignation of the Vice President of the United States.

Relying on the assurances the President had given me at Camp David, I had looked forward to a vigorous administration prepared to control the spendthrift policies of the Congress, reduce the bureaucracy, put an end to enlargement of the federal role, and restore a larger measure of sovereignty to the states.

In January the war in Southeast Asia was ended. If the terms of the Paris accords cannot be considered a victory for the free world, certainly they were not a defeat. They appeared to ensure the independence of South Vietnam. There were solemn assurances all American prisoners of war would be released. The integrity of Laos and Cambodia was recognized.

In my view Nixon had been at least four years late in his decision to employ our real strengths—air and sea power—against

Hanoi, but he had done it. The North Vietnamese had been forced into making concessions. Relations with Russia and China appeared to be improving, and as a Republican I took pride in the Nixon-Kissinger foreign policy moves.

To be sure, there was the problem of the Watergate. Along with many of my colleagues in the Senate, I accepted the White House denials of criminal complicity. I now realize I wanted to believe the President innocent. Even stronger than this partisan urge, my personal experience in prior political campaigns cloaked the whole affair in a perspective not available to the average citizen. In my view, the forced entry into the Democratic party headquarters had been pointless, its commission amateurish. The attempted bugging was an act of extreme naïveté.

I wasn't very shocked by the stories circulating in Washington. In 1958 my telephones had been bugged, my campaign disrupted. In 1972 the Nixon headquarters in Phoenix, Arizona, had been destroyed by arsonists. I could believe that some inexperienced, overeager supporter of the President had engineered the whole thing. Of course, I couldn't know the depth of the White House involvement.

I was puzzled by the President's failure to take the positive steps we had discussed at Camp David, and by mid-March I became alarmed. During this period I had no personal contact with the President, but at every opportunity I attempted to send messages to the White House urging action on the reforms Nixon had promised to initiate. I expressed my concern by Bryce Harlow, who assured me "things were moving." I talked with General Alexander Haig. Nothing happened.

In April I decided to make my discontent public. In an interview with Godfrey Sperling, Jr., of the *Christian Science Monitor* I called on the President to "speak up now and come out in the open and get rid of Watergate once and for all." I said, "It's beginning to smell like Teapot Dome."

I warned that if Watergate weren't settled, GOP candidates all over the country would be at a disadvantage in 1974. I pointed out the Republican National Committee was having difficulty raising money. I reiterated my belief that Nixon was not personally involved and cited as one of my reasons a conversation I had had with John Dean, who at one time had been a roommate of my son

Barry, Jr. I asked Dean if there was any truth to the allegations, and he told me, "No, not at all." It was a long interview, printed on Wednesday, April 11.

On April 30 Nixon went on national television to tell us he had accepted resignations from Bob Haldeman and John Ehrlichman. He had fired John Dean, Gordon Strachan had resigned his position with the USIA, and Richard Kleindienst was leaving the Attorney General's office because of his close personal relationships with some of those involved in Watergate. Nixon named Elliot Richardson the new Attorney General.

The news infuriated me. There was by this time a strong indication that both Ehrlichman and Haldeman had been deeply involved in Watergate.

John Dean told the press that if the White House tried to make him the scapegoat for Watergate, he would drag others down with him. This suggestion that he knew more than he had been telling was a direct contradiction of the assurances he had given me personally and privately. Strachan had been Haldeman's man on CRP. But Kleindienst had not been involved with Watergate or any other impropriety. The President had asked him to resign because of his closeness to John Mitchell, Bob Haldeman, Fred LaRue, and Herbert Kalmbach.

Kleindienst had played a major role in my campaign for the Republican nomination in 1964. He is an astute, experienced politician. Had anyone suggested such a caper as the Watergate to Kleindienst, he would have rejected it and probably announced his decision with some strong profanity and a contemptuous description of anyone stupid enough to suggest such a thing.

I knew Kleindienst had been considering resigning the AG's post in order to enter the private practice of law, where there was an opportunity for him to earn ten times his government salary. We had talked about this. Kleindienst recognized that his continuation as Attorney General created an embarrassing situation for the President and for those of his friends who were suspected of having participated in the Watergate. He didn't merit having his resignation announced in conjunction with the resignations of Haldeman, Ehrlichman, and Strachan and the firing of Dean. Kleindienst had been Nixon's strong supporter. He led the very earliest efforts to persuade Nixon to become a candidate in 1968.

He didn't deserve this cruelty at the hands of the man he had supported, befriended, and defended.

On May 16 I gave a second statement to the press. I said:

It is not easy for me to say this about my country or my President, but I think the time has come when someone must say to both of them, "Let's get going." We are witnessing the loss of confidence in America's ability to govern, we are watching the price of gold go to disastrous heights and having an equally bad effect upon our stock market.

Events at the Pentagon, which is the seat of our ability and responsibility to maintain peace in this world, leave the impression that the Services are suffering... suffering from a lack of civilian direction because of the vacancies not yet filled at the secretariat levels.

In that press release I urged the President to give the country the leadership it needed. I said the questions about Watergate must be answered, but there were more important things.

To my mind the administration appeared to be caught in the grip of some insidious paralysis. In fact, it was, but none of us on Capitol Hill had any indication of the magnitude of the problem.

On May 17, following the release of my statement, I was called to the phone by General Haig. He told me the President was concerned and interested in my press comments. He said he didn't know how the President could act more vigorously because of the Watergate affair. I told him the majority of Americans in my opinion did not associate Mr. Nixon in a guilty way with Watergate, that he should be out in front leading the people.

I pointed out to Haig Nixon's failure to replace the loyalist Kennedy-Johnson Democrats in sensitive policy-making positions with Republicans. There were, I said, a number of vacancies begging to be filled. "It is the second-, third-, and fourth-echelon administrators who operate the federal machine. The President's promised reforms could never be accomplished until we had a lower-level team in government committed to those reforms." He admitted the truth of the charge and said they were getting to work on it.

I reminded Haig of the great slowdown in the reorganization programs Nixon had promised. He admitted this and assured me the President was going to act.

I told him I had been prompted to make the press release and talk to the *Monitor* because of the reaction I was getting from Republicans throughout the country. Haig promised there would be prompt action. Again nothing happened.

On June 20 I sent the President a long letter. This is the way it started:

> Dear Mr. President,
>   Frankly, I think this letter should start out as Dear Dick, because I am writing it myself as you will quickly detect. I'm writing it on my little portable typewriter because I don't want anyone but you to read what I have to tell you. I am doing this, in my opinion, in the best interest of yourself, the office of the presidency and, I think most importantly, the country. And to quite an extent, the Republican party.
>
>   I want you to understand that what I am saying to you comes right from the heart, comes from years of friendship, and comes from a very deep devotion to everything you and I have believed in. You may be angry with me for saying these things, but I have never been one to hold back when I think words are needed, and I think they are needed at this particular point.

In the rest of the letter I urged the President to end his preoccupation with the Watergate problem, come out of the shell into which he had retreated, meet with the members of Congress and push the reforms he had promised to make at our Camp David meeting. I pointed out we were threatened with a fuel shortage—this was long before the Arab boycott. I reminded Nixon he had promised to reorganize the State Department. I praised him for his foreign accomplishments and concluded with a pledge of my continuing support.

Five weeks after I sent that personally typed letter to the White House, Bryce Harlow called to say the President would like to see me the next day. I arrived shortly after 2:00 P.M. and was taken to Harlow's office.

Bryce started the conversation by asking me what I thought the President should do now. As directly and succinctly as I could put it, I said the President's handling of the tapes had been stupid. I didn't agree entirely, but a great many Republicans were beginning to question the President's veracity. He had remained aloof and not consulted the party leaders. I believed he should appear as a volunteer witness before the Ervin committee. Harlow was greatly disturbed. He protested the President's innocence.

I suggested he talk with other party leaders. I said Nixon might be allowed to finish his term—there was already talk of impeachment—but he would be an impotent President, a rejected party leader. I said he should go to the Ervin committee immediately, before the recess. "You can tell the President what I have said, or I will tell him myself." Harlow said he would relay the message.

In August I was vacationing in Newport Beach when I received an invitation from Dr. Henry Kissinger please to come up to San Clemente for a visit. Nine days earlier the President had accepted Bill Rogers's resignation and named Kissinger Secretary of State. This nine-month delay—Nixon had told me in November he planned this change—is a good indication of how the worms of Watergate paralyzed the administration.

Kissinger told me he was determined to take charge of the State Department, which he said was being operated by a tight, small group of career foreign service officers. He was worried over the possibilities of a confrontation with the members of the Senate Foreign Relations Committee.

We discussed Watergate briefly. It was Kissinger's opinion the President had suffered almost irreparable damage but would probably survive. I said he would if he now took hold of the government and began doing the things he had promised me he would do. I told Henry that Nixon had said in November 1972 he intended to make a change in the State Department and was just getting around to it nine months later.

We talked of politics. Kissinger thought Nixon hoped to name his successor. "An aspiration common to all sitting Presidents," I said.

Kissinger told me Nixon favored either John Connally of Texas or Nelson Rockefeller. There was, he said, always the possibility that Ronald Reagan would run. But I gathered that if he did so, he wouldn't have Nixon's support. Apparently Reagan's abortive attempt in 1968 had never been forgiven. Chuck Percy of Illinois, a possible contender, was totally unacceptable to Kissinger and to the President.

We moved from politics to the future. Kissinger was convinced that if the United States continued to weaken itself militarily and economically, the next President would be challenged by the Soviets. The new Secretary of State had a very clear understanding of our military capability. He was worried about inflation, the lack of productivity in the private sector, and believed the Soviets would probe until they discovered a real weakness. It might be a military confrontation. It might be another client war to test our resolution.

Kissinger pointed out the Soviets were not increasing their military strength in order to defend Russia. All their new systems were offensive weapons. He also expressed grave concern about those in the United States who were willing to disarm unilaterally. He said a weakened United States would be isolated in the world, much as we were in the 1920s and 1930s preceding World War II.

I told him of my personal disillusionment and frustration. I described how the Congress had changed and how the bureaucracy had increased. I told him the effective legislators were those bureaucrats who wrote the regulations published in the *Federal Registrar*.

I said, "The Congress considers a bill which is written not by the Senators or the members of the House, but by staff assistants. The bill has a noble, laudable objective, but the language is imprecise." I said what we were passing today was a declaration of intent, and then we authorized the bureaucrats to implement our intentions. Then I emphasized my great disappointment with Nixon's failure to take hold of the government, to shift the reigning bureaucrats, to reduce the spending, to abolish nonproductive programs, and to emphasize the harm overregulation was inflicting on our economy.

Kissinger admitted the validity of my complaint. He said he couldn't do anything about the other departments, but he promised there would be some beneficial changes at State.

Vice President Spiro T. Agnew may have been guilty of everything his accusers claimed. He pleaded no contest to a charge of income tax violation, paid a substantial fine, and resigned his office in disgrace. The circumstances preceding that resignation, the cast of characters involved, and the chronology of events all raise questions which have never been satisfactorily answered.

In response to an urgent invitation, I visited Vice President Agnew at his home in Kenwood on the night of Sunday, September 9. Commencing about May 1 there had been some heavy rumors floating around Washington of a Justice Department investigation of the Vice President.

Agnew told me the first information he had received about the investigation had come to him in a letter from his Maryland attorney, who had been told the United State Attorney in Maryland was questioning former political associates of the Vice President's. Agnew said his inquiries disclosed that President Nixon was fully informed, that the investigation had been prompted by Attorney General Elliot Richardson. Agnew said the allegations of his improper acts were coming from three or four Maryland businessmen, who were themselves being investigated by the Internal Revenue Service.

The Vice President's first act had been to seek an audience with President Nixon. This was denied. Subsequently General Haig and Bryce Harlow had come to him to suggest immediate resignation.

Agnew was puzzled and angry. He could not understand why the Attorney General had not contacted him personally, nor why Nixon had permitted the matter to go this far without any effort to discover Agnew's side of the story.

Ted said he had been told the Attorney General was about to take the case to the grand jury and ask for an indictment. He hadn't been able to learn the exact nature of the charges against him or the names of his accusers. He wanted to ask me what I thought of an idea he had of going to the Speaker of the House to ask for a hearing.

There was a precedent for this move. In 1824 John Quincy Adams had been elected President, and John C. Calhoun of South Carolina Vice President. In 1828 Andrew Jackson ran for President as the candidate of the newly formed Democratic party. John C. Calhoun was campaigning for Vice President on the same ticket. They both were elected. To my knowledge, this is the only time we ever had a President and a Vice President from the same state.

In the course of the campaign it was charged Calhoun had accepted bribes from a cement company. The Vice President immediately went to the House of Representatives to request the House to act in an investigative way to determine if the charges were true. If they were, impeachment proceedings should follow.

Agnew asked me if I thought it would be appropriate for him to go to Speaker Carl Albert firsthand and ask the House to take jurisdiction in the present matter. I found this an interesting proposal. Apparently the Attorney General or the IRS or both had offered immunity to the witnesses in return for their testimony against Agnew.

I suggested he go immediately to the Speaker of the House, that he take with him two Republican and two Democratic House members. I believed he should not tell the White House of his intention, just do it. Agnew thanked me for my sympathy and for the advice and indicated he intended to follow it.

On the way back to my apartment my mind was occupied with a number of questions. Why had I instinctively or intuitively told the Vice President not to tell the White House of his plans? Why had the President permitted his Attorney General to go after the Vice President? Why had no one in the administration asked Agnew his version of the alleged misconduct? I knew that Nixon didn't really like Agnew. This had been made plain in my recent discussion with Henry Kissinger, who didn't even mention the Vice President's name as a possible Republican candidate in 1976. If Nixon wanted either Rockefeller or John Connally nominated, Agnew's presence as Vice President might be a stumbling block.

I knew from my own experience in politics how easy it would be to inspire the kinds of charges being made against Agnew. Every politician must accept campaign contributions. The giver usually wants to hand the donation to the candidate in person. Before the passage of the present strict campaign regulations most of these donations were made in cash. No reports were required, and no records kept.

If the individuals who were now talking to the Attorney General had been in a position to make a contribution to Agnew, whether it was small or large, actually made or not, it would be their word against his word. If, by making charges against the Vice President, they could buy their way out of serious trouble with the IRS, this fact might have inspired their testimony. I have always put very little faith in the statement or claim of an individual who in return for talking about someone else gains immunity from prosecution. I dictated all these thoughts to the Alpha File, including a paragraph to indicate the move to get Ted Agnew might have originated close to the White House. It was representative of the same mentality which had spawned the Watergate.

On September 14 I met again with the Vice President at his request. He told me Nixon had asked him to resign and was making it impossible for him to go to the House of Representatives. Bryce Harlow and General Haig had informed him of the President's decision.

Agnew told me that as governor of Maryland and a candidate for office he had accepted political contributions. Some of the people who had helped him in his campaigns did do business with the state, but the Vice President said all the contributions were small. State contracts had been awarded on merit, and his predecessors in office had established the pattern.

Agnew still didn't know the identity of his accusers, but he had learned they were being granted immunity from more serious charges in return for their willingness to testify against him. He thought he could win acquittal even with the office of the President and the Attorney General against him. But he said a long trial would be a burden for the administration; he thought the press, the public, and perhaps some of the judges were in a vengeful mood because of Watergate. He told me he intended to resign.

I pointed out his resignation might not block prosecution, and if he did have to stand trial, he would be in a much stronger position as the sitting Vice President. He said he wouldn't resign until he had absolute guarantees there would be no prosecution.

That afternoon I flew to Phoenix. When I arrived, there was a message waiting for me. The White House was sending two staff members to Phoenix to brief me on the Agnew situation.

Late that evening Fred Buzhardt and Bryce Harlow came to my home. They told me the Attorney General would drop prosecution on the alleged bribe taking if the Vice President resigned and entered a plea of no contest to one charge of failure to pay income tax.

I thought the arrangement had some inherent drawbacks. It would certainly permit the public to think the White House had forced Agnew to resign with threats of prosecution on the alleged bribery charges. It seemed to me that if he had not taken bribes and they were honestly campaign contributions, he would certainly have no income tax liability. If he accepted the charge on the income violation, it would be construed as a tacit admission he had accepted the payments.

I also said it was well known that Nixon preferred Connally or Rockefeller as a Republican standard-bearer in 1976 and that if either one were appointed Vice-President, it would provoke a split in the party.

Harlow was very sensitive to the political implications. Buzhardt, the President's lawyer, was more concerned with getting rid of Agnew lest his continued presence complicate the President's personal problems with Watergate.

October was the month. Syria and Egypt attacked Israel. Russia provided substantial military supplies to the Arabs. Agnew resigned. The OPEC nations embargoed the shipment of oil to the United States. The Saturday Night Massacre focused the nation's attention on Watergate.

The White House canvassed Republican members of Congress, ostensibly seeking their recommendation for Agnew's replacement. We were asked to consider Connally, Rockefeller, Reagan, and Republican Minority Leader Jerry Ford. I learned Nixon was also asking advice from the Democratic members of the House and the Senate.

I indicated my personal choice would be George Bush, but I understood the complications. Jerry Ford was a highly respected member of Congress. The President might encounter great difficulty in securing the confirmation of Connally. He would be opposed by Democrats who resented his alignment with the Republicans and by the Republicans who thought of him as a Johnny-come-lately. I knew the conservatives in the party would oppose Rockefeller. Bush was an outsider. I think Nixon made a wise political choice when he selected Jerry Ford.

I have not been hesitant to complain about President Nixon's concentration on the Watergate charges and his resultant lack of attention to the affairs of government. But he deserved high credit for his conduct of very sensitive negotiations required as a result of the Yom Kippur War.

The President didn't hesitate. He assured Israel of additional support. He sent Henry Kissinger to Moscow with a stern note warning the Russians of our determination to protect the integrity of Israel. I believe a less skillful or less experienced President might have permitted the hostilities in the Middle East to escalate into a full-scale confrontation between the Soviets and the United States. The press and those who have spoken of this period have made Nixon's failures highly visible. In justice, his accomplishments should not be overlooked.

In this same October period the Congress adopted the War Powers Limitation Act—an ill-conceived piece of crippling legislation flowing out of the bitter aftermath of Vietnam. The principal supporters of this bill in the Senate were Frank Church of Idaho; Richard Clark of Iowa; and Jacob Javits of New York. The bill, Public Law 93-148, limits the war-making powers of the President by requiring congressional approval within sixty days of any presidential use of our military power. It impairs the power of the President to conduct foreign policy and is the first of a series of intrusions by the Senate on the traditional authority of the presidency.

We should remember it was the Congress which cut off supplies to Vietnam and thus opened the door to the complete takeover of that country by the North Vietnamese. In 1976 it was a similar bill authored by Clark of Iowa which prevented us from supplying troops to the anticommunist groups in the Angola conflict.

When President Nixon agreed to the appointment of a special prosecutor, operating under, but outside the Department of Justice, to investigate Watergate, it appeared to be a reasonable move. But when he accepted Archibald Cox as the director of this special effort, it was politically stupid. Cox, a respected member of the legal profession, was so ideologically identified with the liberal Kennedy wing and so obviously a partisan in his selection of staff as to prohibit any kind of an impartial, objective investigation.

There is no doubt in my mind at all that Cox took the job with the intention of destroying the President. Nixon had to fire him. Elliot Richardson resigned in a huff, and his deputy, William Ruckelshaus, followed suit. It gave every anti-Nixon journalist in the country an opportunity to attack Nixon. The stories they wrote were shrill, vengeful, and greatly exaggerated. After the firing of Cox, the possibility of determining the truth of Watergate was lost forever.

By December 1973 the country had reached the nadir of its disillusionment with the 1972 election and the Nixon domestic administration. Watergate had crippled the country. It had also crippled the President.

CHAPTER 31

Tell the Man to Quit

We left the Senate Office Building at 4:30 P.M. on Wednesday, August 7, 1974. The man in the rear seat with me was Hugh Doggett Scott, Jr., of Pennsylvania, the Republican Party's Minority Leader in the United States Senate. We were bound together by party, by common experience, and by the awesome burden of the mission which had been thrust upon us. The driver was instructed to take us to the White House for an audience with the President of the United States, a member of our party, a man for whom we both had campaigned on several occasions.

Ordinarily the trip from the Capitol to the White House takes less than thirty minutes, even in rush-hour traffic. It was a trip we had made many times before, individually and together. Never before in the history of the Republic, and I pray they never will have to again, had two members of the United States Senate made such a journey under such conditions.

Until the preceding Monday, August 5, I had believed the President when he said he had no prior knowledge of the break-in at the Watergate. I had been told by the President himself the newspaper accounts were exaggerated, overblown, an embarrassment which would soon fade from public view.

Between July 27 and July 30 the House Judiciary Committee had voted three articles of impeachment. The first one passed by a vote of 27 to 11; the second 28 to 10; the third 21 to 17. The Democrats held a clear majority in the House, but the vote had not been strictly on party lines. It appeared certain the President would be ordered to stand trial before the Senate of the United States.

On that Monday, August 5, 1974, Dean Burch, counselor to the President, telephoned from the White House and asked to see me around 4:00 P.M. We are the closest of friends. He had served as my administrative assistant and worked on my 1964 presidential campaign. I had named him national chairman of the Republican party. From the tone of his voice I realized something was wrong.

When Dean arrived, he appeared to be under great stress. His face was pale; his speech, almost mechanical. He had come to deliver an advance copy of a statement the President intended to release to the national press within the hour. Dean asked me to read the statement. I looked at it—two legal-size pages, single-spaced.

"What does he say?" I asked.

"He says he hasn't been telling us the truth."

I read the paper slowly. It was carefully worded, as self-serving as such an admission could possibly be. But the message was clear. The President admitted he had deceived the world about Watergate.

In the sixth paragraph the President said:

> In a formal written statement on May 22 of last year I said that shortly after the Watergate break-in I became concerned about the possibility that the FBI investigation might lead to the exposure either of unrelated covert activities of the CIA or of sensitive national security matters that the so-called "plumbers" unit in the White House have been working on, because of the CIA and "plumbers" connections of some of those involved. I, therefore, gave instructions that the FBI should be alerted to coordinate with the CIA and to insure that the investigation not expose these sensitive national security matters.

* * *

In the eighth paragraph the President said:

> The June 23 tapes clearly show, however, that at the
> time I gave those instructions I also discussed the political
> aspects of the situation, and that I was aware of the ad-
> vantage this course of action would have with respect to
> limiting possible public exposure of involvement by persons
> connected with the re-election.

It wasn't necessary for Dean to tell me this was as great a
surprise and shock to him as it was to me. We both had been taken
in by a man to whom we had given our trust.

I have been accused of having a short fuse, of shooting from
the hip, but at the moment my reaction was more sadness than
anger. We had been deceived and dishonored.

There was no sleep for me that Monday night. I have never
knowingly concealed or helped conceal the truth. Now I had been
made a party to the President's deception because I had believed
him and defended him. Up to this moment the charges emanating
from Watergate had severely wounded the President. It seemed
to me his belated admission made those wounds fatal. I knew that
in a matter of hours the press would come demanding a comment.

I told Peggy that I could not and would not defend the cover-
up. Perhaps I should have been outraged by the first reports of
the break-in at the Watergate. Yet our telephones had been bugged
in 1964, when I was running for the presidency. Our security had
been penetrated. The opposition appeared to possess some of the
details of our plans and strategies the minute a decision was made.

The Watergate affair had been so badly bungled it appeared
to some of us the perpetrators were asking for discovery. But to
my mind, the President's admitted deception disqualified him from
continuing to hold that office.

I asked Peggy if she thought I should withdraw as a candidate
for reelection to the United States Senate from Arizona in 1974,
announce that I was retiring from public life, and then go on
television to urge the President to resign. Peggy said to do that
would be running away and hiding, something she had never seen
me do in our almost forty years of life together.

I told her I wasn't thinking about Barry Goldwater. My concern
was for the nation, for the presidency, not the President. I knew

that unless public confidence could be restored in the form and institutions of the Republic, our almost 200 years of effort to create the mechanisms to recognize and preserve the freedom of the individual would be jeopardized.

Some time that night I found what was for me the only acceptable solution to the problem. Nixon would have to resign.

When I reached the office Tuesday morning Republican Party Chairman George Bush called to tell me he had been summoned to the White House to attend an emergency Cabinet meeting, the first in eighteen months. I have great respect for George Bush. When Ted Agnew was forced to resign from the office of Vice President, I urged Nixon to consider Bush as Agnew's replacement. He is an able, articulate, experienced man who has won elective office; he was young enough to be groomed as Nixon's successor.

I told George I didn't think we could get fifteen votes in the United States Senate supporting the President. "I will reserve my right to decide how to vote until the trial is over," I said, "but I will never again defend Richard Nixon, in public or in private."

There had been some speculation in the morning press and on the radio that it would be necessary for Goldwater to lead a delegation of Republicans in the Senate to request Nixon's resignation. Bush and I discussed this. I told him I hoped it wouldn't come to that. "Nixon is a realist. Surely he can see what a Senate trial would do to the country. After yesterday's statement he can't win. With an impotent President we would put this nation at the mercy of our enemies overseas. They are too determined and too shrewd to pass up such an opportunity."

Bush promised to let me know what happened at the White House, and I went on to a scheduled meeting of the Senate Space Committee. About eleven-fifteen that morning an aide brought me a note: General Alexander Haig and Dean Burch at the White House wanted me to call them immediately. It occurred to me that both would be in attendance at the Cabinet meeting.

I had been questioning the witness who was appearing before us. I got up and left the room without a word of apology or explanation. When I returned to the hearing, I tried to make amends for my rudeness. But I couldn't make public the reasons behind my emotional and mental stress.

When I reached the White House on the telephone, I was told General Haig couldn't be disturbed, that I should please hold on.

In a moment Dean Burch came on the line. He asked if I had settled on any course of action. I related my conversation with George Bush and suggested he tell General Haig or perhaps get Haig and Bush together after the Cabinet meeting.

Tuesday noon I went to the Republican Policy Committee luncheon. Vice President Ford was there on one of his infrequent visits. He told us what had transpired at the Cabinet meeting. He said Nixon had admitted deceiving all of us, and the country, about his knowledge of the Watergate affair. But he said the President had no intention of resigning.

There was a prolonged silence when Ford finished. I think some of the members may have been suspicious, may have believed the President hadn't been totally frank with us, but the bluntness of Ford's words were a shock. The Vice President left the meeting.

I told the members of the policy group I felt the President had taken advantage of our loyalty, that I for one would never again defend him, and that it was obvious to me that if he insisted on an impeachment trial, he would be convicted. I thought the best thing he could do for the nation would be to resign.

A number of the other Senators felt the same way. It was decided we would meet late that afternoon in Senator Scott's office to plan a definite course of action.

Just before the luncheon broke up, I received a telephone call from General Haig at the White House. The operator inadvertently said the general was in the Oval Office. There was a slight delay before General Haig came on the wire. I heard a little click just before Haig spoke. It was the kind of noise you hear when someone picks up an extension telephone.

Haig wanted to know what the Senate would do if there should be an impeachment trial. I told him I thought the President would be lucky if he got twelve votes. I said I would not defend the President. "I have been deceived by Richard Nixon for the last time. A majority of the Republicans in the Senate share my feelings."

Haig thanked me for being so direct and said he would get back to me later on. I will always believe Richard Nixon was listening in on an extension.

As the Minority Leader Senator Scott presided at the meeting later that afternoon. The Senators present were Norris Cotton of

New Hampshire, Wallace Bennett, of Utah, Bill Brock of Tennessee, John Tower of Texas, Jacob Javits of New York, and Robert Griffin of Michigan. We reviewed all the facts of the Watergate case as we knew them, in light of what Vice President Ford had told the Policy Committee. It was a solemn session. All of us had campaigned for Richard Nixon, not just in 1972 but in 1968 and 1960 and before that, when he was running for Vice President on the Eisenhower ticket. We had battled our Democratic colleagues in the Senate to enact legislation in support of Nixon's policies.

Other Presidents have been caught in deliberate untruths—Eisenhower over the U-2; Kennedy, the Cuban missile crisis; Johnson, concerning the conduct of the Vietnam War. These deceptions could be defended because they were in support of foreign policy objectives, essential to our national strategy in a time of crisis. It is utterly unthinkable to believe that a President of the United States or a Secretary of State can at all times and under any conditions reveal the full truth to the world. But the Watergate was a penny ante burglary, undertaken for purely political purposes.

All of us at that policy meeting believed that if Nixon had told the truth at the time, if he had condemned the overzealousness of his political operatives, the public would have accepted his explanation and forgiven him. Now it was too late. If an impeachment trial were held, we couldn't defend him. Knowing his guilt, we couldn't ask our colleagues to vote him innocent. We all were sworn to uphold the Constitution of the United States. Loyalty to country transcended loyalty to party. My colleagues commissioned me to call on the President to ask that he resign.

After the meeting I returned to my office and dictated the notes on which this account is based. Ben Bradlee of the Washington *Post* called to ask me if it were true that I had been deputized by Senators Scott, Cotton, Bennett, Brock, Tower, Javits, and Griffin to go to the White House and tell Nixon he should resign.

I told Bradlee I wouldn't answer his question. Then I said, "You know how stubborn Richard Nixon is. If you speculate that anyone is going to tell him to resign, he'll get his back up and refuse. If there's any kind of a story about what happened today or what might happen tomorrow, it will make it very difficult for me."

We talked about other things for a moment or two, and then Bradlee said there would be nothing in his newspaper about any request that the President resign. Because I have been critical of the press when, in my opinion, it deserved to be admonished, I am pleased to record that Ben Bradlee kept his promise.

Early Wednesday morning Dean Burch called to invite me to his home for lunch. He said General Haig was coming and that I should be sure to wear a suit.

August weather in Washington, D.C., is often sultry and uncomfortable. Dean knew I preferred to dress casually. I recognized his suggestion as a clear indication that something momentous would happen that day, something which might take me before the nation's TV cameras.

Over a delicious luncheon served by Dean's wife, Pat, General Haig reviewed the entire dismal situation. He told us the President wanted to do what would be best for the country. An impeachment trial might drag on for months, making headlines every day. Our enemies overseas would recognize that the federal government was paralyzed, incapable of action. The Senate would have no time to carry on its regular duties. The President would be an impotent Commander in Chief. If a crisis should develop, our defense capability would be severely limited.

Listening to Haig's recital, I wondered for a moment if there had been a bug in Senator Scott's office the previous afternoon. Of course, there wasn't. The President and his advisers had merely recognized reality.

I was in no mood to forgive Nixon for his past actions. I did believe, and I do believe, that in this his final hour of agony he was putting the welfare of the nation ahead of every other consideration.

Haig said the President wanted me to come to the White House that afternoon at five o'clock. Republican Representative John Rhodes of Arizona, Minority Leader of the House of Representatives, and Senator Hugh Scott had also been invited.

After lunch I returned to the Senate Office Building to confer with Senator Scott and Senator Griffin. They told me the press had already learned about the meeting. Radio and television reporters were speculating that Goldwater would demand Nixon resign.

Tuesday night NBC falsely reported that I had tried to gain

entrance to the White House and had been refused. About midafternoon Wednesday a reporter for ABC quoted me on national television as having said that Nixon would resign.

These news stories were totally without any foundation in fact. I protested to both networks. Of course, they claimed the information came from reliable sources. In the hysteria surrounding Watergate almost anyone from a janitor to a general was considered a reliable source if he gave a reporter some sensational statement.

When we arrived at the White House on Wednesday afternoon, Scott and I were taken to the office of the President's assistant Bill Timmons, where Congressman Rhodes was waiting for us. John Rhodes represents the First District of Arizona. He and I have campaigned together in election years since we were first elected to the Congress in 1952. My admiration for him is unqualified.

Hugh Scott served two terms in the House, commencing January 3, 1941; then he was defeated for reelection and became chairman of the Republican National Committee. In 1946 he won reelection to the House and was reelected each succeeding two years until 1958, when he ran for the Senate and was elected. Scott, being from a heavily industrialized, long-established eastern state, held views which were somewhat different from mine. But he is a loyal Republican.

When the President received us, he was fresh from having declared to the nation that he would not resign. He was serene, confident, cheerful. He acted as though he had just shot a hole in one. I had never seen him so relaxed. He put his feet on the desk and talked. He didn't mention resignation. He reminisced about the past, recalled how he and I had campaigned together for over twenty years. He made some complimentary remarks about President Lyndon Johnson. He spoke of his deep affection for Dwight Eisenhower. And then, almost casually, he asked me how things stood in the Senate. I told him he could count on about twelve votes, perhaps as many as fifteen. No more. And that it would take thirty-four votes to defeat the impeachment charges in the Senate.

John Rhodes told him the full House was certain to accept the report of the Judiciary Committee. "It won't be a party-line vote, Mr. President. We can't hold all the Republican members."

Senator Scott said the administration's support was rapidly being eroded. He pointed out that Ehrlichman, Kalmbach, Colson, Krogh, and Dean all had been convicted or pleaded guilty.

Throughout my years in public life I have always had reservations about Richard Nixon. Despite our long association, I never felt that I truly knew him. In the moments of tension and stress we shared, he always seemed to be too well programmed, to be carefully calculating the ultimate effect of everything he did or said.

A certain few vengeance seekers have criticized President Gerald Ford for the pardon he granted Nixon. Could they have been with us that afternoon in the White House, they would have understood how impossible it is to imagine a greater punishment than this man was preparing to accept. To be forced to resign from the nation's highest office—one moment the most powerful, respected leader in the world; the next, disgraced and discredited.

The magnitude of the situation brought tears to my eyes. The President knew what he must do. Thank God he did not require us to spell out the message we carried. When we left, he was smiling. Whatever else I may say or think about Richard Nixon, he displayed a quality of courage I have rarely encountered on that Wednesday afternoon.

Scott, Burch, Rhodes, and I returned to Bill Timmons's office to prepare our remarks for the press. It was decided that I would make a short opening statement, and then we would all answer questions.

I told the reporters we had been invited to the White House by the President to disclose to him the political climate in the House and the Senate relative to his situation. I said we were convinced the President intended to do what he believed best for the country, that no decision had been made, that we had made no suggestions.

The first question was to Senator Scott. "How do you evaluate the political climate?"

"The situation is very gloomy," the Senator replied.

I was asked, "Did any of you recommend the President resign?"

I was able to respond truthfully. "No, that subject didn't even come up."

Scott was asked if he thought the President would be impeached. Scott said, "I have made no assessment of that."

They wanted to know if the President had given any indication of when he would announce his decision. We replied, "That wasn't discussed."

We rode back to the Capitol together. Because the President had carefully avoided any discussion of resignation, we had been able to respond truthfully and openly to the reporters' questions. I was suddenly struck with the realization that of the three men who had been selected to carry out this never-before-and-I-hope-never-again mission, two of us were from the same small, remote western state.

It also occurred to me that if we had misjudged the President's intentions—if the President didn't resign—our failure to deal bluntly and openly would prove to be a very grievous error. We had chosen the easy, comfortable way. It might have been a mistake, an understandable, very human mistake, but my colleagues in the Senate might not see it that way. In the past, and many times since the first hint of Watergate, I had given Nixon the benefit of the doubt, and I had been disappointed. I wondered if judgment had been overruled by emotion.

When the Watergate scandal was first exposed, John Rhodes and I urged the President, in public and in private, to take the American people into his confidence. We had no knowledge of the event other than what we read in the newspapers. Nixon had won reelection by an overwhelming majority. The public appeared to approve his renewed negotiations with mainland China and with the Russians. Whatever had happened at Watergate, we told him, tell the truth, come clean. He had chosen to ignore our advice.

The results of that trip to the White House are now history. At 9:00 P.M., Eastern Daylight Time, on the evening of Thursday, August 8, 1974, Richard Nixon resigned the office of President of the United States. In the ninth paragraph of the prepared statement which the President read in a steady, deliberate fashion he spoke these words:

"Therefore, I shall resign the presidency, effective at noon tomorrow. Vice President Ford will be sworn in as President at that hour in this office."

CHAPTER 32

The Nonelected President

Public opinion, influenced, if not controlled, by the mass media, called three strikes on Jerry Ford before he came to the plate. He was the first nonelected President. He was asked to lead an administration which had been paralyzed by Watergate for almost two years. Then he chose, as the second nonelected Vice President, former Governor Nelson Rockefeller of New York.

The press and the partisan Democrats had tasted blood. They had driven the President of the United States from office. When the new President pardoned the former President, they had a new target. The lynch mob had put the noose around the neck of the man they hated. Ford stopped the hanging. It was an act of courage which should have endeared him to every citizen who loves the Republic. It didn't. Had Ford not blocked the avengers, they most certainly would have indicted and then prosecuted Richard Nixon, prolonging the Roman Holiday. Such a trial would have polarized the country, but in my opinion it would have made Jerry Ford an unbeatable candidate for reelection in 1976.

On August 11 I was invited to meet with President Ford at the White House to consider what he described as a "very serious problem of public policy." I was ushered into the Oval Office a little after 5:00 P.M. The President was alone. He offered me a glass of iced tea. He wanted to discuss the selection of a new Vice President. He said he valued my opinion. He thought it would reflect the thinking of the Republicans in the Senate. The President wanted someone experienced in government, capable of carrying on if something happened to him.

The President recognized there might be a problem with confirmation by the Senate. He wanted to choose someone who would be acceptable not only to the Senate but also to the country. He said he would welcome any suggestions I might offer, but he would prefer we discussed categories of choice rather than specific individuals.

I agreed it was important to name someone who would be acceptable to both the Senate and the country, that we needed someone who would be capable of handling the office of President if that became necessary—God forbid. I urged the President to be extremely careful in his travels and public appearances. I said, "The events have provoked extreme feelings." I reminded him there were organized terrorist groups who might very well attempt his assassination.

The President said he understood this. He wasn't going to become a prisoner of the office. He didn't intend to increase security measures. "If I do that now, it will only make matters worse," he said. "We both know they can kill the President, but I'm not going to let them destroy the presidency. That's one reason I must pick the proper person for Vice President and win quick confirmation." Whatever is said about President Gerald Ford, no one can question his courage.

I told the President I thought it was important to pick someone young enough to serve six years as Vice President and then be a potential candidate for the presidency. To my mind that ruled out anyone who was much over fifty.

The President asked me what I thought of appointing a black man. I said I had absolutely no racial prejudice. If he could find a competent man, I would support his choice, but I didn't think Senator Edward Brooke of Massachusetts properly represented either the blacks or the Republican party. He agreed with me.

We talked about the possibility of a woman. I said it would be a radical departure from tradition, but if he could find a highly qualified woman, I would have no objection.

The President thought that if he selected someone from the

Congress, it might be easier to gain prompt confirmation. He said he was sure this was the principal reason Nixon had named him.

I thought it was a good point, worthy of consideration, but I wasn't sure it would be wise to limit his selection to so narrow a field. Then he said that before he made up his mind, he would have to know if the person he selected would be willing to serve. He thought it would create some serious complications if he offered the job to someone and was turned down. We talked about the frustrations and disappointments of the Vice Presidents we had known over the years of our service in the Congress. Then he asked me if I would accept the vice presidency if it were offered.

I had to think about that before I answered. I told the President I was too old and I carried too many scars from the 1964 campaign. I said I could think of a number of younger men who would be more suitable. I told him the person he chose now should be someone who could add strength to the ticket in 1976.

Somehow the conversation switched to my recent knee surgery. I pulled up my trouser leg to show him the scar; then the President did likewise to show me the scar he carried as a result of an old football injury and surgery. It would have made a great memento for both of us had there been a photographer present—two political warriors displaying their wounds.

When I left, the reporters were waiting. I told them we had discussed the problems of the country, the future of the Republican party, and the miseries we shared from our faulty knees. I returned to my office and dictated my notes on the meeting. The President hadn't exactly offered to name me his Vice President. It had been a very iffy question. I hadn't exactly turned it down because it wasn't mine to turn down, but I was sure the President understood I thought he should pick a much younger man.

I wasn't at all pleased when President Ford decided to name Nelson Rockefeller. The former governor was acceptable to the eastern establishment and to the liberals of both parties. The Nixon haters were appeased because Rockefeller had opposed Nixon. He was automatically acceptable to the powerful internationalists who have controlled American foreign policy most of this century.

I didn't mount a campaign of opposition to Rockefeller's confirmation. I did make it clear to my friends in the White House and in the party I would do everything in my power to block his nomination on the Republican party ticket in 1976.

The ramifications of the Watergate scandal are incalculable. Specifically, the uncertainties created by this event compelled me to change my mind. I had concluded I would not be a candidate for reelection to the Senate in 1974, but the Republican party had been brought to its knees. Even before Nixon's resignation, it became obvious to me that unless I changed my mind, a Democrat would be elected to replace me. Subsequently, my friends in Congress and Republican leaders throughout the nation persuaded me I should seek reelection. I have a very clear understanding of the kind of idiotic self-adulation which sometimes leads men in public life to regard themselves as indispensable. Such a notion had no part in my decision.

I have detailed my bitter disillusionment with the Nixon administration. In his first term, my Republican President added fuel to the flames of inflation by increasing spending and increasing the federal debt. He did nothing to block enlargement of the federal establishment. To my mind, his experiment with wage and price controls had been a disaster. He had permitted the Vietnam War to drag on far longer than it should have. He had done nothing to strengthen the Republican party.

Between 1968 and 1974 budgeted federal spending increased by 53 percent. The federal debt increased by 37 percent. The purchasing power of the dollar decreased by 34 percent.

In 1968 candidate Richard Nixon encouraged the voters to believe that if he became President, the deficit-spending, big-government policies of the Kennedy-Johnson years would be drastically altered. The increase in budgeted federal spending had been almost as great over the six-year period Nixon was President as it had been for the eight years of Kennedy-Johnson. During the six years of Nixon, the increase in the federal debt was more than twice what it had been in the eight Kennedy-Johnson years. The decline in the purchasing power of the dollar was almost four times greater under Nixon than it had been under his two predecessors.

This summary might be used to support a charge that Richard Nixon, as President, was the greatest spender in history until the election of Jimmy Carter. The truth is the Congress orders the spending. Democrats have been in control of the Congress, without interruption, since 1955. The President recommends a budget. He can call for prudence and economy. He can use the veto as Gerald

Ford did fifty times. But the Congress has the last word.

I fault Richard Nixon for not being more vigorous, for not making greater use of the power of the White House to bring about the reforms he recognized as essential. But in the final analysis, the blame for inflation, for the increased national debt, for the steadily declining purchasing power of the dollar rests squarely on the Congress.

Throughout his public life, Gerald Ford had been more consistent in his support of prudent domestic fiscal policy than had Richard Nixon. He was committed to working for many of the reforms I have long advocated. As an interim President, he did bind up the nation's wounds. His critics have said he was too low-key. The TV cameras and the commentators unmercifully emphasized the times he physically stumbled in public—a result of his old injured knee. But Jerry Ford never stumbled in principle. He may have lacked charisma. His rhetoric didn't lift an audience out of their chairs. But he was steady. He was faithful. In my opinion, his only failing was the result of his long years in Congress, where he had been forced to accept compromise.

After Nelson Rockefeller's confirmation and into the spring of 1975, I kept after President Ford, urging him to take command, to oppose, to veto, if necessary, any increased spending. In March he came out on television supporting what I considered an inappropriate tax reduction bill. He said he wasn't going to veto it because he might get a worse bill in its place.

I wrote the President a personal letter. I told him we needed leadership, not compromise. I said someone should tell the American people the inevitable results of a $50 billion deficit two or three years in a row. I said, "When the federal government has to start borrowing money from the private sector for the deficits that are coming up, interest rates are going to mount again, building is going to stop, jobs are going to fall off, and we will be right back where we were in December and January."

I didn't expect my protest would change the President's course of action. But I did want him to understand I thought he was making some serious mistakes.

From time to time I was told by my friends close to the administration that President Ford was very anxious to improve his relationship with me. I sent word through Dean Burch that I wasn't opposed to the President personally. I simply disapproved of his willingness to temporize with the Congress, which I thought was committed to bankrupting the country.

Chiang Kai-shek, the leader of free China, died on April 5, 1975. The White House immediately announced we were sending Secretary of Agriculture Earl Butz to represent the United States at the funeral.

I like Earl Butz. I think he was a fine Cabinet officer. But I thought Chiang deserved better from the United States. I raised hell with the White House. I said that if the President wouldn't go, we certainly ought to send the Vice President. Everyone knew I intended to go.

After a little pulling and hauling—as I recall it now, it was about a week—President Ford announced he had decided to ask Vice President Rockefeller to go to Taipei to represent the United States.

I met Rockefeller in Hawaii. We made the rest of the trip together. He was friendly, warm, and most ingratiating. He made it clear to the Chinese on Taiwan that I was responsible for his being there.

Shortly after we returned home we both appeared before the United States Chamber of Commerce. Nelson said a great many kind things about me. In May *Time* magazine ran a picture of the two of us. Nelson had his arm around my shoulders, and the quote attributed to him was very complimentary to me.

It was all very slick and apparently spontaneous. But in the world of politics there is always a reason for everything. I think the White House first nominated Earl Butz because they knew I would object. Then in response to my protest they promptly named the Vice President as our representative. This brought us together on the trip and added materially to the impression that Goldwater and Rockefeller had resolved their differences.

I have been told by a great many insiders that it was my adamant opposition which kept Rockefeller off the ticket in 1976. If so, I am glad. Not because I harbor any resentment over the bitterness developed between us in 1964, but because I am certain the presence of Nelson Rockefeller as a Republican nominee for Vice President in 1976 would have split the party.

As it was, 1976 presented me with the most painful political dilemma of my public life. Jerry Ford was the incumbent Republican President. My dear friend Dean Burch was his closest ad-

viser. While I differed with the President on tactics, we were not
divided on objectives.

On the other hand, Ronald Reagan has been my friend for
many years. His strong support in 1964 is something I will always
cherish. I went to California early in 1968 to offer my support to
Ronald Reagan if he should decide to seek the presidential nomination that year. He had been reluctant to become an announced
candidate. He remained standing in the wings until it was too late
to challenge Nixon.

In 1975, on May 4, Governor Reagan and I had dinner at the
Madison Hotel in Washington. The governor wasn't ready to announce his candidacy. He was particularly interested in knowing
what I would do if Ford insisted on having Rockefeller as his
running mate.

I explained to Ron just how I thought the White House had
used the death of Chiang to create the impression that relations
had improved between me and the Vice President. The governor
didn't ask me if I would support him in the event he decided to
become a candidate. I wasn't sure then, and I'm not sure now,
that he had made up his mind.

Reagan did say we didn't need a third party or a new Republican
party. He thought what we needed was a restatement of fundamental facts of Republicanism which have kept this party together.
He said he thought we had lost elections because we lacked leadership, because the presence of such radical liberals as Jacob
Javits, Clifford Case, Charles Mathias, and others, all wearing the
Republican label, made it impossible for the voters to find any
significant differences between the two major parties. I agreed
with him. We parted on the friendliest of terms. Why then, did
I finally come out in support of Gerald Ford—an act which provoked a flood of bitter letters from many of my former friends?

There is a very simple answer. I believed the incumbent would
be a stronger candidate. I had seen some in-depth polls done by
an organization which in the past has always been right. The men
in charge of the Reagan campaign had never impressed me as
possessing any degree of political skill.

I was anguished and offended when the Democrats in Congress,
using trumped-up false evidence, forced Howard "Bo" Calloway
to resign as head of the Ford campaign. But this unprecedented,
vicious action helped to persuade me the Democrats were more

afraid of Ford than they were of Reagan.

Throughout the primaries that year both candidates made serious errors. Reagan, with his mild approach in New Hampshire and Florida, didn't show much steel until they got to Texas.

The California group advising Ford had handled the Rockefeller primary campaign in that state in 1964. They believed in waging a strong negative effort against an opponent. I thought an incumbent President seeking renomination should be confident and positive.

After the fierce contest for the nomination which climaxed in Kansas City, the loser, Ronald Reagan, generously and without reservation supported the winner, Gerald Ford, but his intensely partisan supporters were emotionally incapable of forgiving and forgetting. Either man would have made a splendid President. The Republicans have a positive talent for self-destruction.

When Gerald Ford agreed to debate candidate Jimmy Carter under the aegis of the League of Women Voters, it was a fatal blunder. And now the country suffers with an indecisive President who brings campaign gimmicks to problem solving. The President's proposals are so ill-advised they are rejected by the members of his own party in the Congress. His administration has been severely damaged by the scandalous failures of the men to whom he has given authority. The record is so incredibly bad I am compelled to suggest it all appears to have been planned.

CHAPTER 33

The Nonelected Rulers

Prior to World War I the people of the United States were preoccupied with internal growth. We were truly isolationists. It was George Washington who, in his Farewell Address, warned us to "keep free of entanglements with other nations." He said, "It is our true policy to steer clear of permanent alliances with any portion of the foreign world."

Until the First World War we were successful in remaining aloof from Europe's quarrels. In the community of nations we were more often debtor than creditor. Our population expanded. Our economic power increased. Under the free enterprise system industry expanded.

After World War I we could no longer remain isolationist. The changing times required us to become a participant in the world community of nations. Scholars turned their attention to foreign affairs. What was to become the American Council on Foreign Relations was organized in Paris in 1919 under the sponsorship of Colonel E. M. House, who had exerted much power in the Wilson administration. This nongovernmental private grouping attracted a variety of individuals who considered themselves to be, or desired to become, specialists in foreign affairs.

In its September 1, 1961 issue, the *Christian Science Monitor* described the Council on Foreign Relations as "probably one of the most influential, semipublic organizations in the field of foreign policy." The *Monitor* said, "The CFR is composed of 1,400 of the most elite names in the world of government, labor, business, finance, communication, the foundations, and the academies. It has staffed almost every key position of every administration since that of FDR."

In September 1939 two members of the Council on Foreign Relations, Hamilton Fish Armstrong and Walter H. Mallory, visited the U.S. State Department to offer the services of the council. They proposed to do research and make recommendations to the State Department without formal assignment or responsibility, particularly in four areas—security armaments, economic and financial problems, political problems, and territorial problems.

The Rockefeller Foundation agreed to finance the operation of this plan. From that day forward the Council on Foreign Relations has placed its members in policy-making positions with the federal government, not limited to the State Department.

Since 1944 every American Secretary of State, with the exception of James F. Byrnes, has been a member of the CFR. Almost without exception the members of the CFR are united by a congeniality of birth, economic status, and educational background.

A number of writers disturbed by the influential role this organization has played in determining foreign policy have concluded the Council on Foreign Relations and its members are an active part of the communist conspiracy for world domination. To support this construction, they cite the fact that since the end of World War II the free world, and the United States in particular, have suffered an unbroken string of defeats at the hands of world communism.

Their syllogistic argument goes something like this: The Council on Foreign Relations has dominated American foreign policy since 1945; all American policy decisions have resulted in losses to the communists; therefore, all members of the CFR are communist sympathizers.

Many of the policies advocated by the CFR have been damaging to the cause of freedom and particularly to the United States, but this is not because the members are communist or communist sympathizers. This explanation of our foreign policy reversals is too pat, too simplistic.

I believe the Council on Foreign Relations and its ancillary elitist groups are indifferent to communism. They have no ideological anchors. In their pursuit of a new world order they are prepared to deal without prejudice with a communist state, a socialist state, a democratic state, monarchy, oligarchy—it's all the same to them.

Rear Admiral Chester Ward, USN (Retd.), who was a member of the CFR for sixteen years, has written, "The most powerful clique in these elitist groups have one objective in common—they want to bring about the surrender of the sovereignty and the national independence of the United States." Their goal is to impose a benign stability on the quarreling family of nations through merger and consolidation. They see the elimination of national boundaries, the suppression of racial and ethnic loyalties as the most expeditious avenue to world peace. Their rationale rests exclusively on materialism. They believe economic competition is the root cause of international tension. This approach dismisses as insignificant the form of government or the political ideology expressed by that form.

It may be that if the CFR vision of the future could be realized, there would be a reduction in wars, a lessening of poverty, a more efficient utilization of the world's resources. To my mind, this would inevitably be accompanied by a loss in personal freedom of choice and the reestablishment of the restraints which provoked the American Revolution.

When we change Presidents, it is understood to mean the voters are ordering a change in national policy. Since 1945 three different Republicans have occupied the White House for a period of sixteen years. Four Democrats have held this most powerful post the world has to offer for a period of seventeen years. With the exception of the first seven years of the Eisenhower administration, there has been no appreciable change in foreign or domestic policy direction.

When a new President comes on board, there is a great turnover in personnel but no change in policy. Example: During the Nixon years Henry Kissinger, CFR member and Nelson Rockefeller's protégé, was in charge of foreign policy. When Jimmy Carter was elected, Kissinger was replaced by Zbigniew Brzezinski, CFR member and David Rockefeller's protégé.

Commencing in the thirties and continuing through World War

II, our official attitude toward the Far East reflected the thinking of the Institute of Pacific Relations. Men of the IPR were placed in important teaching positions. They dominated the Asian Affairs section of the State Department. IPR publications were standard reading material for the armed forces, in most American colleges, and were used in 1,300 public school systems. The IPR was behind the decision to cut off aid to Chiang Kai-shek unless he embraced the communists, and the CFR was the parent organization of the IPR.

In 1962 then Governor Nelson Rockefeller delivered a series of lectures at Harvard University on the future of federalism. In his presentation the governor dwelt at length on the interdependence of nations in the modern world, concluding with this statement: "And so the nation-state, standing alone, threatens in many ways to seem as anachronistic as the Greek city-state eventually became in ancient times."

Everything the governor said was true. We are dependent on other nations for raw materials and for markets. It is necessary to make defense alliances with other nations in order to balance the military power of those who would destroy us. Where I differ from the governor is in the suggestion implicit throughout the lectures that to achieve this new federalism, the United States must submerge its national identity and surrender substantial matters of sovereignty to a new political order.

The implications in Governor Rockefeller's presentation have become concrete proposals advanced by David Rockefeller's newest international cabal, the Trilateral Commission. Whereas the Council on Foreign Relations is distinctly national in membership, the Trilateral Commission is international. Representation is allocated equally to Western Europe, Japan, and the United States. It is intended to be the vehicle for multinational consolidation of the commercial and banking interests by seizing control of the political government of the United States.

Zbigniew Brzezinski and David Rockefeller screened and selected every individual who was invited to participate in shaping and administering the proposed new world order. In the late 1950s Brzezinski, an accepted member of the inner circle of academics, asserting the need for global strategies, was openly anticommunist. By 1964 Brzezinski had modified his criticism of communism. In the book *Political Power: USA-USSR*, Brzezinski and his coau-

thor, Professor Samuel P. Huntington, declare, "When Khrushchev came to power the labor camps were ended, suppression was
relaxed, writers and artists were given more freedom, and the
degree of slavery lessened materially." The recent testimony of
Alexander Solzhenitsyn demonstrates the inaccuracy of Brzezinski's conclusion.

In his book *Between Two Ages*, published in 1970 by Viking
Press, Brzezinski calls for an international community of Japan,
Western Europe, and the United States to supervise and guide the
underdeveloped nations of the world. He declares, "National sovereignty is no longer a viable concept." He calls for a rewriting
of the American Constitution. He condemns the existing federal
system of U.S. sovereign states as no longer necessary or adequate.

In his prospectus describing the Trilateral Commission David
Rockefeller said he intended to bring the best brains of the world
together to bear on the problems of the future. I find nothing
inherently sinister in this original proposal, although the name he
gave his new creation strikes me as both grandiose and presump-
tuous. The accepted definition of a "commission" is a group nominated by some higher authority to perform a specific function.
The trilateral organization created by David Rockefeller was a
surrogate—its members selected by Rockefeller, its purposes defined by Rockefeller, its funding supplied by Rockefeller.

Whether or not the approximately 200 individuals selected for
membership on the commission represent the "best brains in the
world" is an arguable proposition. Examination of the membership
roster establishes beyond question that all those invited to join
were members of the "power elite," enlisted with great skill and
a singleness of purpose from the banking, commercial, political,
and communications sectors.

Invitations were extended to the top executives of Caterpillar
Tractor, Texas Instruments, Exxon, Coca-Cola, Sears, Roebuck,
Shell, Fiat, Hitachi, Soni, and Toyota, among others. From the
world of banking Rockefeller selected representatives from the
Bank of America, Continental Illinois National Bank and Trust
Company, Wachovia Bank and Trust Company, Brown Brothers,
Harriman and Company, Barclay's Bank, and the Bank of Tokyo.
Media support was guaranteed by including the editorial director
of the Chicago *Sun-Times*; the editor in chief of *Time*; directors
of the *New York Times*, the *Wall Street Journal*, the Los Angeles

Times, and the Washington *Post*; and the president of the Columbia Broadcasting System, as well as lesser lights from the field of communications.

The governmental community was not overlooked. Invitations to join were extended to Senator Walter Mondale of Minnesota, Governor Jimmy Carter of Georgia, former Undersecretary of State George Ball, Cyrus Vance, Paul Warnke, and Congressmen Donald Fraser of Minnesota and John Brademas of Indiana, among others.

Most Americans have no real understanding of the operation of the international moneylenders. The bankers want it that way. We recognize in a hazy sort of way that the Rothschilds and the Warburgs of Europe and the houses of J. P. Morgan, Kuhn, Loeb and Company, Schiff, Lehman, and Rockefeller possess and control vast wealth. How they acquired this vast financial power and employ it is a mystery to most of us.

International bankers make money by extending credit to governments. The greater the debt of the political state, the larger the interest returned to the lenders. The national banks of Europe are actually owned and controlled by private interests.

In the early years of the Republic the United States experimented with a central banking system. Jefferson opposed Alexander Hamilton's scheme for the First Bank of the United States, and Andrew Jackson abolished Nicholas Biddle's Second Bank of the United States.

The Wall Street banks contributed the financial muscle to elect Woodrow Wilson President in 1912. Their agent, Colonel E. M. House, became the most powerful figure in the Wilson administration.

Paul Moritz Warburg, scion of the M. M. Warburg Company of Hamburg and Amsterdam, came to the U.S. in 1902. Eight years later he was a partner in the banking house of Kuhn, Loeb of New York. Warburg was the architect of our Federal Reserve System, creating a privately owned mechanism to control the currency and credit of the United States.

The Federal Reserve is a bank of monetary issue. It is empowered to establish a national discount rate and to authorize the printing of the currency of the United States. The accounts of the Federal Reserve System have never been audited. It operates outside the control of Congress and through its Board of Governors manipulates the credit of the United States. Under Franklin D. Roosevelt the original term of office for governors was extended from seven to fourteen years—putting the board beyond the reach of any President.

The powerful European banker Anselm Rothschild once said, "Give me the power to issue a nation's money, then I do not care who makes the laws."

History is more than a record of man's struggle for physical survival. Food and shelter are elementary needs, but in the minds of many, the acquisition of power is more important.

In the world of nature the predator stalks his prey, killing to satisfy hunger. In the society of man the predators pursue sovereignty, not sustenance. If successful, they find easy access to every material indulgence.

The universally recognized power structures are: (1) the state—police power flowing from political control; (2) wealth—economic power flowing from monopoly control; (3) the academy—intellectual authority; and (4) the church—ecclesiastical dictum.

The kings and potentates who seized or inherited power in the Old World were automatically vested with control of the kingdom's riches. Most of the time, by subversion and collusion, they also controlled the church and the academy.

In any contest with these monoliths the individual was at a dreadful disadvantage. The only freedom of choice available was a very limited ability to select which structure he would serve. In all of them opportunity for advancement was generally limited to the rich and the wellborn. The common man was held in bondage by all four authorities.

When rebellions occurred, the oppressed were not attempting to destroy the power structures. Their ambition was to replace the individuals exercising that power. The communist revolution was not an attempt to destroy the state but rather to seize control of the political state and all wealth in private hands. Marxism emerged from the intellectual community. Some of its strongest supporters were found in the academies. The Soviet Union is, without question, a monolith.

In the Western world, particularly in those nations where the people have had some choice in selecting their rulers, citizens invested with political power were not automatically endowed with enormous wealth. Only recently have our political rulers employed the economic power of the public purse to pacify and control the populations.

The method adopted by the Western world to limit the authority of these power centers was to create internal division. Under our federal system political sovereignty was dispersed. The Founding Fathers devised a tripartite system for the central government with equal authority allocated among the executive, the legislative, and the judicial branches. The federal system was made up of a union of sovereign states. The American Constitution is essentially a document of prohibition, specifically limiting the power of the federal government and reserving great areas of sovereignty to the states.

The Industrial Revolution, the development of trade and industry, and, perhaps more than anything else, westward expansion in the United States diluted the authority of concentrated wealth. The homesteaders who brought new land into production, the cattlemen, the miners literally created their own capital without much dependence on those who had hitherto monopolized the money supply.

In this new society the wealthy were not denied or forbidden a voice in the exercise of political authority. But the rich and the well-born were not automatically entitled to a high place in the halls of government as they had been in the Old World.

Personal wealth was not considered a total disqualification for public service, but the people preserved an attitude of healthy cynicism toward all those who were considered too avid in their pursuit of political, economic, academic, or ecclesiastical power. The blacksmith in Iowa, the farmer in Kansas, the dentist in Chicago, and the schoolteacher in Texas probably never said so in so many words, but they all understood that a return to monolithic control of these four power centers would mean the end of individual liberty.

In my view, the Trilateral Commission represents a skillful, coordinated effort to seize control and consolidate the four centers of power—political, monetary, intellectual, and ecclesiastical. All this is to be done in the interests of creating a more peaceful, more productive world community. Throughout my public life and in these pages I have refrained from judging other men's motives. I have no such hesitancy about judging their wisdom and the results of the actions taken.

A report presented at the plenary meeting of the Trilateral Commission May 30–31, 1975, at Kyoto, Japan, called for an enlargement of central authority and expressed a lack of confidence in democratically-arrived-at public decisions. Arguing the need to limit democracy, the report called for:

> Centralized economic and social planning.
> Centralization of power within the Congress.
> Improved working conditions to reduce pressure for industrial democracy modeled on patterns of political democracy.
> A program to lower the job expectations of those who receive a college education.

The report also suggested it would be helpful to impose prior restrictions on the press and restructure the laws of libel to check the power of the press. It seems to me I've suffered as greatly from an abusive press as any man in public life, but I get an itchy, uncomfortable feeling at the base of my spine when someone suggests that government should control the news.

The entire Trilateral approach is strictly economic. No recognition is given to the political condition. Total reliance is placed on materialism. The Commission emphasizes the necessity of eliminating artificial barriers to world commerce—tariffs, export duties, quotas—an objective I strongly support. What it proposes to substitute is an international economy managed and controlled by international monetary groups through the mechanism of international conglomerate manufacturing and business enterprise.

Most of our foreign aid channeled through the Export-Import Bank, the International Monetary Fund, the Corporation for Overseas Investment, and Jimmy Carter's new International Stabilization Fund is now being used to advance this objective. Populations are treated as nothing more than producing and consuming units. No attempt has been made to explain why the people of the Western world enjoy economic abundance. Freedom—spiritual, political, economic—is denied any importance in the Trilateral construction of the next century.

The final paragraph of that Trilateral Commission report is an admission of the commission's true aims: "Close Trilateral co-operation in keeping the peace, in managing the world economy, in fostering economic redevelopment and alleviating world poverty will improve the chances of a *smooth and peaceful evolution of the global system*." (Emphasis added.)

What the Trilaterals truly intend is the creation of a worldwide economic power superior to the political governments of the nation-states involved. They believe the abundant materialism they propose to create will overwhelm existing differences. As managers and creators of the system they will rule the future.

CHAPTER 34

Jimmy Who?

The Roman emperor Augustus created the Praetorian Guard, an elitist, privileged, protective corps. Over the years the Praetorians accumulated sufficient power to destroy any emperor they opposed. They blocked efforts to reestablish a true republic. They were able to select and elevate their candidate to the position of emperor.

The Trilateral Commission is a modern Praetorian Guard. David Rockefeller and Zbigniew Brzezinski found Jimmy Carter to be their ideal candidate. They helped him win the nomination and the presidency. To accomplish this purpose, they mobilized the money power of the Wall Street bankers, the intellectual influence of the academic community—which is subservient to the wealth of the great tax-free foundations—and the media controllers represented in the membership of the CFR and the Trilateral.

Their candidate, a relatively unknown, relatively unsuccessful, one-term Georgia governor, captured the machinery of the Democratic party and parlayed a not very successful series of primary campaigns into the nomination. Carter won the New Hampshire primary with 28 percent of the vote. He lost in Massachusetts, running fourth behind Jackson, Udall, and Wallace. He was the winner in Vermont, Florida, and Illinois, but in none of these states was he able to capture a majority of the party vote.

Not until North Carolina, on March 23, did Jimmy Carter win a primary by more than 50 percent of the votes cast. He won in Wisconsin and Pennsylvania with 37 percent of the vote. He lost Maryland and Nebraska. He wasn't on the ballot in West Virginia. He lost Nevada; then he won Arkansas and lost Oregon. He won Tennessee and Kentucky and lost Idaho. In Rhode Island he ran second behind the "uncommitted delegates." Overall, he lost eight primaries, managed to eke out victories in seventeen. In ten of those seventeen states his victory was by much less than 50 percent. Despite this unimpressive record, the *New York Times* and *Time* magazine and most of the nation's media projected Jimmy Carter as the invincible, super-popular candidate for the Democratic nomination.

In the twenty-five presidential primary states a total of 16,032,192 Democrats expressed a preference for a presidential candidate. Jimmy Carter got only 6,235,609 votes—or 39 percent. To put it another way, 61 percent of the Democrats who went to the polls in the presidential primaries voted for some candidate other than Jimmy Carter.

Before the Trilateral settled on Jimmy Carter, Brzezinski described the kind of candidate it was seeking. In a speech in October 1973, he said, "The Democratic candidate will have to emphasize work, family, religion, and increasingly, patriotism, if he has any desire to be elected." Of course, it also wanted a candidate who would embrace its devotion to world trade, diminishing nationalism, and one-world government.

It was Hamilton Jordan, Carter's closest political adviser, who suggested his boss, then governor of Georgia, establish trade missions abroad which would provide a legitimate excuse to travel overseas. Jordan understood the need for visibility.

Gerald Rafshoon, who served the Carter campaign as media expert, has said, "One of the most fortunate accidents in the early campaign and critical to his building support where it counted was Jimmy Carter's membership in the Trilateral Commission." It was no accident. Brzezinski and Rockefeller invited Carter to be a member of the Trilateral Commission in 1973. They immediately commenced grooming him for the presidency.

In those early stages Rockefeller and Brzezinski weren't ready to bet all their chips on Governor Jimmy Carter. They made him a founding member of the Trilateral Commission; but to keep their options open, they brought in Senator Walter Mondale, Democrat of Minnesota, and Elliot Richardson, a highly visible Republican member of the Nixon administration, and they looked at other potential nominees.

London Sunday *Times* reporter Peter Pringle quotes Brzezinski in a frank and far-ranging interview as having told him, "It was a close thing between Carter and Reubin Askew of Florida, but we were impressed that Carter had opened up trade offices for the state of Georgia in Brussels and Tokyo. That seemed to fit perfectly into the concept of the Trilateral." When the full membership of the Trilateral met in Kyoto, Japan, May 30–31, 1975, Jimmy Carter's blatant efforts to enlist support for his candidacy inspired *Newsweek* to begin its story with a reference to Carter's campaign activities, an ambition which Brzezinski publicly supported from the podium.

Jimmy Carter campaigned for election to the office of President of the United States as a moralistic critic of the policies and practices of the federal government. He was the outsider running against the insider. His posture on the major questions of the moment was an adjustable reflection of majority opinion as determined by a series of highly sophisticated continuous public opinion polls.

Carter called our national taxing laws a "disgrace to the human race" when he was asking to be the leader of the national political party which has controlled the Congress since 1956 and is therefore responsible for writing those onerous tax laws. The voters applauded candidate Carter because they, too, found the tax laws burdensome, illogical, and in many cases counterproductive.

Carter called the welfare system "a mess" and got away with it, even though his party had served as the controlling architect of the system which the people recognize as wasteful, inefficient, and riddled with loopholes. Carter displayed enormous indignation over what he called the secrecy surrounding the conduct of our foreign affairs, and he promised that if he were elected, these negotiations would be conducted in public with citizen participation.

The columnists and commentators confessed difficulty in their efforts to catalogue the philosophical position of the candidate.

At one moment he appeared to them to be conservative and the next—extremely liberal.

James Wooten, White House correspondent of the *New York Times*, who covered the Carter campaign, says Carter told a reporter, "I don't give a damn about abortion or amnesty or right to work laws. They are impossible political issues. In fifty years people will still be arguing about them, and they won't be any closer to resolving them then than they are now. It can't possibly help anyone, including myself, if I'm out on the edge of such volatile things; and I don't intend to be. It would be foolish. If I'm going to lose, it's not going to be because I staked my whole candidacy on a ban on abortions or the right to have them."

As a newcomer on the national scene Jimmy Carter was free of the burden of defending any past errors. His managers carefully cultivated the public image of the unsophisticated farm boy, cloaked in innocence and righteousness, prepared to slay the evil dragons responsible for our discontent.

The blurred, imprecise, often contradictory image Jimmy Carter offered to the public in the 1976 presidential campaign was no accident. The basic strategy Carter followed was to tell each particular audience what it wanted to hear. It was an expansion of the cynical formula which had made him a successful candidate for governor of Georgia in 1970. The employment of this policy reveals Carter's complete contempt for the intelligence and integrity of the voters.

Purists in the art of communication maintain that the communicator is responsible both for what he says and for what his audience believes it heard him say. This requirement places a heavy responsibility on the communicator, suggests the message must be direct, understandable, and unequivocal: no hedging; no qualifications; no use of language susceptible to more than one interpretation.

In 1966, as a candidate for the Democratic gubernatorial nomination in Georgia, Carter campaigned as a candidate with a strong, fixed philosophical position considerably to the left of the Georgia constituents.

In that campaign he appeared to be an enlightened southern liberal, opposed to segregation and discrimination. There were three candidates in the Democratic primary—Ellis Arnall, a former governor who enjoyed a moderate image; Lester Maddox, the militant, racist restaurant owner; and Carter. The Republican candidate was Howard "Bo" Calloway.

Carter, who had originally intended to run for the Congress against Calloway, who had been elected in 1964, turned his sights on the governor's chair when Calloway announced that instead of running for reelection to the national legislature, he would seek the governorship of Georgia. Maddox won the Democratic party nomination. Jimmy Carter ran a poor third.

In the general election Arnall ran as a write-in candidate. Calloway received a plurality of the votes cast for the office, but not a majority. Under Georgia rules, this threw the contest into the Georgia legislature for resolution. Maddox was declared the winner.

Carter, deeply in debt, physically and mentally exhausted, entered a period of deep depression. He was forced to seek psychiatric help. Dr. Peter Bourne and his wife, Mary, came to Georgia to treat the disturbed loser. It was at this time that Carter sought the help of his sister Ruth and ultimately became a born-again Christian.

In January 1971 *Time* magazine named Jimmy Carter "Man of the Year," put his picture on the cover, and devoted five whole pages of glowing tribute to the man they hailed as "the prophet of the New South." The article was so wholehearted in its praise and so devoid of any criticism as to inspire one commentator to say *Time* canonized Jimmy Carter. *Time* commenced its puff piece with the portion of Governor Jimmy Carter's inaugural speech in which he said, "I say to you quite frankly that the time for racial discrimination is over."

The *Time* magazine writers ignored the glaring inconsistency between the statements of candidate Carter and Governor Carter. The controlling wisdom of gubernatorial candidate Jimmy Carter and Governor Jimmy Carter demonstrated his belief that "it is often just as important to be perceived as something as actually to be that something and, as a matter of fact, a candidate need not be anything ideological at all."

Throughout that campaign there was the reassuring spectacle of a candidate with all the earthy virtues of Plains, Georgia: the railway station campaign headquarters; the modest home; the friends and neighbors pitching in to help. In actuality, the Carter campaign headquarters was located in Atlanta, staffed by sophisticated experts, employing every device and strategy of proved worth in a campaign for public support.

Jimmy Carter, the man of the people, emerging from the airplane carrying his own garment bag. Jimmy Carter, the simple farmer condemning political insiders and professionals, saying, "The people are better than the government"; asking, "Why not the best?"; saying, "Trust me, I will never lie to you."

James Wooten, in his revealing book *Dasher*, tells us that during the campaign when reporters confronted Carter with his inconsistencies, he always said he had been misinterpreted. Believing in his heart that he was innocent of any prevarication, he could maintain with a righteous countenance that it was the reporters, not Carter, who were guilty of misstatements.

During that period Carter frequently praised the music of his "good friend Bob Dylan." Actually, he had met Dylan only once. John Denver, at Carter's request, flew to Georgia in order to be able to fly back with the candidate to Los Angeles. Nearing the end of that four-hour flight Carter summoned Denver to the front of the airplane. They had a ten-minute conversation. When Carter stepped to a waiting microphone at the Los Angeles airport, he told his audience he had "just flown out with his good friend John Denver." A single-meeting, ten-minute conversation hardly support the "good friend."

When Copley newspaper columnist Jeffrey St. John offered documentation to prove Carter lieutenants had rigged the straw poll taken at the Democratic party convention in Florida, Jody Powell didn't deny it. His response: "That's politics."

The reporters who had relentlessly penetrated every privacy of the Republican administration somehow never got around to telling us the man from Plains was a certified member of the New York establishment group closely tied to banker David Rockefeller. Jerry Ford, President by appointment, burdened by the misdeeds of the Nixon administration, for which he was not in any way responsible, surrounded by advisers who were in position when he came on board, challenged almost daily by a hostile Congress, never had a chance.

When the subject of negotiations for a new canal treaty with the Republic of Panama came up during the campaign, candidate Carter appeared to be opposed to any surrender of U.S. rights or sovereignty. He encouraged the producers of oil and natural gas to believe that he favored deregulation. He emphasized what he perceived to be the necessity of strengthening our military ties with friendly allies. He was very much in favor of a balanced budget. He didn't endorse the make-work program of Humphrey-Hawkins. We all believed he intended to enlarge the military capability of our defense establishment. We saw him going to church regularly with little Amy and teaching Sunday school. When his churchly brethren refused admission to a black militant seeking to join the congregation and worship, Carter managed to maintain a sort of precarious neutrality. Truly the voters of the United States, those who supported Carter and those who opposed him, had reason to believe the new administration would move swiftly to correct some of the errors and redress some of the injustices of the past.

When Jimmy Carter strolled the length of Pennsylvania Avenue after having been sworn in as President, the world in general and the United States in particular were in considerable disarray. Most of the problems were related to the economy, public and private. We faced both inflation and unemployment—more deficit financing despite tax rates so high they were stifling business expansion. More than 30 million Americans were dependent on benefits from the Social Security system, and the so-called trust fund from which these benefits are paid was approaching insolvency.

We were confronted with obvious and confusing contradictions. On the one hand, more people than ever before were working at regular jobs. The national unemployment rate was about 8 percent. Among some groups, teenagers and particularly black teenagers, the rate was scandalously higher.

We were building more new homes, making more television sets, more automobiles, more household appliances, and more recreation equipment than ever before. Yet there were many pockets of genuine hardship. There appeared to be general affluence. There was also unmistakable miserable poverty. Inflation was pushing up the prices of luxuries and necessities until, like that delightful character in *Through the Looking Glass*, we had to run faster and faster just to keep from falling behind.

There was no first-class shooting war going on. But tensions in the Middle East and southern Africa, in the Orient and the southern half of the Western Hemisphere threatened to explode into hostilities which might engulf the world.

All who understood the true dimension of the problems facing the new administration wished Carter well and prayed for his success. We believed the outsider—the non-Washington politician, the anti-establishment peanut farmer—would challenge the bureaucracy, end unnecessary waste, strengthen national defense. In short, we thought he would turn the rascals out and lead an administration of fresh faces. All the old coaches and all the old players would be sent to the showers. There would be a new team, unfettered by past failures. Indeed, Carter's Hamilton Jordan told us, "If after the inauguration you find a Cy Vance as Secretary of State and Zbigniew Brzezinski as head of national security, then I would say we failed and quit."

Jimmy Carter chose Walter F. Mondale to be his Vice President, Brzezinski his foreign affairs advisers, Cy Vance, Secretary of State—all members of the Trilateral Commission. The outsider had been co-opted by the insiders.

Accepting the Democratic presidential nomination in New York, Carter denounced those "unholy, self-perpetuating alliances that have formed between money and politics." After election he staffed his administration with members of either the CFR or the Trilateral Commission.

Five of his twelve Cabinet members and all nineteen of his top advisers are Trilateral members. In addition to Mondale, Brzezinski, and Vance, he named Harold Brown Secretary of Defense; Michael Blumenthal Secretary of the Treasury; Andrew Young Ambassador to the United Nations; Warren Christopher Deputy Secretary of State; Lucy Benson Wilson Undersecretary of State for Security Affairs; Richard Cooper Undersecretary of State for Economic Affairs; Richard Holbrooke, Assistant Secretary of State for East Asian and Pacific Affairs; W. Anthony Lake Undersecretary of State for Policy Planning. The American Department of State is clearly dominated by members of the Trilateral Commission.

Carter also named Sol Linowitz co-negotiator on the Panama Canal treaties; Gerald Smith Ambassador at Large for Nuclear Power Negotiations; Elliot Richardson delegate to the Law of the Sea Conference; Richard Gardner Ambassador to Italy; Anthony Solomon Undersecretary of the Treasury for Monetary Affairs; C. Fred Bergsten Assistant Secretary of the Treasury for International

Affairs; and Paul Warnke Director, Arms Control and Disarmament Agency.

One reporter, in a moment of sarcasm, said, "It would be unfair to say the Trilateral Commission dominates the Carter administration. The Trilateral Commission *is* the Carter administration."

Most of us understand there is a vast difference between the politics of election and the politics of governing. The inconsistencies and contradictions of past Presidents have been called to our attention by their critics.

Woodrow Wilson campaigned for reelection in 1916 on the slogan "He kept us out of war." Roosevelt was reelected in 1940 partly on his promise to American mothers that he would "never send their sons to fight in a foreign war." When he was first elected in 1932, he ran on a platform promising to reduce federal spending and the size of the federal government.

John F. Kennedy promised to close the missile gap, to reestablish our superiority in defense capabilities. Kennedy's Secretary of Defense, Robert McNamara, instituted a deliberate program to downgrade our military power until we reached a parity with Russia.

In 1964 Lyndon Johnson pictured me as a reckless warrior who would enlarge hostilities in Vietnam. Before his election he secretly escalated the war in Southeast Asia.

Richard Nixon ran as the conservative, opposed to increased federal spending and deficit financing. Then he embraced the policy of Lord Keynes and increased both the spending and the deficit.

Jimmy Carter said he would never lie to us. We believed him.

CHAPTER 35

Strength Through Weakness

The President of the United States is the supreme architect of American foreign policy. The Congress plays a subordinate, supporting role. Appropriations for defense must originate in the House and be approved by the Senate. Two-thirds of the Senate must concur in any formal treaty arrangements. The War Powers Limitation Act adopted in the aftermath of the Vietnam War was, in my opinion, an ill-advised attempt to limit presidential power in foreign affairs. Even so, American foreign policy at any given moment is whatever the President declares it to be. And since 1945, our foreign policy has been an inconsistent pattern of compromise and accommodation punctuated briefly by moments of temporary resistance.

For the past thirty-four years the Russian communists have relentlessly pursued their announced objective of world domination. With each passing year they have enlarged their control over land area and populations. Keep in mind that the Soviet communists understand it is not essential to incorporate the subjugated lands into the Soviet Union in order to establish their communist hegemony. Count the countries—Poland, Czechoslovakia, Rumania, Hungary, Austria, Yugoslavia, Bulgaria, Albania, East Germany, all China, most of Southeast Asia, half of Korea, Mozambique, Angola, Ethiopia, Somalia, West Pakistan, Afghanistan, South Yemen, and, in the Western Hemisphere, Cuba.

History is the recital of the rise and fall of nations. If in our minds we mark the dissolution of empire by some singular military defeat, we are misreading history. In every case the climactic act has been preceded by internal failures, by a lessening of devotion to the principles and beliefs which created and sustained the rise to power and prominence. Great nations do not disappear into the dustbin of history without broadcasting in advance the direction they are taking.

Concessions made at Teheran and Yalta brought Russia into the war against Japan just eight days before the Japanese surrendered and established Russia as a Pacific power. American Secretary of State George C. Marshall ordered Chiang Kai-shek to form a coalition government with the communists Mao Tse-tung and Chou En-lai. When Chiang refused, we withdrew logistic support, the nationalist Chinese retreated to Formosa, and communism was firmly established in mainland China.

American foreign policy denied MacArthur victory in Korea. We settled for an armistice and a communist government in North Korea. When the Hungarian freedom fighters attempted to overthrow their communist masters in 1956, we refused to act, and the revolt was crushed by Russian tanks.

Fidel Castro came to power in Cuba on January 1, 1959, because American foreign policy had denied assistance to the government of Fulgencio Batista. The American press and the American State Department told us Castro was a freedom-loving democratic reformer. Two years later the man Senator John Kennedy once described as the "new South American Simón Bolívar" dropped his masquerade and proclaimed Cuba a communist nation ruled by a communist dictator. In 1961 we betrayed the Cuban freedom fighters, and in 1962, as an aftermath of the Cuban missile crisis, we guaranteed the unmolested continuation of Castro's communist dictatorship.

When the communist troops of Ho Chi Minh drove the French out of Indochina, we remained aloof. Later, we entered the Vietnam War in an effort to prevent the communist takeover of all Southeast Asia and then refused to use our military power to win that war.

In 1968 the North Koreans seized the USS *Pueblo* and its

eighty-three-man crew. With the capture of the ship, top-secret electronic devices fell into the hands of the enemy. Eleven months later, after having been brutally mistreated, the crew was released. We took no action.

An unarmed U.S. reconnaissance plane flying over the Sea of Japan, 100 miles from North Korea, was shot down by North Korean jets on April 15, 1969. The United States made no response.

The war in Vietnam was finally ended with the Paris agreements in 1973. The pacts appeared to guarantee the integrity of both North and South Vietnam. In 1974 Congress cut off all military aid to South Vietnam. The North Vietnamese took over the country.

The first Strategic Arms Limitation Treaty (SALT I), engineered by Henry Kissinger and Richard Nixon, permitted the Soviets to expand their weapons systems—nuclear, air, sea, and conventional—and placed restrictions on the United States.

In 1977 President Jimmy Carter halted the construction of the B-1 bomber, and postponed development of the MX missile and the cruise missile. After persuading our NATO allies to accept deployment of the neutron artillery shells, Carter changed his mind and stopped development of this new weapons system.

In December 1978 President Carter granted full diplomatic recognition to the People's Republic of China and announced his intention to abrogate the mutual defense treaty with the free Chinese government on Taiwan. American diplomats have been kidnapped and murdered; American embassies, attacked and pillaged. We make no response.

The American economy is burdened with inflation. The federal budget has not been balanced since 1960. Federal spending has increased from $93 billion in 1965 to an estimated $530 billion in 1979. Inflation is the result of excessive federal spending and an inflationary increase in the supply of money. Since 1960 the money supply has increased 300 percent.

The breakup of the Bretton Woods Fixed Rate System in 1971 (President Nixon took the U.S. dollar off the gold standard) has produced a disastrous decline in the value of the U.S. currency abroad. Since 1970 the U.S. dollar has depreciated 50 percent against the German mark, 44 percent against the Japanese yen.

The annual rate of growth of international trade has been cut in half from 10 percent in the 1960s to only 5 percent in 1978.

In the early days of the Carter administration Secretary of the Treasury Michael Blumenthal and his assistant, Anthony M. Solomon, made public statements encouraging a drop in the dollar's value overseas.

In 1977 President Carter called for the moral equivalent of war to meet the energy shortage and reduce our dependence on foreign oil. He created a new Department of Energy, which is costing the taxpayers about $10 billion per year. We are worse off today than we were two years ago. Government policies have discouraged domestic production. Secretary James Schlesinger vetoed an effort by private industry to import natural gas from Mexico. The rules and regulations promulgated by the Energy Department are contradictory and defeatist.

Because of government regulations and red tape, it takes ten years to build a nuclear power plant. Regulations of the Environmental Protection Agency have added hundreds of billions of dollars to the cost of our mineral products, electric power, highway construction, food, automobiles, and housing. It almost seems as though the government regulators were determined we should all freeze to death in the dark.

Over the past twenty-five years American productivity per manhour worked has steadily declined. In a burst of generosity we built new plants for West Germany and Japan while American taxing policies and governmental borrowing blotted up the sources of investment capital needed to modernize our own industrial machinery.

In January 1979 the Russian capacity to wage nuclear war was substantially greater than the capacity of the United States to defend itself against such a war. We are outnumbered in ICBMs. The Russians are ahead of us in throw weight and overall delivery systems. The Soviets are producing and have deployed a first-rate intercontinental bombing aircraft they call the Backfire.

Until 1961 American defense policy was committed to maintaining a capability superior to that of the Russians. Under Kennedy and his Defense Secretary McNamara, we opted to settle for parity. Under Richard Nixon we adopted a new concept—"sufficiency." Under President Carter we are asked to believe the cause of world peace will best be served by continuing to allow the American defense system to deteriorate.

If the American people do not penetrate the fog of propaganda which has led us to our present position of military weakness, if we don't discard the policy of appeasement and accommodation which has controlled our foreign policy since the end of World War II, the days of the Republic are numbered. And if the United States falls as the result of internal economic collapse or external military threat, the hopes of mankind for freedom throughout the world will fall with us.

The truth is available. Foy D. Kohler, former U.S. Ambassador to the Soviet Union and one of America's foremost Russian experts, gave us this warning in 1977:

> The essential assumption underlying U.S. optimism is that the Soviet leaders fundamentally share U.S. views on the necessity and utility of achieving a balance of mutual deterrent and recognize the political futility and destabilizing effects of efforts to attain military superiority.
>
> In fact, as Soviet leaders have repeatedly made it clear, the purpose of arms control efforts on the part of the U.S.S.R. is to set unilateral constraints on western defenses while, at the same time, maintaining the ability to continue the buildup of Soviet military might.

Former Secretary of Defense Donald Rumsfeld concluded his Fiscal Year 1978 Report with these words: "It should now be evident that the Soviets have taken the initiative in a wide range of programs, that restraint on our part—for whatever reason—has not been reciprocated."

Commenting on SALT I and the proposed SALT II, Dr. Fred Eickel, Director of the Arms Control and Disarmament Agency under President Gerald Ford, addressed the problem of Russian war-making capabilities vis-à-vis the United States in an article which appeared in the October 1977 issue of *Fortune* magazine. He said:

> . . . In the early 1950's our deliverable nuclear weapons outnumbered Soviet weapons at least ten to one. In the early

'60's the ratio was still easily two to one in our favor. By about 1970, however, the Russians had reached approximate equality overall. In addition, they had pressed ahead to surpass us on several counts.

Today they have more missiles and larger ones and a far more vigorous program for replacing and upgrading their land and sea based missile forces.

Paul H. Nitze, chairman of the Policy Studies Committee on the Present Danger, speaking to an audience in Chicago on December 5, 1978, concluded with these statements:

> The Soviet leaders have a full understanding of the potential destructiveness of nuclear weapons. . . . They do not want a nuclear war. The best way to avoid a nuclear war is to have overwhelming superiority. As Clausewitz put it, "The aggressor never wants war. He would prefer to enter your country unopposed."
>
> The Chinese communists who know the Kremlin will tell us that the current focus of Soviet strategy is on western Europe—that they aim to outflank Europe by achieving dominance over the Middle East—that they propose to outflank the Middle East by achieving controlling positions in Afghanistan, Iran, and Iraq on one side—South Yemen, Eritrea, Ethiopia, and Mozambique on the other—and by achieving the neutrality of Turkey to the north. Currently they are attempting to encircle China by pressure on Pakistan and India, by alliance with Vietnam, and dominance over North Korea.
>
> We're heading into a different, more ominous world. It will call for prudence, nerves of steel, foresight, and a sense of strategy in our leaders. Above all, it will call for a willingness to pull together and work together for our common *survival*. We have a country, a history, and a potential future in which we can take pride.
>
> Some say that because of inflation we cannot afford an adequate defense. If we recognize that there is a threat— a serious, multisided threat, calling for unity and sacrifice— there is no reason why we cannot handle both inflation and assure out nation's security. If we don't, we can't handle either.

* * *

I am convinced the present movement can be reversed. I have confidence in the courage of the American people. The cynics claim we have gone soft—that we are a self-indulgent society dedicated to material affluence. Not so! We have arrived at our present position of peril in the world and at home because our leaders have refused to tell us the truth.

When the Japanese attacked Pearl Harbor, the peril was plain to be seen. Hundreds of thousands of young men volunteered for the armed services. Housewives went to work in offices and factories. United, we cheerfully accepted sacrifice. I am persuaded the cause of human freedom is in greater jeopardy today than it was on that December morning in 1941.

It is very difficult for a free people in a society rooted in the Judeo-Christian ethic to comprehend the nature of the enemy or truly to understand the incredible arsenal of weapons deployed against us. The Russians are determined to conquer the world. They will employ force, murder, lies, flattery, subversion, bribery, extortion, and treachery. Everything they stand for and believe in is a contradiction of our understandings of the nature of man. Their artful use of propaganda has anesthetized the free world. Our will to resist is being steadily eroded, and this is a contest of will.

I am not suggesting we should wage a nuclear war. God forbid. It isn't necessary. What I am saying is that unless we, who profess to believe in freedom, wake up, the world is headed for a period of slavery.

Twenty-six years ago I took an oath to support and protect the Constitution of the United States and all the virtues that document symbolizes. As a member of the U.S. Senate I have been faithful to that promise. The Constitution protects the people from the government and the government from the people. It is the catalogue of freedom. The Constitution created the Republic. The people, in that divine climate of freedom ordered by the Constitution, made the nation.

At Gettysburg Abraham Lincoln, describing the agony of the War between the States, said, "Now we are engaged in a great civil war, testing whether that nation . . . so conceived [in liberty] and so dedicated [to the proposition that all men are created equal], can long endure." The sweeping changes—political, economic, and military—which have taken place since the end of World War II require us to face and answer that question now. Can the Republic long endure?

CHAPTER 36

"There is Only the Fight to Recover What has been Lost and Found and Lost Again and Again."

What then shall we say to these things—this alarming decline in American military power, this runaway inflation? This centralization of power in an ever-expanding, paternalistic federal government with a national debt of more than $800 billion?

We are the "can-do" people. We crossed the oceans; we climbed the mountains, forded the rivers, traveled the prairies to build on this continent a monument to human freedom. We came from many lands with different tongues united by our belief in God and our thirst for freedom. We said governments derive their just powers from the consent of the governed. We said the people are sovereign.

We can put aside apathy, turn our backs on disappointment, relegate the errors of the past to the past, and face the future unafraid. An aroused America, an informed America, can overcome the perils of the present moment and rescue freedom for our nation and for the world. It will not be easy. We must be prepared to make the necessary sacrifices, to discipline ourselves, to demand a quality of leadership equal to the undertaking.

The foreign policy of the United States is determined by the President. Domestic policy is largely the work of the Congress.

If the Republic is to survive, we must find and follow new leaders. We will have that opportunity in 1980.

In the beginning we were thirteen colonies perched precariously along the Atlantic seaboard. We had no army. We had no navy. We had no manufacturing capacity. We had no wealth. What we did have was the belief that God intended men to be free, and on the strength of that belief we challenged the greatest commercial and military power in the world. In times of tribulation we have found among the people leaders—uncommon men whose understanding, whose courage, whose devotion to the Republic lifted us up to meet the challenge. They promised us nothing more than a chance to retain our freedom, to preserve the Republic, to continue this most noble experiment.

We must have a President who will speak the truth, who will not attempt to gloss over or conceal the magnitude of the threats confronting us. We must have a President who will employ our technological, scientific, economic, and productive superiority to reestablish confidence in the power of freedom to defend the United States and to overwhelm and defeat tyranny in every arena where freedom is now threatened.

We must build the B-1 or a comparable intercontinental supersonic bomber. We must develop the MX missile. We must perfect the neutron artillery shell. We must strive to improve the cruise missile in both range and accuracy. All this will cost a great deal of money, but better spend what it takes now than sacrifice needlessly the lives of American defenders in the future.

Those who oppose spending for defense argue that building weapons is a total waste. Not so. The wages paid go to American laborers. The results of engineering research have application in nondefense production. The technological advancement which accompanies the development of any new system benefits all of our industrial efforts.

We must find a President who will order a foreign policy of enlightened self-interest supported by a defense system of superior weapons strong enough to deter the most reckless aggressor. Such a foreign policy will make it clear to all the nations of this world that we have no desire to expand our territory or to impose our type of government or our way of life on any other people.

Would such a foreign policy make a nuclear confrontation with the Soviets inevitable? The history of the past thirty-five years supports my belief that it would materially lessen the possibility of a nuclear war.

Communist expansion since the end of World War II has been accomplished without any direct military involvement on the part of the Russians. They have used client troops: North Koreans in Korea; North Vietnamese in Southeast Asia; Cubans in Angola, Ethiopia, and Somalia.

Deprived of Western technology and Western agricultural production, life for the citizens of the Soviet Union would be even more miserable than it is now. There is room for nation-to-nation cooperation, but we must make this a two-way street. There must be a meaningful quid pro quo.

Freedom is a fragile thing. Its enemies are human greed, lust, envy, vanity, and selfishness. We should also be aware that noble motives can destroy freedom. The charitable instinct to improve the lot of the less fortunate may be accompanied by acceptance of the need to control, to regulate, to subtract from the substance of the more productive members of society, to employ the bayonets of governmental compulsion. Perhaps the most dangerous notion of all is the belief that given the proper amount of power and the ability to manipulate and manage, well-intentioned men can create heaven on earth.

We must put aside the childish notion that we can spend ourselves into prosperity. Every householder, every laborer, every business manager, every professional man in this nation knows in his heart that if we continue year after year to spend more than we take in, bankruptcy is inevitable.

The capitalistic system, as developed in the United States of America, has demonstrated an ability to provide more goods and more services for more people at reasonable prices than any other economic system ever devised. Investment capital and profits are the necessary supports of the capitalistic system. As our technology has improved, the capital requirements have increased. Unfortunately the egalitarian socialists are waging war against both profits and capital. It may not have been intended, but the American taxing system discriminates against capital formulation. Excessive federal spending and federal borrowing consume great amounts of capital. The private sector suffers.

We have used the tax policy offering both incentive and penalty to shape the bright new world envisioned by the social planners.

We should use both incentive and penalty to encourage capital formulation and plant modernization, to make U.S. products more competitive, and to improve the productivity of our labor.

The government should remove all the limits on interest payments by banks and other savings institutions. We should eliminate the double taxation on business profits which are taxed now at the company level when they are earned and taxed again when the company pays out dividends to the investors who provided the capital to form the company.

Even before the Arab oil boycott we were aware of the approaching energy shortage. There is new oil and new gas to be discovered in the continental United States and in identified offshore fields. We can manufacture methyl alcohol from a variety of wasted products. We can burn it in our internal-combustion engines with some modification. We can mix it with gasoline, as much as 30 percent, and use it without any engine modification. Nuclear generation is the cheapest, safest way to produce the electric power we need. Geothermal and solar energy must be explored. We must rip aside the stultifying federal controls, do away with red tape, eliminate imposed governmental price ceilings, and permit American ingenuity and the American economic system to solve the energy crisis.

It's been done before. We made the transition from whale oil to kerosene, from wood to coal to manufactured gas to natural gas to petroleum products. Remember, we are the "can-do" people.

We must restore the restraints on the federal government which the framers of the Constitution intended to impose. By so doing, we will restrict the federal government to its proper role, reduce the unbearable tax burden, eliminate the unnecessary controls which are stifling the economic system, and improve the opportunity for every American citizen to enjoy an ever-increasing share of that can-do productivity which has made us the envy of all the nations on earth.

Three amendments to the Constitution are needed:

1. to require a balanced budget except in times of war or national emergency;

2. to limit the amount of money the federal tax collector can take from the people to a percentage of the gross personal income;

3. to reestablish the convertibility of our currency.

The first proposed amendment, requiring a balanced federal budget, would bring a halt to deficit spending, stop our borrowing against the future to indulge our appetites today. Obviously, we cannot move in one year from a deficit of $60 or $70 billion to a balanced budget. Here gradualism is called for. We could order that within six or eight years the budget must be balanced. But standing by itself, this amendment would do nothing to reduce the tax burden.

Nobel laureate Dr. Milton Friedman reminds us that in 1928 total government spending was about 10 percent of the national income. The federal share was 3 percent; local governments claimed 7 percent. In 1978 taxes claimed more than 46 percent of total personal income. The division between federal and local spending has been drastically reversed, with the federal government claiming between 25 and 30 percent, local governments the balance.

By limiting the federal tax collector to a fixed percentage of total personal income, taxes would be controlled, and there would still be room for growth in government as our incomes increased. Because we have been on a forty-year binge of excessive government spending, a sudden cutoff might result in severe economic dislocation. I would propose an initial percentage limit of 30 percent to be decreased by two percentage points each year until we arrived at an ultimate limit of 20 percent or less.

Money has three functions: It is a medium of exchange necessary to commerce; it is a measure or standard of value, prices, fees, etc.; it is also a store of value. This last function is crucial to a stable and productive economy. Unless the future purchasing power of the currency is guaranteed to be approximately equal to the current purchasing power of the currency, this third function of money is destroyed.

In the final days of the Roman Empire the rulers clipped coins. This reduced the intrinsic value and permitted the government to mint more coins with the material it had stolen by clipping. Hyperinflation preceded the French Revolution of 1789. It opened the way for Hitler in Germany after World War I. It preceded the Russian Revolution in 1917. A number of observers believe inflation made it possible for Mao Tse-tung to conquer mainland China.

Government can build streets and highways and armies and navies and order the education of children in specific locations. It can claim and redistribute the nation's substance. It cannot produce and never has produced any real wealth.

The root of the problem lies in the Congress of the United States—535 men and women who have been taught to believe they are competent to control every aspect of our complicated, inventive society. Congress assumes it knows more about banking than bankers and has written millions of words of regulation. Congress believes it is competent to run every service station, barbershop, library, bus company, construction crew, airline, manufacturing plant, extractive operation, pharmaceutical house, dairy, and dog kennel. Common sense condemns this assumption as ludicrous, yet we do nothing about it.

I am not suggesting all the members of the House of Representatives or the Senate have been meanly motivated or are egotistical seekers after enlarged personal power. It is the fatal overestimation of the competency of the Congress to oversee every woodcutter and every wine merchant, every dentist, doctor, and automobile mechanic in this great heterogeneous citizenry which is responsible for our present discontent.

Nowhere is it written that freedom must succumb to slavery. There is no inevitable historical imperative which says that we, who have known freedom, must now surrender our lives to governmental domination. We are being seduced by those who have no confidence in the ability of the American people to face reality.

If the present Congress fails to act and continues to temporize and compromise, we can elect a new Congress in 1980. And if that Congress fails to act, we can initiate the amendments I propose through the various state legislative bodies.

By the end of March 1979 twenty-eight states had petitioned the Congress for an amendment to require a balanced budget. The Carter administration immediately organized a task force to resist this expression of the will of the people. You can be sure that long before the required two-thirds of the states have passed measures in support of this balanced budget proposal, the federal Congress will act.

To my mind, the most destructive change flowing from the war in Vietnam has been the legitimization of public protest groups. When a mob of emotionally excited antinuclear zealots use their bodies to block the construction of a needed, legally authorized nuclear power generation plant, it is anarchy, not what some critics have called an "excess of democracy."

Single-interest political groupings—antiabortion, proabortion, ERA supporters—have demonstrated a capacity to effect the outcome of elections. Let us then unite in a single-interest group determined to preserve freedom and use the process available to us for achieving this objective.

About one-half of all the Americans eligible to do so don't bother to register to vote. We call it a good turnout if 60 or 70 percent of those registered go to the polls. I can understand their apathetic attitude. Time after time they have voted for change, and there has been no change.

Most recently candidate Jimmy Carter displayed enormous indignation over what he called the secrecy surrounding the conduct of foreign affairs. He promised that if he were elected, these negotiations would be conducted in public with citizen participation.

The Panama Canal treaties which provoked such acrimonious division in 1977 and 1978 were written in secret. No details of the language of the treaties were released to the Congress or to the country until just twenty-four hours before they were signed by President Carter. In December 1978, without any prior consultation with the Congress, the President announced the abrogation of our mutual defense treaty with Taiwan and full diplomatic recognition of Red China.

If, in the campaigns of 1980, the people are told the truth about the dangers we face, we may be blessed with a new President and a new majority in the Congress possessing the courage and the wisdom to take the necessary steps to save the Republic. We can make that happen.

I see our young people searching for enduring values. I find tradition gaining new respect. Our society is badly flawed, but there is a remnant. The mechanics for reform are available. Understanding our weaknesses will give us new strength. To serve that purpose, this book has been written.

The world may seem dark and cold and beyond redemption for a moment—but only for a moment. We know Almighty God intended His children to be free. We know the pursuit of freedom has been a relentless quest. We should also know that despite our scientific, technological sophistication, this is still God's world.

> ...And what there is to conquer...has already been
> discovered
>   Once or twice or several times...
>   There is only the fight to recover what has been lost
>   And found and lost again and again.

Acknowledgments

This book, I hope, offers more than a recital of personal struggles, individual triumph and disaster, or a rationalization of the controversy which has surrounded me since I entered public life.

If it appears I have devoted too much space to World War II, the Korean War, the McClellan Committee, Eisenhower, the Bay of Pigs, and the Cuban Missile Crisis, it was necessary because at least one-half the people of the United States will have no personal recollection of these events. To comprehend adequately the present we must first understand the past. The undiagnosed malignancy is never treated. The problem is recognition.

During my years in politics many people across the country have asked me where I find the time to perform my duties as a Senator and still prepare speeches, write books, and perform numerous other tasks. That is a very good question and one which I believe I should answer.

Most of my speeches are extemporaneous, based on hastily written notes usually confined to the back of dinner menus, envelopes, napkins and what have you. I try to gauge the interest and the temper of my audience and fashion my words accordingly. When I feel a prepared speech is needed, my friend, Tony Smith, who has worked in my office for many, many years as a press representative, helps me to put together the appropriate words.

During my Presidential campaign in 1964, numerous speeches were written for me by Karl Hess, a man who has been around the liberal-conservative bush so many times he would make Walter Lippmann look as though he had walked a perfectly straight line all of his life. The man whose genius helped me in putting together my earliest speeches and finally drew them into my first successful book, Brent Bozell, was formerly an editor of the publication, *National Review*.

For input and advice over the years, I have called upon a wide range of friends and experts in many fields. Names that come readily to mind at the moment are William F. Buckley, the columnist and TV personality; William Baroody, Sr., of the American Enterprise Institute; Phoenix attorneys Denison Kitchel and Frank Ryley; Dr. Warren Nutter of the University of Virginia; Professor Milton Friedman, the Nobel Prize-winning economist from the University of Chicago; Bert Fireman, Arizona's leading historian and one of my most constant and severest critics.

In a special category are people like my personal secretary, Judy Eisenhower, and Stephen Shadegg, a friend of many years' standing who masterminded my first campaign for the Senate and who helped immensely in my campaign for President. And it is Steve who has drawn together in this book the thousands of words which I dictated on tape. He has corrected my grammar, weeded out unnecessary words, and helped organize the material in readable form.

There are many others whom I have depended on, men and women whose advice I seek on what to say and how to say it. I think one of the most steadfast and dependable of these has been my legal assistant, Terry Emerson. I am not a lawyer and, even after all of these years in the Senate, I still require much legal help. Over the years, Terry has done brilliant research for me on many subjects. In addition, he has written papers for law reviews and other publications which always appeared under my name even though I have repeatedly asked him to take credit for what he has accomplished.

Others upon whom I rely include my Administrative Assistant, Jack Murphy; Earl Eisenhower, my chief man on the Senate Intelligence Committee; Bob Old, my advisor on the Senate Armed Services Committee; Charles Lombard, who was of great assistance when I was a member of the Space Committee; and, of course, retired General William Quinn, who reads what I write and offers good criticism and suggestions. As I think it over, the list would be much longer if I were to name all of the people who had been of assistance to me over the many years I have served in public office.

The question is sometimes asked whether the use of such help by a public official is really an appropriate and honest way to perform his duty. All I can say is that any man, particularly one like myself, who thinks he can handle the requirements of serving in Congress without help and advice is a man so egotistical that he would go to his grave with the firm conviction that he probably dug it himself. And you know, he might be right.

Barry Goldwater
Be-Nun-I-Kin—1978

INDEX

A distinguished conservative's bold
challenge to America

WILLIAM E.
SIMON
A TIME FOR
TRUTH

Not since Tom Paine's COMMON SENSE
in 1775 has the case for Free Enterprise
been stated so boldly or so well. Not since
Barry Goldwater's THE CONSCIENCE
OF A CONSERVATIVE in 1964 has the
call to Liberty rung so clearly across the
nation.

This outspoken and alarming bestseller is a
book about our Freedom—what is happening
to it and what we can do about it. Before it is
too late!

66S